Arms Trade Registers
The Arms Trade
with the Third World

Arms Trade Registers
The Arms Trade
with the Third World

A SIPRI PUBLICATION

Stockholm International Peace Research Institute

The MIT Press
Cambridge, Massachusetts and
London, England

Almqvist & Wiksell International
Stockholm, Sweden

First published by Almqvist & Wiksell International
26 Gamla Brogatan, S-111 20 Stockholm

In collaboration with

The MIT Press
28 Carleton Street
Cambridge, Mass. 02142

and

126 Buckingham Palace Road
London SM 1W 9SD

ISBN 0 262 19138 5

Library of Congress Catalog
Card Number: 75–868

HD9743
A2
S76
1975

Printed in Sweden by
Tryckindustri AB, Solna, 1975

PREFACE

This SIPRI publication is a register of deals in major arms with 97 third world countries. The information is as complete as the open literature allows up to 1 January 1974 and there is preliminary information on deals and orders up to mid-1974.

The register should be read in conjunction with the SIPRI volume *The Arms Trade with the Third World* (Stockholm, 1971) for information on the mechanisms governing this trade.

The register was prepared by Eva Grenbäck, a member of the SIPRI research staff.

December 1974 *Frank Barnaby*
Director

CONTENTS

North Africa

Sub-Saharan Africa

South Africa

Central America

TABLES, CHARTS AND FIGURES

The arms trade registers

The arms trade registers were not originally conceived as a project of their own; nor, in fact, were they intended for publication. They are a spin-off product of SIPRI's major study, *The Arms Trade with the Third World,* (Almqvist & Wiksell, 1971). When this study was undertaken, considerable effort was spent on finding reliable statistics on the flow of weapons from the industrialized countries to the third world. However, normal international and national trade statistics do not identify the transactions adequately and it soon became clear that the only way to get a reliable picture of the trade over the past twenty years or so was to construct our own statistics. These registers represent an attempt to provide as complete a list as possible of the major arms imported by the countries in the third world. The transactions were also valued in appendix 2 in order to permit conclusions to be drawn about trends and relative magnitudes of the flow of arms. (The methods used in compiling the registers and in valuing them, as well as their limitations and shortcomings, are described in appendix 3, p. 170.)

The arms trade registers were thus intended originally as background material for a more thorough study of the structures and mechanisms governing the trade in arms, and this is still their main function. A list of deliveries from one set of countries to another or the corresponding value figures, has little meaning except when studied in the context of the totality of relations between these countries.

The registers make no claim to be official, complete or final. They are based entirely on open sources and published on our responsibility. When there were conflicting reports – and this was often the case for the number of items supplied – we have used our judgement, based on general experience of the reliability of different sources. Any corrections, additions or deletions, from official or unofficial sources, would be welcome.

The registers include information on arms supplies to the third world countries which are reported to have imported major arms over the period 1950–73. They also include preliminary information on the orders and deliveries of weapons up to mid-1974. The information provided in the registers and value tables of *The Arms Trade with the Third World* and the *SIPRI Yearbooks 1972, 1973* and *1974* has been revised and updated.

The information is arranged by importing country and chronologically under four main headings of major weapons: aircraft, missiles, naval vessels and armoured fighting vehicles.

A description of the individual items is given in appendix 1. The dates provided are those of delivery. When deliveries have been spread over a number of years and it is not known how they have been divided among the years, the whole trans-

1

action has been entered, and the years over which the supplies were spread are shown in the delivery column: thus: *1954–57*. Displacement figures are provided for all naval vessels; the figures refer to standard weight, except where otherwise stated. Figures for the actual cost to the recipient of particular deals are included where these are available and are recorded as "cost" or "u.c." (unit cost).

Whether an item is second-hand or refurbished or whether it has been provided as military aid has only been included when our sources explicitly state that this is the case. SIPRI estimates of delivery dates, numbers and so on, are placed in brackets.

Conventions

. . .	Information not available; refers only to items on order
( )	A greater degree of uncertainty about, for example, the date of an order or delivery, the number of items supplied or the identity of a supplier
[ ]	Conflicting reports as to whether a delivery took place
+	When + is added to a figure, it means at least the number given, and probably more
u.c.	Unit cost
Displ:	Displacement of naval vessels, in numbers of tons
t	Tons
1969–	1969 and subsequent years
Mk	Mark
AA	Anti-aircraft
AAM	Air-to-air missile
AC	Armoured car
AF	Air Force; thus: USAF – United States Air Force; RAF – Royal Air Force (UK); RCAF – Royal Canadian Air Force
APC	Armoured personnel carrier
ASM	Air-to-surface missile
ASW	Anti-submarine warfare
ATM	Anti-tank missile
COIN	Counter-insurgency
MAP	(US) Military Assistance Program
SAM	Surface-to-air missile
SAR	Search and rescue
SSM	Surface-to-surface missile
STOL	Short take-off and landing
T.S.	Official national trade statistics

Far East

Register 1. Arms supplies to Brunei

Date	Number	Item	Supplier	Comment
		Aircraft		
1965	3	Westland Whirlwind Series 3	UK	Part exchanged in 1967 for Westland Wessex
1967	2	Westland Wessex Mk 54	UK	
(1968)	1	Bell 206A Jet Ranger	USA	
(1970)	2	Bell 205A Iroquois	(USA)	
1971	2	Bell 212 Twin-Pac	USA	
1971	1	HS748	UK	
(1971)	3	Bell 206A Jet Ranger	USA	
1974	2	Bell 212 Twin-Pac	USA	
		Missiles		
1972	(48)	Nord SS.12	France	2 quadruple launchers on Vosper patrol boat purchased 1967
		Naval vessels		
1967	1	Vosper fast patrol boat	UK	Displ: 95 t; completed 1967; fitted with Nord SS.12 missiles 1972
1970–71	2	Fast patrol boat	UK/Singapore	Displ: 25 t; new
(1971)	1	Hovercraft, SR.N6 Winchester	UK	Displ: 10 t
1972	1	Vosper fast patrol boat	UK/Singapore	Displ: 25 t; new
		Armoured fighting vehicles		
(1965)	(15)	Ferret	UK	
(1966)	(15)	Saracen	UK	

Register 2. Arms supplies to Burma

Date	Number	Item	Supplier	Comment
		Aircraft		
1954	6	Hunting Provost T.53	UK	
1954	4	DH Vampire T.55	UK	Refurbished
1954–55	2	Bristol 170 Mk 31M	UK	
(1954–56)	20	Supermarine Spitfire Mk 9	Israel	
1955	4	DH Vampire T.55	UK	Refurbished
1955	3	Hunting Provost T.53	UK	
(1955)	2	Douglas C–47	(UK)	War surplus
1956	6	Kawasaki-Bell 47	Japan	Cost: $250 000
1956–60	31	Hunting Provost T.53	UK	
1957	6	Beech D-18S	USA	
1957	10	Cessna 180	USA	
1957–58	18	Hawker Sea Fury FB.11	UK	
1957–58	3	Hawker Sea Fury T.61	UK	
1958	7	Kawasaki-Bell 47	Japan	
(1959–60)	10	DHC–1 Chipmunk	Canada	

Date	Number	Item	Supplier	Comment
1960	(10)	Douglas C–47	USA	
1960	8	DHC-3 Otter	Canada	
(1961)	(4)	Sud Alouette III	France	
(1962)	12	Lockheed T–33	USA	
1963	5	Kaman HH–43B Huskie	USA	
(1963)	(3)	Mi–4	USSR	
(1963)	(3)	Sud Alouette III	France	
1964	(3)	Sud Alouette III	France	
(1965)	3	Sud Alouette III	France	
1968	12	Kaman HH–43B Huskie	USA	
1968	12	NA F–86F Sabre	USA	MAP
1968	3	Kawasaki-Vertol KV–107–11	Japan	
1971	12	Cessna T–37C	USA	MAP
		Naval vessels		
1950	1	Tug	UK	Displ: 800 t; completed 1940; on loan
1950–51	10	Motor gunboat, "CGC" class	USA	Disp: 45 t; completed 1938–42
1951	4	Patrol vessel	USA	Displ: 50 t; completed 1940
1956–57	5	Motor torpedo boat	UK	Displ: 50 t; completed 1956–57; total cost: $4.4 mn iclusive
1957	1	Escort minesweeper, "Algerine" class	UK	Displ: 1 040 t; completed 1943
1958	10	River gunboat	Yugoslavia	Displ: 120 t; completed 1958
(1959–61)	6	Motor gunboat, "PGM" class	USA	Displ: 100 t
(1963–64)	8	Landing craft, "LCM" type	USA	Displ: 28 t
(1964–65)	7	Motor gunboat, "CGC" class	USA	Displ: 49 t; completed 1960; ex-US; new hulls built in Burma
1965	1	Patrol vessel	USA	Displ: 640 t; launched 1943; completed 1964
1967	1	Transport vessel, "UCL" class	USA	Displ: 200 t
1967	1	Patrol vessel	USA	Displ: 650 t; launched 1944
1968	4	Tug	USA	Displ: (534 t); MAP
		Armoured fighting vehicles		
(1954–57)	(15)	Ferret	UK	
(1960–64)	(15)	Comet	UK	
(1961–65)	(10)	Humber	UK	

Register 3. Arms supplies to Indonesia

Date	Number	Item	Supplier	Comment
		Aircraft		
1950	30	NA F–51D and F–51K Mustang	Netherlands	

Date	Number	Item	Supplier	Comment
1950–52	(8)	Convair PBY–5A Catalina	Netherlands	
(1950–54)	(10)	Hiller 360	USA	
(1950–54)	(15)	Convair Vultee BY–13A Valiant	USA	
(1950–55)	40	Douglas C–47	USA	
(1950–55)	(10)	Lockheed 12	USA	
(1950–55)	18	NA B–25D and B–25J	USA/Nether-lands	
(1950–55)	(10)	Auster (light aircraft)	(Netherlands)	
(1951–55)	(15)	NA T–6 Harvard	USA	
(1951–55)	(20)	Piper L–4J Cub	Netherlands	
(1953–55)	(10)	Cessna 180	UK	
1955	10	Sikorsky S–58	USA	
1955	8	DH 115 Vampire	UK	
(1956)	4	Bell 47	USA	
1957	8	Grumman HU–16 Albatross	USA	
1958	2	DHC–3 Otter	Canada	
1958–60	(30)	MiG–15 UTI	Czechoslova-kia	
1958–60	(30)	MiG–17	Czechoslova-kia	
1959	2	DHC–3 Otter	Canada	Amphibian
1959	28	Il–14	Czechoslova-kia	
1959	1	Fuji-Beech T–34 Mentor	Japan	
1960	4	Mi–4	USSR	
1960	3	DHC–3 Otter	Canada	Land plane
1960	40	Il–28	Czechoslova-kia	
(1960)	5	Lockheed C–130B	USA	
1960–63	(20)	MiG–19	USSR	
1961	5	Lockheed C–130B	USA	
1961	15	Douglas B–26B Invader	USA	Surplus
1961	35	NA F–51D Mustang	USA	20 from US surplus stocks; 15 from private source
1961	3	An–12	USSR	
1961	14	Fairey Gannet AS.4	UK	
1961	2	Fairey Gannet T.5	UK	
1961	1	HAL HT–2 Marut	India	Gift
(1961–62)	16	Mi–4	USSR	
1962	2	Fairey Gannet AS.4	UK	
1962–63	25	Tu–16	USSR	
1962–64	40	Fuji-Beech T–34 Mentor	Japan	
1963	2	Bell 204B	USA	
1964	1	Sikorsky S–61A	USA	
1964	6	An–12	USSR	
1964	12	L–29 Delfin	Czechoslova-kia	
(1964)	18	MiG–21	USSR	
1965	2	Aero Grand Commander	USA	
1965	8	Mi–6	USSR	
1965	3	Sud Alouette III	France	
1965	9	Pilatus Porter PC–6	Switzerland	

Date	Number	Item	Supplier	Comment
(1965)	(10)	MiG–21	USSR	
1967	1	Beech Super H–18	USA	
1968	3	Lockheed C–140 Jet Star	USA	
1969	7	Sud Alouette III	France	
1969	5	Cessna 401A	Australia	
1969	2	Cessna 402A	Australia	
1969	(2)	Cessna 310P	Australia	
1970	3	Short Skyvan	UK	
1970	5	Cessna T.207 Turbo Skywagon	Australia	Cost: $332 000+, incl spares
1971	12	Scottish Aviation Twin Pioneer	Malaysia	Ex-RMAF; gift with pilot training
1972	(10)	Douglas C–47	USA	
1972	(2)	AESL Airtourer T6	New Zealand	
1972–73	10	Sikorsky S–55	USA	
1973	14	NA F–51 Mustang	USA	
1973	16	Lockheed T–33	USA	MAP
1973	16	Avon Sabre	Australia	Value: $11.9 mn, incl spares and training; ex-RAAF; gift
1973	2	Douglas C–47	Australia	Military aid
. . .	4	GAF Nomad	Australia	On order for Navy; delivery Oct 1974 – Mar 1975; gift

Missiles

Date	Number	Item	Supplier	Comment
1961–63	6	SA–2	USSR	1 battery
1961–65	(72)	SS–N–2 "Styx"	USSR	
1962–63	(150)	AS–1 "Kennel"	USSR	For use with Tu–16
1964	108	K–13 "Atoll"	USSR	For use with MiG–21
1965	60	K–13 "Atoll"	USSR	For use with MiG–21
1968	(200)	Nord Entac 58	France	

Naval vessels

Date	Number	Item	Supplier	Comment
1950	25	Patrol boat	Netherlands	Displ: 46 t; built 1943–46
1950	2	Australian corvette, "Banteng" class	Netherlands	Displ: 815 t; built 1941
1950	5	Landing craft	Netherlands	Displ: 250 t; built 1935; ex-US
1950–51	12	Auxiliary patrol craft, "Alkai" class	Netherlands	Displ: 134 t; new
1951	6	Landing craft	USA	Ex-US
1951	1	Destroyer, "N" class	Netherlands	Displ: 1 760 t; built 1941; ex-British; scrapped 1961
1951	1	Oiler	Sweden	Displ: 1 372 t; built 1949
1952	1	Surveying vessel	Netherlands	Displ: 1 200 t; built 1952
1952	1	Lighthouse tender	Netherlands	Displ: 1 250 t; completed 1952
1952	2	Minesweeper	Netherlands	Displ: 254 t; ex-British
1953	1	Training ship	FR Germany	Displ: 810 t; built 1953
1953	1	Surveying vessel	Netherlands	Displ: 200 t; completed 1953
(1953)	3	Submarine chaser, auxiliary patrol craft	USA	Displ: 116 t; completed 1943; ex-US; refitted
1954–57	10	Coastal minesweeper	FR Germany	Displ: 139 t; built 1954–57
(1956)	2	Submarine chaser, "PC" class	USA	Displ: 280 t; built 1943; ex-US
1957	2	Transport	(Netherlands)	Displ: 5 614 t; old

Date	Number	Item	Supplier	Comment
1958	1	Submarine chaser, "PC" class	USA	Displ: 280 t; built 1943; ex-US
1958	8	Submarine chaser "Kronstad" class	USSR	Displ: 300 t; built 1951–54, ex-Soviet
1958	2	Frigate, "Swapate" class	Italy	Displ: 1 150 t; completed 1958; cost incl 2 Pattimura: $18.5 mn
1958	2	Frigate, "Pattimura" class	Italy	Displ: 950 t; completed 1958
1958	1	Oiler	Singapore	Displ: 1 412 t
1958	6	Submarine chaser, "Kraljeca" class	Yugoslavia	Displ: 190 t
1958	4	Landing craft	Yugoslavia	Displ: 100 t; ex-Yugoslav "LCT" type
1958–59	6	Auxiliary patrol craft	FR Germany	Displ: 140 t; built 1958–59
1959	2	Oiler	USSR	Displ: 2 170 t; ex-Soviet
1959	4	Destroyer, "Skoryi" class	Poland	Displ: 2 600 t; built 1951–56; ex-Soviet
1959	2	Submarine, "W" class	Poland	Displ: 1 030 t surface, 1 180 t submerged; ex-Soviet; 1 overhauled 1960
1959–60	8	Motor Torpedo boat, "Jaguar" class	FR Germany	Displ: 150 t; built 1959–60
1960	3	Submarine chaser, "PC" class	USA	Displ: 280 t; built 1942–43; ex-US
1960	3	Landing ship	USA	Displ: 1 653 t; ex-US
1960–62	8	Submarine "W" class	USSR	Displ: 1 030 t surface, 1 180 t submerged
1961	1	Tug, "Apache" class	USA	Displ: 1 235 t; built 1942; ex-US
1961	3	Landing ship	USA	Displ: 1 653 t; ex-US
1961	8	Motor torpedo boat, "P6" class	USSR	Displ: 75 t; ex-Soviet
1961	10	Motor gunboat	USSR	Ex-Soviet
1961	1	Submarine support ship	Japan	Displ: 3 200 t; built 1961
1961	1	Landing ship	Japan	Displ: 2 200 t; built 1961
1961	1	Ocean tug	Japan	Displ: 250 t; built 1961
1961–63	6	Patrol boat, "Komar" class	USSR	Displ: 75 t; built 1960–61; ex-Soviet
1962	4	Destroyer, "Skoryi" class	USSR	Displ: 2 600 t; built 1951–56; ex-Soviet
1962	1	Cruiser, "Sverdlov" class	USSR	Displ: 15 540 t; ex-Soviet
1962	2	Frigate, "Riga"class	USSR	Displ: 1 200 t; probably built 1955–58; ex-Soviet
1962	4	Submarine, "W" class	USSR	Displ: 1 030 t surface, 1 180 t submerged
1962	6	Motor torpedo boat, "P6" class	USSR	Displ: 75 t; ex-Soviet
1962	4	Fleet minesweeper, T53	USSR	Displ: 500 t; ex-Soviet
1962	1	Coastal minesweeper, "T.301" class	USSR	Displ: 130 t; ex-Soviet
1962	18	Motor gunboat, "BK" class	USSR	Displ: 120 t; probably built 1956–63; ex-Soviet
1962	1	Submarine support ship, "Don" class	USSR	Displ: 4 750 t; ex-Soviet
1962	1	Submarine support ship, "Artrek" class	USSR	Displ: 3 500 t; built 1955–57; converted from mercantile freighter
1963	2	Frigate, "Riga" class	USSR	Displ: 1 200 t; ex-Soviet

Date	Number	Item	Supplier	Comment
(1963)	3	Motor gunboat, "PGM" class	USA	Displ: 100 t; built for MAP
1963–64	10	Patrol vessel	Italy	Displ: 140 t; for police; cost: $7.6 mn
(1963–64)	10	Motor torpedo boat, "P6" class	USSR	Displ: 75 t; ex-Soviet
1964	2	Destroyer, "Skoryi" class	USSR	Displ: 2 600 t; built 1951–56; ex-Soviet
1964	4	Patrol boat "Komar" class	USSR	Displ: 75 t
1964	2	Frigate, "Riga" class	USSR	Displ: 1 200 t; ex-Soviet
1964	2	Fleet minesweeper, "T43" class	USSR	Displ: 500 t; built 1948–57
1965	2	Patrol boat, "Komar" class	USSR	Displ: 75 t; built 1960–61
1970	2	Tank landing ship	USA	Displ: 1 653 t
1971	1	Tank landing ship	USA	Displ: 1 653 t
1971	6	Minesweeper	USA	Displ: 320 t light, 370 t full load
1971	1	Destroyer tender, "Klondike" class	USA	Displ: 8 165 t; launched 1944–46
1971	1	Repair ship	USA	Displ: 1 625 light, 4 100 t full load; built during WW II
1973	1	Escort ship, "Claud Jones" class	USA	Displ: 1 450 t; commissioned 1959; refitted before transfer
1973–74	2	Patrol boat, "Attack" class	Australia	Displ: 146 t full load; part of $30 mn military aid programme
. . .	6	Patrol boat	Australia	51 ft. Military aid
Armoured fighting vehicles				
(1955)	(15)	Saracen	UK	
(1956)	20	M–3 Stuart	(UK)	
(1958)	(30)	Ferret	UK	
(1960)	(15)	Saladin	UK	
(1962)	(50)	AMX–13	France	
(1963–65)	(30)	BTR 152	USSR	
(1964)	(50)	PT–76	USSR	

Register 4. Arms supplies to Khmer Republic (Cambodia)

Date	Number	Item	Supplier	Comment
		Aircraft		
1954	7	Fletcher FD–25A/B Defender	Japan	Built under licence by Toyo in Japan; cost: $184 000
1955	(15)	Morane-Saulnier M.S. 733 Alcyon	France	
(1955)	6	Curtiss C–46	USA	
1956–57	12	Douglas C–47	USA	
1956–57	8	Cessna 0–1 Birddog	USA	
1956–57	2	DHC–2 Beaver	(Canada)	
(1959)	3	Sikorsky S–58	USA	
1960	2	Sud Alouette II	France	

Date	Number	Item	Supplier	Comment
(1961)	6	NA T–6G Texan	USA	
1961–62	4	Fouga Magister	France	Gift
(1962)	15	NA T–28D	USA	
1963	3	Sud Alouette II	France	
1964	5	MiG–17	USSR	
(1964)	2	Il–14	USSR	
(1964)	1	Mi–4	USSR	
(1964)	5	Sud Alouette II	France	
1965	12	Morane Saulnier M.S. 733 Alcyon	France	
1965	6	Dassault M.D. 315 Flamant	France	
1965	30	Douglas A–1D Skyraider	France	
(1955)	8	MiG–15	China	
1966	6	Cessna T–37B	USA	MAP
1966	3	MiG–17	China	
1967	2	An–2	USSR	
1967	5	MiG–17	USSR	
1968	3	MiG–17	China	
1968	4	(An–2) transport	China	
1968	4	(MiG–15 UTI) trainer	China	
1968–69	12	Sud Horizon	France	
(1969)	2	Sud Alouette III	France	
1970	6	Bell UH–1 Iroquois	USA	MAP
1971	(5)	NA T–28D	USA	MAP
1972	14	Cessna T–41	USA	
1972	2	Cessna 0–1 Birddog	USA	MAP
1972	(3)	Cessna 185 Skywagon	USA	
1972	6	Douglas C–47	Australia	5 ex-RAAF; 1 ex-Jet Air; military aid
1972–73	(36)	NA T–28D	USA	
1972–73	(32)	Bell UH–1 Iroquois	USA	
1973	4	Douglas C–47	USA	
1973	(22)	Fairchild C–123 Provider	USA	Previously operated in Viet-Nam
1973	14	Helio Stallion AU–24	USA	Under USAF "Credible Chase" COIN programme
1973	(35)	Cessna 0–1 Birddog	USA ⎫	Probably part of batch of 82 aircraft
(1973)	8	DHC–3 Otter	(USA) ⎬	transferred from Viet-Nam
. . .	24	Cessna A–37	USA ⎫	Promised after cessation of US
. . .	15	NA T–28D	USA ⎭	bombing, Aug 1973
		Naval vessels		
1954–56	2	Landing craft	France	Displ: 180 t; ex-US; transferred from USA to France
1955–56	2	Patrol vessel	France	Displ: 325 t; ex-US sub chasers; transferred from USA to France 1951
1956	2	Small harbour tug	France	Built 1940; ex-US
1956	1	Patrol boat	France	Displ: 46 t; ex-British harbour defence launchers (1942); transferred from UK to France 1944
1956–57	2	Landing craft	France	Displ: 160 t; ex-US tank landing craft
1957	1	Support gunboat	France	Displ: 230 t; former US infantry landing ship

Date	Number	Item	Supplier	Comment
(1957)	2	Patrol boat	France	Displ: 46 t; ex-British harbour defence launchers (1942); transferred to France 1950
1962	2	Landing craft	France	Displ: 130 t; ex-US utility landing craft
1964	1	Patrol boat	USA	Displ: 100 t; ex-US
1965	2	Torpedo boat	Yugoslavia	Displ: 55 t; ex-Yugoslav "108" type
1968	3	Coastal patrol boat	China	Displ: 7.7 t; ex-Chinese; gift
1969	1	Landing craft, "Edic" type	France	Displ: 292 t
1971	1	Ferry boat	Japan	For troop transport
1973	21	River patrol boat	USA	
		Armoured fighting vehicles		
(1954–55)	(15)	M–3 A1 White	France	
(1958)	(10)	M–24 Chaffee	USA	
(1961)	(5)	M–8 Greyhound	USA	
(1962)	(15)	M–20	USA	
1964	20	AMX–13	France	Gift
(1964–65)	(15)	AML–60	France	Gift
1965	(30)	BTR 152	USSR	Gift
1969	50	Military vehicle	France	
1973	(50)	M–48 Patton	USA	
1973	30	(M–113) APC	USA	
1973	8	M–109	USA	

Register 5. Arms supplies to North Korea

Date	Number	Item	Supplier	Comment
		Aircraft		
1950–51	(100)	MiG–15	China	Built in USSR
(1950–51)	(35)	La–9	USSR	
(1951–52)	(35)	Tu–2	USSR	
(1951–52)	(10)	Il–12	USSR	
1953	(100)	MiG–15	USSR	
1953	(5)	Il–28	USSR	
1953	(70)	La–11	USSR	
(1953)	(2)	Il–28 U	USSR	
(1953)	(8)	Li–2	USSR	
(1953)	(5)	Mi–1	USSR	
(1953)	(15)	Yak–17 UTI	USSR	
(1953)	(15)	MiG–15 UTI	USSR	
(1954)	(10)	Yak–11	(USSR)	
1955	(30)	Il–28	USSR	
1956–58	(100)	MiG–17	USSR	
1957	(4)	Fong Shou No. 2	China	An–2 produced under licence in China
1958	(80)	MiG–15	China	
1958–59	(40)	Il–28	China	

Date	Number	Item	Supplier	Comment
(1958–59)	(4)	Il–28 U	(China)	
(1958–59)	(20)	Shenyang Yak–18	China	In addition to those supplied by the Soviet Union before 1950
(1958–60)	(300)	Shenyang F–4	China	MiG–17 produced under licence in China
(1959–60)	(20)	MiG–19	China	
1965	14	MiG–21	USSR	
(1965)	(15)	Il–14	USSR	
(1965)	(3)	MiG–21 UTI	USSR	
(1965–66)	(5)	An–24	USSR	
1966	21	MiG–21	USSR	
(1966)	20	Mi–4	USSR	
(1968–71)	65	MiG–21	USSR	
1971	28	Su–7	USSR	
		Missiles		
(1966)	(360)	SA–2	USSR	
(1968–71)	(390)	K–13 "Atoll"	USSR	To arm MiG–21
(1969–72)	(132)	SS–N–2 "Styx"	USSR	To arm "Osa" and "Komar" class patrol boats
1971	(3)	"Samlet"	USSR	
1971	(40)	"Frog–5"	USSR	
1972–73	(20)	"Frog–7"	USSR	
1972–73	(200)	SA–7	USSR	
		Naval vessels		
1954	4	Patrol boat, "MO 1" type	USSR	Displ: 50 t; completed (1939); ex-Soviet
(1954–55)	8	Fleet minesweeper, "Fugas" type	USSR	Displ: 440 t; completed 1935-42; ex-Soviet
(1956)	(12)	Motor torpedo boat, "P4" type	USSR	Displ: 50 t; completed 1951–57; ex-Soviet
(1957–60)	24	Inshore minesweeping boat	(China)	Displ: 20 t
(1959)	2	Patrol boat "Artillerist" type	USSR	Displ: 240 t; completed 1943; ex-Soviet
(1963)	2	Fleet minesweeper, "T43" type	USSR	Displ: 500 t; completed 1954; ex-Soviet
(1963)	(9)	Motor torpedo boat, "P4" type	USSR	Displ: 50 t; completed 1957; ex-Soviet
1967	2	Submarine, "W" class	USSR	Displ: 1 030 t; completed 1950–57
1967	7	Motor gunboat, "MGB" type	(USSR)	
1967	3	Motor torpedo boat, "PTF" type	(USSR)	Displ: 160 t approx
1967	4	Patrol boat, "Shanghai" type	China	Displ: 100 t
(1967)	(18)	Motor torpedo boat, "P4" type	USSR	Displ: 50 t; completed 1951–57; ex-Soviet
1968	4	Motor gunboat, "PTG" type	(USSR)	
(1969–71)	6	Missile boat "Komar" class	USSR	Displ: 75 t
(1971–72)	2	Submarine, "W" class	USSR	Displ: 1 030 t
(1971–72)	4	Missile boat, "Osa" class	USSR	Displ:165t

11

Date	Number	Item	Supplier	Comment
		Armoured fighting vehicles		
(1950–51)	(200)	Ba–64	USSR	
(1950–53)	(100)	Su–76	USSR	
(1950–57)	(100)	BTR 40	USSR	
(1950–59)	(150)	BTR 152	USSR	
(1950–62)	(450)	T–34	USSR	
(1965–68)	(100)	Su–100	USSR	
(1965–71)	(250)	BTR 152	USSR	
(1965–71)	(250)	BTR 40	USSR	
(1966–68)	150	PT–76	USSR	
(1967)	(70)	T–54/55	USSR	
(1968–70)	(250)	T–54/55	USSR	
1972–73	(50)	T–55	USSR	

Register 6. Arms supplies to South Korea

Date	Number	Irem	Supplier	Comment
		Aircraft		
1950–52	75	NA F–51 Mustang	USA	
1950–52	(15)	Piper L–4	USA	
(1950–52)	(15)	Douglas C–47	USA	
(1950–53)	20	Curtiss C–46D	USA	
1954	3	Aero Commander 520	USA	
1955	5	NA F–86F Sabre	USA	10–20 were converted to reconnais-
1956	75	NA F–86F Sabre	USA	sance versions
(1956)	6	Sikorsky S–55	USA	
1957	9	Lockheed T–33A	USA	
(1957)	(5)	Cessna 0–1A Birddog	USA	
1958	30	NA F–86F Sabre	USA	
1960	(30)	NA F–86D Sabre	USA	Ex-USAF; equipped with Side-winder AAMs
(1960)	(5)	Cessna LC–180	USA	
(1962)	(30)	NA F–86D Sabre	USA	Ex-USAF; equipped with Side-winder AAMs
(1962)	(16)	NA T–28	USA	
(1964)	(8)	Cessna 185 Skywagon	USA	
(1965)	(15)	Cessna 0–1E Birddog	USA	
1965–66	30	Northrop F–5A Freedom Fighter	USA	
1965–66	4	Northrop F–5B Freedom Fighter	USA	
1965–66	(2)	Curtiss C–46D	USA	MAP
1966	2	Kawasaki-Bell KH–4	Japan	
(1966)	(10)	DHC–2 Beaver	Canada	
(1967)	(5)	Douglas C–54	USA	
1967–68	(2)	Curtiss C–46	USA	MAP
1967–68	(5)	Cessna 0–1A Birddog	USA	MAP
(1968)	2	Northrop F–5B Freedom Fighter	USA	MAP; agreement in Feb 1968

Date	Number	Item	Supplier	Comment
1968–71	(40)	Northrop F–5A Freedom Fighter	USA	
1969	18	McDonnell-Douglas F–4E Phantom	USA	Part of $100 mn aid package; agreement in Feb 1968
1969	5	Bell UH–1D	USA	Cost: $2.4 mn, incl spares for 1 year
1971	(10)	Grumman S–2 Tracker	USA	
(1971)	2	Bell 212 Twin-Pac	USA	
1972	1	Pazmany PL–2	US/S. Korea	Built for evaluation
(1972)	18	McDonnel-Douglas F–4 Phantom	USA	On lease; 2 years rent paid by MAP; in return for F–5s provided by S. Korea to S. Viet-Nam
. . .	3	Pazmany PL–2	US/S. Korea	Being built for evaluation
. . .	. . .	Northrop F–5E Tiger II	USA	On order
		Missiles		
(1959)	(12)	Usamicon MGR–1 Honest John	USA	
1960–62	(360)	NWC Sidewinder	USA	To arm ex-USAF F–86D
1965	(25)	Western Electric Nike Hercules	USA	
1965	(150)	Raytheon MIM–23 Hawk	USA	
1971	(12)	Usamicon MGR–1 Honest John	USA	
		Naval vessels		
1950	2	Frigate, "Tacoma" class	USA	Displ: 1 430 t; completed 1944; on loan
1950	1	Patrol boat "PC" type	USA	Displ: 280 t; completed 1941–42; cost: $18 000
1951	2	Frigate, "Tacoma" class	USA	Displ: 1 430 t; completed 1944
1951	4	Patrol boat, "PC" type	USA	Displ: 280 t; completed 1941–42
1952	4	Patrol boat, "PCS" type	USA	Displ: 251 t; completed 1943–44
1952	4	Motor torpedo boat	USA	Displ: 33 t; completed 1945
1953	1	Frigate, "Tacoma" class	USA	Displ: 1 430 t; completed 1944, replacement
1953	2	Oiler	Norway	Displ: 1 400 t; completed 1951
1955	1	Oiler	USA	Displ: 893 t; on loan
1955	2	Tank landing ship	USA	Displ: 1 635 t; ex-US
1955	2	Escort "180 ft" PCE type	USA	Displ: 640 t; completed 1942–45; on loan
1955–57	6	Supply ship	USA	Displ: 520 t; ex-US
1956	2	Escort, "180 ft" PCE type	USA	Displ: 640 t; completed 1942–45
1956	1	Tank landing ship	USA	Displ: 1 635 t; ex-US
1956	2	Frigate, "Bostwick" type	USA	Displ: 1 240 t; completed 1944; MAP
1956	9	Medium landing ship	USA	Displ: 743 t beaching, 1 095 t full load; ex-US
1956	3	Coastal minesweeper, "YMS" type	USA	Displ: 270 t; completed 1941–42; ex-US
(1957)	4	Coastal minesweeper, "YMS" type	USA	Displ: 270 t; completed 1941–42; 1 decommissioned 1962, 1 scrapped 1964
(1957)	3	Medium landing ship	USA	Displ: 743 t beaching, 1 095 t full load
1958	3	Tank landing ship	USA	Displ: 1 635 t; ex-US

Date	Number	Item	Supplier	Comment
1959	(2)	Tank landing ship	USA	Displ: 1 635 t; ex-US; at least 1 delivered in 1959
1959	1	Escort transport	USA	Displ: 1 400 t; completed 1945; ex-US; modified destroyer escort
1959	3	Coastal minesweeper, "Bluebird" class	USA	Displ: 320 t; new; built specially for MAP transfer
1960	1	Rocket landing ship	USA	Displ: 1 102 t
1960	2	Patrol boat, "PC" type	USA	Displ: 280 t; completed 1941–42
(1960)	1	Landing craft repair ship	USA	Displ: 2 366 t; completed 1944
1961	4	Escort, "180 ft" PCE type	USA	Displ: 640 t; completed 1942–45
1962	2	Tug, "Maricopa" class	USA	Displ: 538 t; completed 1944–45
1963	1	Destroyer, "Fletcher" class	USA	Displ: 2 100 t; completed 1943
1963	1	Frigate, "Rudderow" class	USA	Displ: 1 450 t; completed 1944
1963	1	Escort, "Auk" class	USA	Displ: 890 t; completed 1945
1963	2	Coastal minesweeper, "Bluebird" class	USA	Displ: 320 t; new; built specially for MAP transfer
1964	1	Patrol boat, "PC" type	USA	Displ: 280 t; completed 1941–42
1966	2	Escort transport	USA	Displ: 1 400 t; launched 1944; ex-US modified destroyer escort
1967	3	Escort transport	USA	Displ: 1 400 t; launched 1943–44; ex-US modified destroyer escorts; 2 transferred under MAP
1967	2	Escort, "Auk" class	USA	Displ: 890 t; completed 1942–43
1968	1	Coastal minesweeper, "Bluebird" class	USA	Displ: 320 t; new; MAP
1968	2	Destroyer, "Fletcher" class	USA	Displ: 2 100 t; launched 1943
1968	1	Hydrographic survey vessel	USA	Displ: 267 t; built 1943
1968–69	9	Patrol boat, Ex-CGC "95 ft" type	USA	Displ: 106 t; completed 1958–59
1971	1	Patrol boat	USA	Displ: 225 t; ex-US; rebuilt 1969
1971	1	Oiler	USA	Displ: 1 400 t
1971	1	Supply ship	USA	Displ: 700 t approx; completed 1960
1972	2	Destroyer, "Gearing" class	USA	Displ: 2 425 t; completed 1945; modernized; on loan
1973	1	Patrol boat	USA	Displ: 70 t approx; new
. . .	2	Coastal minesweeper, "Bluebird" class	USA	Displ: 320 t; being built under MAP

Armoured fighting vehicles

Date	Number	Item	Supplier	Comment
(1950–51)	(100)	M– Sherman	USA	
(1950–51)	(50)	M–5 Stuart	USA	
(1950–53)	(50)	M–24 Chaffee	USA	
(1950–53)	(70)	M–10	USA	
(1950–59)	(200)	M–8 Greyhound	USA	
(1951–66)	(500)	M–47/M–48 Patton	USA	
(1954–60)	(70)	M–36	USA	
(1961–65)	(150)	M–113	USA	
1965–66	(50)	(M 52) 105 mm howitzer	USA	
1965–66	(50)	(M–109) 155 mm howitzer	USA	MAP
1966–67	(60)	(M–110) 203 mm howitzer	USA	MAP
1971	(50)	M–110	USA	MAP

14

Date	Number	Item	Supplier	Comment
1971	(50)	M–113A APC	USA	MAP
1971	(50)	M–107	USA	MAP
1971	(50)	M–48A2C Patton	USA	MAP

Register 7. Arms supplies to Laos

Date	Number	Item	Supplier	Comment

Royal Lao

		Aircraft		
1955	10	Morane Saulnier M.S.500 Criquet	France	
1955–56	4	Aero Commander 520	USA	1 as aid
1955–58	20	Cessna 0–1 Birddog	USA	10 as aid
1955–59	10	Douglas C–47	USA	Aid
1955–60	6	DHC–2 Beaver	USA	Aid
1959	2	Sud Alouette II	France	Cost: $200 000
1961	4	Sikorsky S–58	USA	
1961	10	NA T–6 Texan	USA	
(1961–62)	(40)	NA T–28D	USA	
1962	1	Cessna 185 Skywagon	France	
(1963)	4	Sud Alouette III	France	
(1964)	20	NA T–28D	USA	
(1966)	(20)	NA T–28D	USA	
1967	(4)	On Mark B–26 K Counter Invader	USA	
1968	(20)	NA T–28D	USA	
(1969)	(2)	Bell UH–1 Iroquois	USA	
1969–70	10	Douglas AC–47	USA	After use in Viet-Nam
(1970)	(10)	NA T–28D	USA	
1971	3	Douglas DC–3	Australia	Ex-Jetair
(1972–73)	7	Cessna T–41D	USA	Aid
(1972–73)	6	Cessna 185 Skywagon	USA	
(1972–73)	24	Sikorsky S–58	USA	Transferred from Viet-Nam; aid
(1972–73)	(5)	Douglas C–47	USA	Transferred from Viet-Nam; aid

		Armoured fighting vehicles		
(1954)	(15)	M–3 Al White	France	
(1955)	(15)	M–8 Greyhound	France	
(1960)	(10)	M–24 Chaffee	USA	
(1970–71)	(15)	M–113	USA	

Pathet Lao

		Aircraft		
1960–62	10	Po–2	(USSR)	
(1960–62)	6	Il–12	(USSR)	

		Armoured fighting vehicles		
1960–62	(10)	PT–76	USSR	
1962	(10)	BRT 40	USSR	

Register 8. Arms supplies to Malaysia

Date	Number	Item	Supplier	Comment
		Aircraft		
1958	2	Cessna 310	USA	
1958	4	Scottish Aviation Pioneer	UK	Ex-RAF
1958	4	Scottish Aviation Twin Pioneer	UK	
1958	6	DH Chipmunk	UK	Ex-RAF
1961	3	DH Dove	UK	
1961	2	Scottish Aviation Pioneer	UK	
1961–62	12	Hunting Provost T.51	UK	
1962	10	Scottish Aviation Twin Pioneer	UK	
1963	2	DH Heron	UK	
1963–64	8	Handley Page Herald	UK	
1963–64	16	Sud Alouette III	France	
1964	3	Hunting Provost T.51	UK	
1965	4	DHC–4 Caribou	Canada	U.c.: $750 000; military aid
(1965)	3	Hunting Provost T.51	UK	
(1966)	8	Sud Alouette III	France	
1967	2	DH Devon	New Zealand	Ex-RNZAF; refurbished
1967–68	10	Sikorsky S–61A–4	USA	
1967–68	20	Canadair CL–41G Tutor	Canada	
1969	5	Sud Alouette III	France	
1969	9	DHC–4A Caribou	Canada	
1969	10	CAC CA–27 Avon-Sabre Mk 32	Australia	
1970	2	HS 125	UK	
(1970)	1	DHC–4 Caribou	Canada	
1971	6	Sikorsky S–61A–4	USA	
1971	1	(Westland Wasp)	UK	For use on "Yarrow" type frigate
1971–72	6	CAC CA–27 Avon-Sabre	Australia	
1972	15	Scottish Aviation Bulldog	UK	
1972	4	DHC–4 Caribou	Canada	
...	14	Northrop F–5E Tiger II	USA	On order; delivery to begin 1976
...	2	Northrop F–5B	USA	On order; delivery in 1975
...	2	Fokker-VFW F–28	Netherlands	Ordered via Indonesian company
		Missiles		
1971	(96)	Nord SS.12 (M)	France	2 quadruple launchers on 4 "Perkasa" patrol boats
1971	(20)	Short Seacat	UK	To arm "Yarrow" type frigate
1973	(40)	Aérospatiale MM–38 Exocet	France	4 on each of 4 fast patrol boats
		Naval vessels		
1958	2	Landing craft	UK	Displ: 350 t
(1958)	7	Seaward defence boat	UK	Displ: 46 t
1958–59	4	Inshore minesweeper, "Ham" class	UK	Displ: 120 t
1960	1	Coastal minesweeper, "Ton" class	UK	Displ: 360 t; transferred under Defence Agreement
1963	6	Patrol boat, "Kedah" class	UK	Displ: 96 t; new
1963	1	Coastal minesweeper, "Ton" class	UK	Displ: 360 t; refitted before transfer

Date	Number	Item	Supplier	Comment
1964	1	Frigate, "Lock" class	UK	Displ: 1 575 t; completed 1944; refitted before transfer
1964	4	Patrol boat, "Sabah" class	UK	Displ: 96 t; new
1964	2	Coastal minesweeper, "Ton" class	UK	Displ: 360 t; refitted before transfer
1965	1	Tank landing craft	UK	Displ: 657 t; refitted before transfer
1965–66	5	Minor landing craft	Australia	Displ: 55.5 t; new
1966	2	Coastal minesweeper, "Ton" class	UK	Displ: 360 t; refitted before transport
1966	2	Inshore minesweeper, "Ham" class	UK	Displ: 120 t
1966–68	14	Patrol boat, "Kris" class	UK	Displ: 96 t; new; cost: $8.4 mn approx
1967	4	Patrol boat, "Perkasa" class	UK	Displ: 95 t; new
1970	1	Survey vessel	UK	Displ: 360 t; converted 1964
1971	1	Support ship	USA	Displ: 1 653 t; completed 1945
1971	1	Frigate, "Yarrow" type	UK	Displ: 1 250 t; new; cost: $11.2 mn; armed with Seacat SAMs
1971	1	Diving tender	Singapore	Displ: 120 t; new
1973	4	Fast patrol boat, "La Combattante II" class	France	Displ: 234 t; new; armed with Exocet SSMs
		Armoured fighting vehicles		
(1962)	(15)	Daimler AC	UK	
(1963–64)	(30)	Ferret	UK	
1971	100	V–100 Commando	USA	
(1971–72)	44	Panhard AML-VTT	France	

Register 9. Arms supplies to the Philippines

Date	Number	Item	Supplier	Comment
		Aircraft		
(1952)	1	Aero Commander 520	USA	
1956	6	Lockheed T–33	USA	
(1956)	1	Bell 470	USA	
(1956–57)	4	Grumman HU–16A Albatross	USA	
1957–58	40	NA F–86F Sabre	USA	
(1957–58)	5	Sikorsky S–55	USA	
(1958)	18	NA F–86 D Sabre	USA	
1958–59	36	Fuji-Beech T–34 Mentor	Japan	War reparations; value: $2.98 mn
1959	(15)	NA T–28A	USA	
(1961)	(2)	Cessna 0–1 Birddog	USA	
(1961–62)	3	Fokker Friendship	Netherlands	
(1963)	(2)	Piper L–4 Cub	USA	
(1964)	(2)	Cessna 310	USA	
1965–66	3	Northrop F–5B Freedom Fighter	USA	MAP; value: $2.2 mn

Date	Number	Item	Supplier	Comment
(1965–66)	2	Sikorsky S–58	USA	MAP; value: $1.3 mn
1965–67	19	Northrop F–5A Freedom Fighter	USA	MAP; value: $13.3 mn
1965–67	4	NAMC YS–11	Japan	
1966–67	2	Mitsubishi-Sikorsky S–62A	Japan	War reparations; value: $1.5 mn
1967	8	Fairchild-Hiller FH–1100	USA	
1967	8	Cessna 185 Skywagon	USA	
(1968–71)	12	Bell UH–1 Iroquois	USA	Value of 4: $1.02 mn
(1969–70)	(6)	Hughes 300	USA	
(1970–71)	18	Douglas C–47	USA	
1972	(10)	Cessna T–41D	USA	
(1972)	4	NT T–28A	USA	
(1972)	7	Lockheed T–33	USA	
1973	(10)	Bell UH–1 Iroquois	USA	
1973	4	Lockheed L100–20 Hercules	USA	Acquired for development purposes with $8 mn Ex-Im bank loan; used for troop transport
1973	120	DHC–2 Beaver	USA	Acquired for development purposes; Viet-Nam surplus, purchased for cost of shipping; armed with machine-guns
1973–74	48	Siai-Marchetti SF.260	Italy	16 of armed version for COIN
...	...	Lockheed C–130 Hercules	USA	On order; delivery from 1975
...	5	MBB BO 105	FR Germany	Delivered complete; more to be supplied in components for local assembly
...	12	GAF Nomad	Australia	On order
Missiles				
(1957–58)	200	NWC Sidewinder	USA	
Naval vessels				
(1950)	7	Landing ship	USA	Displ: 1 625 t light, 4 080 t full load; ex-US
(1950)	1	Oiler	USA	Displ: 521 t; ex-US
(1950)	1	Rescue tug	USA	Displ: 534 t; ex-US; ex-British
(1950–51)	5	Escort patrol vessel	USA	Displ: 640 t; completed 1943–44
1951	8	Coastguard vessel	USA	Completed 1940
(1951)	1	Lighthouse tender	USA	Displ: 162 t; ex-US
1953	7	Coastguard vessel	USA	Ex-US
(1954)	2	Infantry landing craft	USA	Displ: 173 t; ex-US
(1954–55)	2	Lighthouse tender	USA	Displ: 470 t; ex-US
1955	4	Patrol boat	USA	Displ: 95 t; new
(1955)	1	Water carrier	USA	Displ: 1 235 t full load; ex-US
1956	2	Patrol boat	USA	Displ: 95 t; new
1956	2	Coastal minesweeper, "Bluebird" class	USA	Displ: 335 t; new
1958	1	Patrol boat	USA	Displ: 280 t; completed 1942
1959	1	Command ship	Japan	Displ: 2 200 t gross; war reparations
(1959)	3	Patrol boat	USA	Displ: 95 t; new
1960	4	Patrol boat	USA	Displ: 95 t; new
1961	1	Repair ship	USA	Displ: 1 625 t light, 4 100 t full load; ex-US; MAP

Date	Number	Item	Supplier	Comment
1961	1	Landing ship	USA	Displ: 743 t beaching, 912 t full load; ex-US
(1961)	2	Landing ship	USA	Displ: 743 t beaching, 912 t full load; ex-US
1963	3	Harbour tug	USA	Ex-US; MAP
1965	1	Fleet minesweeper, "Auk" class	USA	Displ: 890 t; launched 1944; ex-US; used as escort patrol vessel
1965	2	Hydrofoil patrol boat	Italy	Displ: 28 t; new; u.c.: $400 000
1966	6	Patrol boat, "Swift" type	USA	Displ: 22,5 t full load; new
1966	2	Hydrofoil patrol boat	Japan	Displ: 60 t gross; new; for smuggling prevention
1967	1	Command ship	USA	Displ: 1 240 t; completed 1943; ex-US; destroyer escort
1967	1	Fleet minesweeper, "Auk" class	USA	Displ: 890 t; launched 1943 ex-US; used as escort patrol vessel
1967	1	Oiler	USA	Displ: 521 t; ex-US; MAP
1968	8	Patrol boat, "Swift" type	USA	Displ: 22.5 t full load; new
1968	1	Patrol boat	USA	Displ: 280 t; completed 1942
1968	1	Patrol boat	USA	Displ: 330 t; completed 1942–44
1968	1	Dry dock	USA	Capacity: 2 800 t; built during WW II
1969	3	Landing ship	USA	Displ: 1 625 t light, 4 080 t full load; ex-US
(1969)	1	Patrol boat, "Swift" type	USA	Displ: 22.5 t full load; new
1970	3	Patrol boat, "Swift" type	USA	Displ: 22.5 t; new
1970	1	Repair ship	USA	Displ: 2 366 t; launched 1945
1972	1	Lighthouse tender	USA	Displ: 935 t; launched 1943
1972	1	Supply ship	USA	Displ: 4 900 t light, 5 636 t full load; launched 1945
1972	3	Tank landing ship	USA	Displ: 2 366 t beaching, 4 050 t full load; 2 completed 1943–44
1972	2	Ocean minesweeper, "Agile" class	USA	Displ: 665 t light, 750 t full load; completed 1953
. . .	6	Inshore patrol craft	USA	On order; displ: 33 t full load
		Armoured fighting vehicles		
(1956–57)	(25)	M–4 Sherman	USA	
(1959–60)	(25)	M–24 Chaffee	USA	
(1964–65)	(25)	M–41 Walker Bulldog	USA	
(1965–66)	15	M–3	USA	
(1973)	(15)	M–113	USA	

Register 10. Arms supplies to Singapore

Date	Number	Item	Supplier	Comment
		Aircraft		
1963	1	HAL HT–2 Marut	India	
1967	2	HAL Pushpak	India	
1969	8	Cessna T–41	USA	

Date	Number	Item	Supplier	Comment
1969–70	16	BAC 167 Strikemaster	UK	Cost: $7.2 mn, part of which contributed by UK
1969–70	8	Sud Alouette III	France	
1970	1	Cessna 402	(USA)	
1970	4	HS Hunter T.75	UK	Refurbished
1970	2	AESL Airtourer 150	New Zealand	Gift under military aid programme
1970–71	12	HS Hunter FGA.74	UK	Refurbished
1970–71	4	HS Hunter FR.74A	UK	Refurbished
1971	16	Siai-Marchetti SF.260X	Italy	U.c.: $48 000
1972–73	22	HS Hunter FGA.74	UK	Refurbished
1972–73	5	HS Hunter T.75	UK	Refurbished
1973	4	AESL Airtourer	New Zealand	Option for 2 more; cost: $157 000
1973–74	40	McDonnell Douglas A–4B Skyhawk	USA	Refurbished in Singapore
1973–74	6	Short Skyvan	UK	Cost: $3.5 mn; 3 specially equipped for SAF
Missiles				
1971	56	BAC Bloodhound Mk 2	UK	Ex-RAF; refurbished; cost: $24 mn, incl spares, after sales services and training
(1972)	36	IAI Gabriel	Israel	To arm 3 fast patrol boats
(1973)	(24)	BAC Rapier	UK	
Naval vessels				
1970	2	Landing ship	UK	Displ: 657 t
1970–71	2	Fast patrol boat	UK	Displ: 100 t; new; cost: $9.6 mn for 6, of which remaining 4 being built in Singapore
1971	1	Landing ship	USA	Displ: 1 653 t; modernized 1960; ex-US
1972	2	Missile boat	FR Germany	Displ: 120 t; new; one more built in Singapore
Armoured fighting vehicles				
(1964–66)	(15)	Ferret	UK	
1969	50	AMX–13	Israel	
(1970)	(30)	V–100 Commando	USA	

Register 11. Arms supplies to Taiwan

Date	Number	Item	Supplier	Comment
		Aircraft		
(1951)	(15)	Beech C–45	USA	
(1951)	(12)	NA T–6 Texan	USA	
(1951–55)	(15)	Douglas C–47	USA	
(1954–55)	25	Republic RF–84F	USA	Replaced by RF–104G
(1954–55)	(70)	Republic F–84G	USA	Replaced by F–100A in 1960

Date	Number	Item	Supplier	Comment
1954–58	320	NA F–86F Sabre	USA	
1954–58	7	NA RF–86F Sabre	USA	
(1955)	(12)	Lockheed T–33A	USA	
(1955)	7	Sikorsky S–58	USA	
(1957)	25	NA F–86D Sabre	USA	
(1957)	(5)	Grumman HU–16 Albatross	USA	
(1958)	25	McDonnell RF–101C Voodoo	USA	US surplus
(1958)	(15)	Convair PBY–5A Catalina	USA	
1958–59	2	Kawasaki-Bell 47	Japan	
1959	25	McDonnell RF–101A Voodoo	USA	
(1959)	(10)	NA T–28D	USA	
1960	25	Lockheed F–104A Starfighter	USA	Ex-USAF; refurbished; now withdrawn from service
1960	(3)	Lockheed F–104B Starfighter	USA	
1960	80	NA F–100A Super Sabre	USA	
1960	2	Lockheed U–2	USA	In return for share in resulting intelligence
1960	(8)	NA F–100F Super Sabre	USA	
(1960)	(15)	Fairchild C–119G Packet	USA	
(1960)	7	Sikorsky S–55	USA	
(1960)	25	Martin RB–57 B/D Canberra	USA	
1962	1	Douglas DC–6B	USA	
(1962)	15	Martin B–57 B/D Canberra	USA	
(1962)	1	Lockheed U–2	USA	
(1962)	10	Bell HH–13	USA	
(1963)	1	Lockheed U–2	USA	
1963–64	50	Lockheed F–104G Starfighter	USA	
1964	(5)	Lockheed TF–104G Starfighter	USA	
(1964)	1	Lockheed U–2	USA	Lost 1 in 1964
(1964)	15	Lockheed RF–104G Starfighter	USA	
1965	7	Northrop F–5A Freedom Fighter	USA	
1965	2	Northrop F–5B Freedom Fighter	USA	
(1965)	1	Lockheed U–2	USA	Lost 1 in 1965
(1965)	(6)	Lockheed T–33A	USA	US excess stocks
(1965)	(1)	Sikorsky S–55	USA	US exsecc stocks
1966	18	Northrop F–5A Freedom Fighter	USA	
1966	(1)	Northrop F–5B Freedom Fighter	USA	
1966	(15)	Fairchild C–123B Provider	USA	
(1966)	(2)	McDonnell RF–101A Voodoo	USA	US excess stocks

Date	Number	Item	Supplier	Comment
[1966	9	Republic F–105 Thunder-chief	USA]	Delivery uncertain
(1966)	(2)	Grumman HU–16 Albatross	USA	US excess stocks
(1966–67)	19	Grumman S–2A Tracker	USA	Purchased FY 1966 under $3.1 mn credit
1967	2	Sikorsky S–62	USA	U.c.: $200 000 approx
(1967)	(5)	Cessna 0–1 Birddog	USA	US excess stocks
(1967)	(2)	Bell 205 Iroquois	USA	US excess stocks
(1967)	1	Lockheed U–2	USA	Lost 1 in 1967; had 2 in 1968
1968	2	Pazmany PL–1	USA	1 purchased, 1 built under licence
1968	6	Bell 205 Iroquois	USA	Purchased FY 1968 under $3.3 mn credit
(1968)	(2)	Hughes OH–6A	USA	US excess stocks
1969	70	Northrop F–5 Freedom Fighter	USA	
1969	20	Lockheed F–104 Starfighter	USA	US excess stocks
1969	35	NA F–100 Super Sabre	USA	US excess stocks
1969	30	Fairchild C–119 Packet	USA	US excess stocks
1969–71	45	Northrop F–5A Freedom Fighter	USA	MAP; credit for 19 FY 1968: $19.3 mn
1969–71	9	Northrop F–5B Freedom Fighter	USA	MAP
1970	34	NA F–100 Super Sabre	USA	MAP; surplus
1970	6	Hughes OH–6A	USA	MAP
1970–72	50	Pazmany PL–1	USA/Taiwan	Built in Taiwan from US design
1971–73	50	Bell 205 Iroquois	USA/Taiwan	Built under licence in Taiwan
(1972)	1	Boeing 720	USA	Ex-Northwest Airlines; for VIP
. . .	(100)	Northrop F–5E Tiger II	USA	On order; agreement may include licence and offset production
. . .	68	Bell 205 Iroquois	USA/Taiwan	To be built under licence in Taiwan
		Missiles		
(1954–58)	(1050)	NWC Sidewinder	USA	For use with F–86
(1954–58)	(1050)	Hughes HM–55 Falcon	USA	
(1959–60)	(250)	Western Electric Nike Hercules	USA	1 battalion
(1960)	(150)	Raytheon MIM–23 Hawk	USA	1 battalion
(1961)	(12)	Usamicon MGR–1 Honest John	USA	1 battalion
1970	(25)	Western Electric Nike Hercules	USA	1 battery; MAP
. . .	. . .	Raphael Shafrir	Israel	On order
		Naval vessels		
1951	7	Submarine chaser	USA	Displ: 95 t
1951	1	Tug	USA	Displ: 1 312 t; completed 1944
1951	2	Frigate, "Castle" type	Canada	Displ: 1 100 t; completed 1944; reconverted from merchant ships
1953	1	Transport	Japan	Displ: 950 t
(1953)	1	Oiler	USA	Displ: 1 400 t full load; built 1945
(1953–56)	9	Submarine chaser	USA	Displ: 280 t; completed 1943
1954	2	Destroyer, "Mayo" class	USA	Displ: 1 620 t; completed 1940
1954	1	Gunboat	USA	Displ: 295 t; completed 1945

Date	Number	Item	Supplier	Comment
1954	5	Landing craft, "LSSL" type	USA	Displ: 227 t; incl 2 transferred under MDAP formerly on loan to France in Indo-China; for cannibalization
(1954)	9	Landing craft, "LSIL" type	USA	Displ: 227 t; incl 3 transferred under MDAP, formerly on loan to France in Indo-China; for cannibalization
(1954)	1	Tug	USA	Displ: 1 312 t; completed 1944
1955	2	Coastal minesweeper	USA	Displ: 335 t; ex-US
1955	1	Destroyer, "Gleaves" class	USA	Displ: 1 630 t; completed 1942; on loan
1955	5	Tank landing ship	USA	Displ: 1 653 t; acquired from merchant service
(1955)	2	Landing craft	USA	Displ: 143 t
1957	1	Repair ship	USA	Displ: 1 625 t; completed 1943
1957	4	Submarine chaser	USA	Displ: 280 t; launched 1941–43
1957	2	Patrol craft	Japan	Weight 52 t; completed 1957
1958	6	Tank landing ship	USA	Displ: 1 653 t
1959	1	Destroyer, "Gleaves" class	USA	Displ: 1 700 standard; completed 1940
1959	1	Submarine chaser	USA	Displ: 280 t; completed 1943
1959	1	Medium landing ship	USA	Displ: 743 t
1959	5	Medium landing ship	USA	Displ: 743 t; in addition to 8 delivered before 1950
1960	1	Fast transport	USA	Displ: 1 400 t; ex-US destroyer escort
1960	1	Dock landing ship	USA	Displ: 295 t; completed 1943
1960	1	Tank landing ship	USA	Displ: 1 653 t
1961	1	Tank landing ship	USA	Displ: 1 653 t
1961	1	Oiler	USA	Displ: 1 850 t; completed 1945
1962	1	Tug	USA	Displ: 534 t; completed 1944
1962	1	Medium landing ship	USA	Displ: 743 t
(1962–65)	16	Landing craft	USA	Displ: 143 t; 5 formerly on loan to France in Indo-China
(1963)	1	Tug	USA	Displ: 534 t
1963–64	5	Small harbour tug	USA	
1964	1	Amphibious flag ship	USA	Completed 1964
1964	7	Landing craft	USA	Displ: 143 t; MAP transfer
1964	1	Escort patrol vessel	USA	Displ: 890 t
1965	2	Patrol boat	USA	Displ: 890 t; ex-US
1965	2	Coastal minesweeper	USA	Displ: 335 t; ex-US
1965	2	Fast transport	USA	Displ: 1 400 t; built 1940–45; ex-US destroyer escort
1966	7	Fast transport	USA	Displ: 1 400 t; built 1940–45; ex-US destroyer escort
1966	1	Coastal minesweeper	USA	Displ: 335 t
1966	1	Tug "Apache" type	USA	Displ: 1 235 t; completed 1942; on loan
1967	2	Fast transport	USA	Displ: 1 400 t; built 1940–45; ex-US destroyer escort
1967	1	Destroyer, "Fletcher" class	USA	Displ: 2 100 t; built 1943; MAP transfer
1968	1	Frigate, "Bostwich" class	USA	Displ: 1 450 t; completed 1944
1968	1	Fleet minesweeper	USA	Displ: 650 t; built 1942; ex-US

Date	Number	Item	Supplier	Comment
1968	1	Destroyer, "Fletcher" class	USA	Displ: 2 100 t; completed 1943
1969	8	Coastal minesweeper	USA	Displ: 330 t light, 380 t full load; completed 1953–55; ex-Belgian
1969	1	Fast transport	USA	Displ: 1 400 t; completed 1943; ex-US destroyer escort
1969	1	Tug-surveying ship	USA	Built 1945; converted 1969
1969	1	Oiler	Japan	Displ: 1 049 t light, 4 150 t full load; new
1970	5	Destroyer, "Allen M Sumner" class	USA	Displ: 2 200 t; completed 1943–44
1970	1	Destroyer, "Gleaves" class	USA	Displ: 1 700 t; completed 1942
1970	1	Destroyer	USA/Japan	Displ: 1 630 t; completed 1941; for cannibalization
1971	2	Destroyer, "Fletcher" class	USA	Displ: 2 100 t; completed 1943
1971	1	Destroyer, "Gearing" class	USA	Displ: 2 425 t; completed 1945; modernized mid-1960s
1971	1	Cargo ship	USA	Displ: 700 t approx; built 1944; transferred from Indo-China
1971	1	Oiler	USA	Displ: 1 850 t light, 4 335 t full load; launched 1944; transferred from New Zealand
1972	1	Destroyer, "Allen M Sumner" class	USA	Displ: 2 200 t; completed 1944; cost: $153 000; FY 1973 ship sale
1972	1	Oiler	USA	Displ: 1 850 t light, 4 570 t full load; completed 1944; FY 1973 ship lease
1972	1	Tug	USA	Displ: 435 t; launched 1944
1972	1	Repair ship, "Liberty" type	USA	Displ: 5 766 t; completed 1944
1972	1	Surveying ship	USA	Displ: 6 090 t; built 1945; refitted 1966–67
1972–73	5	Destroyer, "Gearing" class	USA	Displ: 2 425 t; commissioned 1945–47; 4 modernized; cost: $229 500; FY 1974 ship sale; 1 to be used for parts
1973	2	Submarine, "Guppy II" type	USA	Displ: 1 870 t; completed 1945–46; modernized; on loan; for ASW training
		Armoured fighting vehicles		
(1951–53)	(25)	M–24 Chaffee	USA	
(1952–54)	(60)	M–3	USA	
(1954–56)	(25)	M–41 Walker Bulldog	USA	
(1955–58)	(50)	M–48 Patton	USA	
(1959–61)	(60)	M–18	USA	
(1967)	(25)	(M–24) light tank	USA	US excess stocks
1968–69	146	M–113	USA	Purchased FY 1968–69 under $6.5 mn credit
1969	50	M–41 Walker Bulldog	USA	US excess stocks; cost: $5.4 mn for parts and transportation

Register 12. Arms supplies to Thailand

Date	Number	Item	Supplier	Comment
		Aircraft		
1950	50	Grumman F–8F–1D Bearcat	USA	
(1950–54)	(10)	Douglas C–54	USA	
1951	63	NA T–6 Texan	USA	For COIN and training
(1951–52)	50	Grumman F–8F–1D Bearcat	USA	
(1951–52)	(5)	Cessna 170	USA	
(1951–52)	(5)	Convair Stinson L–5	USA	
(1951–53)	4	Westland S–51 Dragonfly	UK	
(1951–55)	(10)	Beech C–45	USA	
(1952)	(6)	Curtiss SB2C–5 Helldiver	USA	For Navy
(1952–53)	29	Grumman F–8F–1B Bearcat	USA	Broken up for spares
(1952–53)	(5)	Fairchild 24 W	USA	
(1953)	(10)	Piper L–18 Super Cub	USA	
(1954)	(5)	Cessna 0–1 Birddog	USA	
(1955–56)	13	Sikorsky S–55	USA	
(1956)	4	Hiller 360	USA	
1957	75	NA T–6 Texan	USA	For COIN and training
1957	30	Republic F–84G	USA	
(1957)	6	Lockheed T–33A	USA	
(1957)	6	Lockheed RT–33A	USA	
(1959)	(3)	Grumman S–2 Tracker	USA	
(1960)	6	Fairchild C–123B Provider	USA	
1961	38	Cessna 0–1 Birddog	USA	
1961	4	DHC–2 Beaver	Canada	
(1961)	(5)	Helio U–10A Courier	USA	
1961–62	47	NA F–86F Sabre	USA	MAP
1961–62	17	NA F–86L Sabre	USA	MAP
(1961–62)	(7)	Grumman HU–16 Albatross	USA	2 for Navy
1962	8	Cessna T–37B	USA	
(1962–64)	55	NA T–28D	USA	For COIN
1963	3	Kaman HH–43B Huskie	USA	
1963–64	6	Kawasaki-Bell KH–4	Japan	Cost of first 3: $2.9 mn
(1965)	1	HS 748	UK	For VIP transport
1966	7	Kawasaki-Bell KH–4	Japan	
(1966)	2	Northrop F–5B Freedom Fighter	USA	MAP
1966–67	20	Northrop F–5A Freedom Fighter	USA	MAP
1967	6	Bell 205 Iroquois	USA	
1968	2	BHC–4 Caribou	Canada	
(1968)	5	Northrop F–5A Freedom Fighter	USA	MAP
(1968)	4	Kawasaki-Vertol 107–11	Japan	
(1968–69)	35	Sikorsky S–58	USA	
(1969)	3	Bell 206 Jet Ranger	USA	For Army
(1969)	3	Kawasaki-Bell KH–4	Japan	
1969–71	19	Bell 205 Iroquois	USA	
(1970–71)	7	Fairchild C–123 Provider	USA	

Date	Number	Item	Supplier	Comment
1971	16	NA–Rockwell OV–10 Bronco	USA	
1972	4	Boeing-Vertol CH–47 Chinook	USA	
1972	25	Bell UH–IH Iroquois	USA	
1972	2	Pazmany PL–2	USA	Built for evaluation
1972	1	HS 748	UK	
1973	16	Fairchild-Hiller FH–1100	USA	For Army
(1973)	13	Fairchild AU–23A Peace-maker	USA	Under USAF "Credible Chase" COIN programme
1973–74	16	NA–Rockwell OV–10 Bronco	USA	
1973–74	12	SIAI-Marchetti SF.260	Italy	
1973–74	24	AESL CT4 Airtrainer	New Zealand	
...	...	Northrop F–5E Tiger II	USA	On order
...	30	McDonnell Douglas A–4 Skyhawk	USA	On order; some overhaul to be done in Thailand
		Missiles		
(1961–62)	(200)	NWC Sidewinder	USA	For use with F–86
(1969–70)	36	Raytheon MIM–23 Hawk	USA	
1973	(12)	Short Seacat	UK	1 quadruple launcher on "Yarrow" type frigate
		Naval vessels		
1950	4	Landing craft, "LCT" type	USA	Displ: 130 t; ex-British
(1950)	1	Oiler	USA	Displ: 422 t
1951	2	Frigate, "PF" class	USA	Displ: 1 430 t; completed 1943–44
1954	4	Coastguard cutter	USA	Displ: 95 t; completed 1953
1954	7	(Patrol boat)	Japan	Displ: 48 t; cost: $220 000
(1954)	1	Tank landing ship	USA	Displ: 1 625 t
(1954–55)	4	Patrol boat	USA	Displ: 280 t; completed 1941–43
(1955)	2	Inshore landing craft	USA	Displ: 230 t; ex-US
(1955–56)	2	Medium landing craft	USA	Displ: 743 t; completed 1945
1957	6	Landing craft, "LCT" type	UK	Displ: 130 t; ex-British
(1958–59)	3	Patrol boat	USA	Displ: 110 t; built 1954–55; ex-US sub chasers
1959	1	Destroyer escort, "Bostwich" class	USA	Displ: 1 240 t; completed 1944; on loan under MAP
1959	2	Coastguard cutter, "YP" class	USA	Displ: 44.5 t; launched 1938–42; ex-US
1961	1	Surveying vessel	FR Germany	Displ: 870 t; launched 1960
1962	1	Tank landing ship, "LST" type	USA	Displ: 1 625 t; completed 1944
1962	1	Medium landing ship	USA	Displ: 743 t; completed 1945
1963	1	Coastal minesweeper	USA	Displ: 330 t; ex-US
1965	3	Coastal minesweeper	USA	Displ: 330 t; launched 1964
1965	2	Gunboat	USA	Displ: 130 t; launched 1965
1965	2	Patrol boat	FR Germany	Built by Lürssen
1966	1	Tank landing ship, "LST" type	USA	Displ: 1 625 t
1966	1	Gunboat	USA	Displ: 233 t; ex-US, ex-Japanese

Date	Number	Item	Supplier	Comment
1966–70	9	Coastal gunboat	USA	Displ: 130 t
1967	1	Minesweeper support ship	Japan	Displ: 586 t; built 1944
1968	1	Fast patrol boat	USA	
(1968–69)	6	River patrol boat	USA	Displ: 10.4 t
1970	(4)	Fast patrol boat, "Swift" class	USA	Displ: 20 t
1970	1	Landing ship, "LST" type	USA	Displ: 1 625 t; ex-US
1972	10	River patrol boat	USA	Displ: 10.4 t
(1972)	2	Fast patrol boat, "Swift" class	USA	Displ: 20 t
1972–73	2	Frigate "Corvette" type	USA	Displ: 900 t; new
1974	1	Frigate, "Yarrow" type	UK	Displ: 1 780 t; new; cost: $16 mn; armed with Seacat SAMs
. . .	1	Frigate "Corvette" type	USA	Displ: 900 t; being built
		Armoured fighting vehicles		
1955–59	(100)	Scout car M–3 A1 and M–8	USA	
(1960–62)	(100)	M–24 Chaffee	USA	
(1962–63)	(100)	M–2	USA	
(1964–65)	(18)	M–41 Walker Bulldog	USA	
1966–67	32	M–41 Walker Bulldog	USA	
1967	200	M–113	USA	
(1968)	(50)	M–6 Staghound	USA	
1971–72	(32)	Shorland Mk 3	UK	

Register 13. Arms supplies to North Viet-Nam

Date	Number	Item	Supplier	Comment
		Aircraft		
(1954–55)	20	Li–2	USSR	
(1955–56)	6	Il–12	USSR	
(1956–57)	8	An–2	USSR	
(1958–59)	(10)	Mi–1	USSR	
(1961–62)	12	Il–14	USSR	
(1964–65)	(15)	Mi–4	USSR	
(1964–55)	(5)	MiG–17	China	
(1964–65)	10	MiG–15	China	
1964–67	(50)	MiG–15	USSR	
1964–67	(30)	MiG–17	USSR	
1966–67	20	MiG–21	USSR	
1967	8	Il–28	USSR	
1967	6	Mi–6	USSR	
(1967)	(5)	An–24	USSR	
1967–72	(35)	MiG–19/F6	China	
1968	(30)	MiG–17	USSR	
(1968)	(5)	Il–28	USSR	

Date	Number	Item	Supplier	Comment
1968–72	(95)	MiG–21	USSR	
1969–72	(40)	MiG–17	USSR	
1969–72	(20)	MiG–17	China	
(1970)	6	Mi–6	USSR	
(1970)	12	An–2	USSR	
		Missiles		
1966–68	(5000)	SA–2	USSR	With about 300 launchers
1966–72	(690)	K–13 "Atoll"	USSR	To arm MiG–21
1969–70	(200)	SA–2	USSR	
1971–72	(3200)	SA–2	USSR	
1972	(1000)	SA–7	USSR	
1972	(500)	AT–3 "Sagger"	USSR	
1972	(24)	SS–N–2 "Styx"	USSR	To arm 4 "Komar" class patrol boats
		Naval vessels		
1957	3	Motor torpedo boat, "P6" type	China	Displ: 50 t; new
1958	30	Motor gunboat, "Swatow" type	China	Displ: 67 t full load; new
1960–61	2	Patrol boat, "SO1" type	USSR	Displ: 250 t; ex-Soviet sub chasers
(1960–66)	30	Patrol craft	USSR/China	
1961	9	Patrol boat, "P4" class	USSR	Displ: 50 t
1964	3	Patrol boat, "P4" class	USSR	Displ: 50 t
1964	3	Motor torpedo boat, "P6" class	China	Displ: 50 t; completed
1964	20	Motor gunboat, "Swatow" class	China	Displ: 67 t full load; to replace losses
1964–65	2	Patrol boat, "SO1" type	USSR	Displ: 250 t; completed 1957–60; ex-Soviet sub chasers
1966	4	Motor gunboat, "Shanghai" class	China	Displ: 100 t; new
1967	(3)	Motor gunboat, "P6" class	USSR	Displ: 50 t; new
(1968)	1	Landing craft, "LCT 6" class	China	
(1969)	7	Landing craft	(China)	Displ: 743 t
(1970)	5	Landing craft	(China)	Displ: 230 t light, 387 t full load
1972	4	Patrol boat, "Komar" class	USSR	Displ: 75 t
1972	3	Motor torpedo boat, "P6" class	USSR	Displ: 50 t
		Armoured fighting vehicles		
(1955–60)	(30)	T–34	USSR	
(1960–62)	(50)	BTR–152	USSR/China	
(1964–68)	(100)	BTR–40	USSR	
(1965–68)	(150)	PT–76	USSR	
(1970)	(50)	JSU–122	USSR	
(1970)	(50)	Su–76	USSR	
(1970–72)	75	T–54	USSR	
(1970–71)	(50)	BTR–50	USSR	
1971–72	(100)	Light tank	China	Version of PT–76

Register 14. Arms supplies to South Viet-Nam

Date	Number	Item	Supplier	Comment
		Aircraft		
1954	(20)	Cessna 0–1 Birddog	USA	
1954	16	Douglas C–47/RC–47	France	
1954	4	Fletcher FD–25 Defender	Japan	Cost: $105 000; produced under licence in Japan
(1954)	(10)	Beech C–45	USA	
1954–56	(25)	Grumman F–8F Bearcat	France	Ex-US; transferred to France for use in Indo-China
(1954–56)	55	NA T–6	USA	MAP
1956	16	Douglas C–47	(USA)	
1958	(5)	Sikorsky S–55	USA	
1958–59	2	DHC–4 Caribou	Canada	
(1960)	2	Bell 47	USA	
1960–62	70	NA T–28	USA	
1961	4	Douglas B–26 Invader	USA	
(1961)	(15)	Bell UH–1A	USA	
1961–62	150	Douglas A–1E/H Skyraider	USA	
1961–62	5	DHC–4 Caribou	Canada	
1962	(5)	Sikorsky S–55	USA	
1962–63	(20)	Douglas C–47/RC–47	USA	
(1962–63)	25	Cessna 185 Skywagon	USA	
1962–64	80	Sikorsky S–58	USA	
1963	(6)	On Mark B–26K Counter Invader	USA	New COIN version of B–26
1964–65	(40)	Cessna 0–1 Birddog	USA	
(1964–65)	7	DHC–6 Beaver	(USA)	For psychological warfare unit
(1965–67)	25	Douglas C–47/RC–47	USA	
1966	4	Martin B 57B Canberra	USA	
1966	1	Douglas DC–6	USA	For use by the President
1966–67	48	Cessna 0–1 Birddog	USA	
1967	17	Northrop F–5 Freedom Fighter	USA	MAP
1967	2	Northrop F–5B	USA	
1968	16	Fairchild C–119 Packet	USA	
1969	60	Cessna A–37	USA	
1969–70	150	Bell UH–1H Iroquois	USA	
1970	16	Fairchild AC–119 Packet	USA	Gunship version
1970	20	Boeing-Vertol CH–47 Chinook	USA	
1970–71	48	Fairchild C–123 Provider	USA	
1970–72	104	Cessna A–37B	USA	
1971	200	Bell UH–1H Iroquois	USA	
1971	1	Pazmany PL–2	USA/S. Viet-Nam	
1971–72	30	Boeing-Vertol CH–47 Chinook	USA	Incl some delivered in Nov airlift
1972	20	Douglas A–1 Skyraider	USA	Transferred from USAF in Thailand
1972	120	Northrop F–5 Freedom Fighter	USA	Delivered in Nov airlift; 20 supplied by USA, 30 on loan from Iran and 70 on loan from S. Korea and Taiwan

Date	Number	Item	Supplier	Comment
1972	90	Cessna A–37B	USA	Delivered in Nov airlift
1972	549	Bell UH–1H Iroquois	USA	270 delivered in Nov airlift; remainder turned over by departing US units
1972	20	Fairchild AC–119 Packet	USA	Delivered in Nov airlift; gunship version
1972	32	Lockheed C–130 Hercules	USA	Delivered in Nov airlift
1972	(5)	Douglas EC–47	USA	Delivered in Nov airlift; for electronic warfare
1973	20	Boeing-Vertol CH–47 Chinook	USA	
1974–	126	Northrop F–5E Tiger II	USA	On order; incl at least 28 F–5F trainers
		Missiles		
1972	(1000)	Hughes TOW	USA	
		Naval vessels		
1954	5	Utility landing craft	USA/France	Displ: 180 t; French reparations
1954	3	Coastal minesweeper, "YMS" type	France	Displ: 232 t; ex-US
1955	1	Training ship	USA/France	Displ: 950 t; adapted as training ship 1966
1955	2	Landing ship	USA/France	Displ: 743 t beaching, 1 095 t full load; sold by USA to France 1954
1955	1	Landing ship	USA/France	Displ: 227 t; transferred from USA to France 1951
1956	1	Patrol vessel	USA/France	Displ: 280 t; completed in USA 1944
1956	7	Landing ship	USA/France	Displ: 227 t; transferred from USA to France 1951–53
1956	1	Oiler, "Yog" class	USA/France	Displ: 450 t; transferred from USA to France 1950
1957	1	Landing ship	USA/France	Displ: 227 t; transferred from USA to France 1951
1958	2	Utility landing craft	USA/France	Displ: 180 t; MAP; offshore procurement
1959–60	3	Coastal minesweeper, "Bluebird" class	USA	Displ: 320 t; transferred under MAP; ex-US
1960	1	Patrol vessel	USA	Displ: 280 t; completed 1945
1960–63	10	Motor gunboat	USA	Displ: 95 t beaching, 143 t full load; new
1961	1	Escort	USA	Displ: 640 t; completed 1944
1961	1	Landing ship	USA	Displ: 743 t beaching, 1095 t full
1962	2	Escort	USA	Displ: 650 t beaching, 945 t full load; completed 1944
1962	2	Landing ship	USA	Displ: 2 366 t beaching, 4080 t full load; completed 1944–45
1962	1	Landing ship	USA	Displ: 743 t beaching, 1 95 t full load
1963	1	Landing ship	USA	Displ: 2 366 t beaching, 4 080 t full load; completed 1944
1963	12	Minesweeper and mine-layer	USA	

Date	Number	Item	Supplier	Comment
1963	1	Oiler, "Yog" type	USA	Displ: 450 t;
1963	13	Tug	USA	
1964	2	Escort	USA	Displ: 650 t; completed 1944
1964	2	Patrol gunboat	USA	Displ: 95 t; new
1965	1	Landing ship	USA	Displ: 743 t beaching, 1 095 t full load
1965	4	Landing ship	USA	Displ: 227 t; built in Japan
1965	(20)	River patrol craft, "RPC" type	USA	
1965	150	Minor landing craft	USA	For river force
1965–70	22	Monitor	USA	Displ: 75 t full load; ex-US landing craft
1965–71	700	Small river and coastguard craft	USA	
1966	1	Escort	USA	Displ: 640 t; completed 1944
1966	1	Landing ship	USA	Displ: 227 t; built in Japan
1967	4	Motor gunboat	USA	Displ: 95 t; new
1968–69	(7)	River patrol craft, "RPC" type	USA	Mostly new
1968–70	(150)	Landing craft	USA	
1968–70	107	Inshore patrol craft, "Swift" type	USA	Displ: 22.5 t full load
1968–70	293	River patrol boat, "FBR" type	USA	Displ: 7.5 t
1969	100	Armoured troop carrier, "ATC" type	USA	Displ: 66 t full load
(1969)	4	Tug, "YTL" type	USA	
1969–70	8	Tank landing ship	USA	Displ: 2 366 t; completed 1943–44
1969–70	42	River monitor	USA	Displ: 80 t full load
1969–70	9	Command control boat "CCB" type	USA	Displ: 80 t full load
1969–70	26	Patrol gunboat, "Point" class	USA	Displ: 64 t
1969–70	84	Assault support patrol boat, "ASPB" type	USA	Displ: 36 t full load
1970	1	Patrol vessel, "MSF" type	USA	Displ: 650 t; completed 1944
1970	1	Escort, "PCE" type	USA	Displ: 640 t; completed 1944
1970	1	Oiler, "Yog" type	USA	Displ: 450 t light, 1 253 t full load
1970	14	Minesweeping launch	USA	8 launches of 56 ft and 6 of 50 ft
1971	4	Frigate	USA	Displ: 1 766 t; completed 1944
1971	2	Destroyer escort	USA	Displ: 1 590; completed 1943–44
1971	1	Surveying ship	USA	Displ: 534 t; launched 1944
1971	1	Light ship	USA	Ex-US
1972	3	Frigate	USA	Displ: 1 766 t; commissioned 1943–44

Armoured fighting vehicles

(1954–55)	(10)	M–24 Chaffee	USA/France	
(1954–56)	(50)	M–41 Walker Bulldog	USA	
(1958–60)	(50)	AMX–13	France	
1965	(125)	V–100 Commando	USA	
(1965–67)	(300)	M–113	USA	
(1968–69)	(100)	M–59	USA	
1969–72	(350)	M–41 Walker Bulldog	USA	

31

Date	Number	Item	Supplier	Comment
1969–72	1100	M–113	USA	
(1970)	(125)	M–8 Greyhound	USA	
(1970)	(30)	M–3	USA	
1971	24	M–107	USA	
1971	24	M–109	USA	
1971–72	(107)	M–48 Patton	USA	Incl a number delivered after being repaired in Japan
1972	(50)	M–60	USA	
1973	35	(M–60) tank	USA	
1973	35	(M–113) APC	USA	

South Asia

Register 15. Arms supplies to Afghanistan

Date	Number	Item	Supplier	Comment
		Aircraft		
1956	1	Il–14	USSR	Gift
1957	7	MiG–17	USSR	
1957	(3)	Il–28	USSR	
1957	6	MiG–15 UTI	USSR	
1957	10	An–2	USSR	
1957	6	SM–1	Poland	Mi–1 helicopters built under licence in Poland
(1957–58)	(6)	Yak–18	USSR	
(1958)	(10)	Yak–11	USSR	
1958–59	32	MiG–17	USSR	
(1959–61)	(43)	Il–28	USSR	To have received a total of 46
1960–61	(60)	MiG–17	USSR	
(1960–63)	25	Il–14	USSR	
(1964–65)	12	MiG–19	USSR	
(1964–65)	18	Mi–4	USSR	
(1966–68)	30	MiG–21	USSR	
(1968)	1	Il–18	USSR	
(1970)	1	Il–18	USSR	
(1970)	10	MiG–21	USSR	
(1971)	(4)	Mi–8	USSR	
(1972)	(15)	Su–7	USSR	
		Missiles		
(1962–64)	(150)	AT–1 "Snapper"	USSR	
(1966–67)	120	SA–2	USSR	
(1966–68)	(180)	K–13 "Atoll"	USSR	To arm MiG–21
(1970)	(60)	K–13 "Atoll"	USSR	To arm MiG–21
		Armoured fighting vehicles		
(1956–58)	(25)	T–34	USSR	
(1959–61)	(25)	PT–76	USSR	
(1962–64)	(50)	T–54	USSR	

Register 16. Arms supplies to Bangladesh

Date	Number	Item	Supplier	Comment
		Aircraft		
1971	4	DHC–3 Otter	India	
(1971)	1	DHC–4 Caribou	India	
1971–72	3	Sud Alouette III	India	
(1972)	1	An–12	(India)	
1973	10	MiG–21 MF	USSR	
1973	2	MiG–21 UTI	USSR	
1973	1	An–24	USSR	
1973	(3)	An–26	USSR	
(1973)	(3)	Sud Alouette III	(India)	
		Naval vessels		
1972	1	Patrol boat "Poluchat" class	(India)	Displ: 100 t

Register 17. Arms supplies to India

Date	Number	Item	Supplier	Comment
		Aircraft		
1949–53	62	HAL/Percival Prentice	UK/India	Produced under licence in India
1950	10	Short Sealand	UK	
(1950–51)	(20)	DHC–1 Chipmunk	Canada	
1953	5	Fairey Firefly T.T.1	UK	
1953	(10)	DH Vampire N.F. 54	UK	Ex-RAF
1953–54	71	Dassault M.D. 450 Ouragan	France	
1953–59	230	HAL/DH Vampire FB. 9	UK/India	Produced under licence in India
1954	6	Sikorsky S–55	USA	
1954	26	Fairchild C–119G Packet	USA	
1955	2	Il–14	USSR	Gift
1955	2	Vickers Viscount 730 and 723	UK	
1955	10	Auster AOP. 9	UK	
1956	30	NA T–6G Texan	USA	
1956	20	Auster AOP. 9	UK	
1956–60	50	HAL/DH Vampire T.55	UK/India	Produced under licence in India
1957	6	DHC–3 Otter	Canada	
(1957)	33	Dassault M.D. 450 Ouragan	France	
1957–58	6	Bell 47G–3B	USA	
1957–61	160	Hawker Hunter F.56	UK	
1957–61	22	Hawker Hunter T.66	UK	
1958	5	Fairey Firefly T.T.4	UK	
1958	66	English Electric Canberra B(1)58	UK	
1958	8	English Electric Canberra PR.57	UK	

Date	Number	Item	Supplier	Comment
1958	6	English Electric Canberra T.4	UK	
1958	25	Folland Gnat	UK	
1958	110	Dassault Mystère IV A	France	
1958	20	DHC–3 Otter	Canada	
(1959)	15	Folland Gnat	UK	In component form for local assembly
1960	2	Sikorsky S–62	USA	Cost: $540 000; supplied for evaluation
1960	24	Il–14	USSR	
1960–63	24	Armstrong Whitworth Seahawk	UK	Partly new, partly ex-RAF
1960–(65)	100	HAL/Folland Gnat	UK/India	Produced under licence in India
1961	29	Fairchild C–119G Packet	USA	
1961	6	Bell 47–G–3B	USA	
1961	10	Mi–4	USSR	U.c.: $150 000; sold for cash
1961	8	An–12	USSR	
1961	15	Brequet 1050 Alizé	France	
1961–65	12	Armstrong Whitworth Seahawk	UK	Refurbished
1962	2	DHC–4 Caribou	USA	MAP
1962	16	Mi–4	USSR	For cash
1962	8	An–12	USSR	
1962	8	DH Vampire T.55	Indonesia	
(1962)	(23)	Fairchild C–119G Packet	USA	
1962–64	12	Lockheed C–130 Hercules	USA	Free loan basis with air and ground crews provided
1963	5	Auster AOP. 9	UK	
1963	24	Fairchild C–119G Packet	USA	MAP
1963	6	MiG–21	USSR	
1963	6	Mi–4	USSR	For cash
1963	8	An–12	USSR	
1963	20	Sud Alouette III	France	
1963	5	DHC–3 Otter	Canada	Emergency aid
1963	8	Douglas C–47	Canada	Emergency aid
1963	36	CCF T–6 Harvard	Canada	Emergency aid
1963–64	16	DHC–4 Caribou	Canada	On loan
1965	36	Mi–4	USSR	On deferred payments
1965	6	BAC Canberra B(1)58	UK	
1965–67	(90)	MiG–21	USSR	Direct purchase
1965–67	10	HAL/HS–748	UK/India	Produced under licence in India
1966	40	Mi–4	USSR	U.c.: $120 000; on deferred payment terms
1966	24	Armstrong Whitworth Seahawk Mk 100 and 101	FR Germany	
(1966)	14	MiG–21 UTI	USSR	
(1966)	10	An–12	USSR	
1966–69	100	HAL/HS Gnat	UK/India	Production expanded due to Gnat success in Indo-Pakistani War 1965
1966–73	120	HAL/Sud Alouette III	France/India	Produced under licence in India; indigenous content 96 per cent; Indian export price: $235 000
1967	3	Tu–124	USSR	

Date	Number	Item	Supplier	Comment
1967	36	HS Hunter F.56	UK	Refurbished
1967	12	HS Hunter T.66D	UK	Refurbished
1967–74	196	HAL/MiG–21FL	USSR/India	Produced under licence in India; indigenous content 60 per cent 1972
1968	3	Breguet 1050 Alizé	France	
1968	4	DHC–4 Caribou	Canada	
1968–69	4	HAL/HS–748	UK/India	Continued licence production
1968–70	100	Su–7B	USSR	U.c.: $1 mn
1970–71	12	BAC Canberra B.15 and 16	UK	Ex-RAF; refurbished
1970–71	5	HAL/HS–748	UK/India	Continued licence production
1970–71	10	BAC Canberra B(1)12	New Zealand	
1971	50	Su–7B	USSR	
1971	6	Westland Sea King	UK	Cost: $4.8 mn, incl spares and support equipment; for ASW
(1971)	10	Hughes 300	USA	For Navy
(1971)	20	Mi–8	USSR	
1972	7	MiG–21M	USSR	Delivered prior to start of licence production
(1972)	5	HS Hunter	UK	Refurbished
1972	150	HAL/MiG–21MF	USSR/India	Improved version produced under licence in India
1972–	26	HAL/HS–748	UK/India	Continued licence production to meet IAF order for 45
1972–	8	Aérospatiale Alouette III	France	For use on "Leander" class frigates
1972	200	HAL/Aérospatiale SA–315 Cheetah	France/India	Produced under licence in India
1973–74	6	Westland Sea King	UK	Option for 3; for ASW
. . .	. . .	HAL/HS Gnat Mk 2	UK/India	Production to be resumed of improved version
. . .	20	HAL/HS–748	UK/India	Freighter version to be produced under licence

Missiles

Date	Number	Item	Supplier	Comment
1963	(36)	K–13 "Atoll"	USSR	To arm MiG–21
1965–66	102	SA–2	USSR	17 sites; cost: $112 mn
1966–67	(540)	K–13 "Atoll"	USSR	To arm MiG–21
1967–73	(1120)	K–13 "Atoll"	USSR/India	Produced under licence in India; to arm MiG–21
(1968)	(50)	Nord AS.30	France	
1968–72	(75)	SA–2	USSR	8 batteries on 50 sites
1969	(50)	Nord Entac	France	
1969	(50)	Nord SS.11	France	
1971–72	(96)	SS–N–2 "Styx"	USSR	4 missile launchers in 2 pairs on motor torpedo boats
1971–73	(750)	Nord SS.11	France/India	Produced under licence in India; indigenous content 70 per cent by 1973/74
(1972)	(20)	Short Seacat	UK	2 quadruple launchers on frigate "Leander" class
1972–73	40 systems	Short Tigercat	UK	Cost: $10.4 mn
. . .	(100)	Short Seacat	UK	2 quadruple launchers on each of remaining 5 frigates "Leander" class

Date	Number	Item	Supplier	Comment
		Naval vessels		
1950	3	Destroyer, "R" class	UK	Displ: 1 725 t; completed 1942; refitted 1949
1953	3	Destroyer escort, "Hunt" class	UK	Displ: 1 050 t; 1 completed in 1941, 2 in 1944; on loan
1953	1	Oiler	Italy	Displ: 3 500 t
1954–55	2	Inshore minesweeper, "Ham" class	UK	Displ: 120 t; launched 1954
1956	4	Coastal minesweeper, "Ton" class	UK	Displ: 360 t; completed 1956
1957	1	Cruiser, "Colony" class	UK	Displ: 8 700 t; completed 1940; refitted 1954
1957–58	4	Seaward defence craft, "Savitri" class	Italy	Displ: 63 t; 1 completed in 1957, 3 in 1958
1958	1	Anti-aircraft frigate, "Leopard" class	UK	Displ: 2 251 t; completed 1958
1958	3	Anti-submarine frigate, "Backwood" class	UK	Displ: 1 180 t; 1 completed in 1958, 2 in 1959
1959	2	Seaward defence craft, "Sharada" class	Yugoslavia	Displ: 86 t; completed 1959
1960	2	Anti-aircraft frigate, "Leopard" class	UK	Displ: 2 251 t; completed 1960
1960	2	Anti-submarine frigate, "Whitby" class	UK	Displ: 2 144 t; completed 1960
1961	1	Aircraft carrier, "Majestic" class	UK	Displ: 16 000 t; launched 1945; sold to India 1957; completed 1961
1966	2	Landing craft, "Polnocny" class	USSR	Displ: 900 t
1967	5	Fast patrol boat, "Poluchat" class	USSR	Displ: 100 t
1968	1	Submarine tender, modified "Ugra" type	USSR	Displ: 6 000 t light
1968	2	Landing craft, "Polnocny" class	USSR	Displ: 900 t
(1968)	1	Fast patrol boat, "Poluchat" class	USSR	Displ: 100 t
1968–69	2	Submarine, "F" class	USSR	Displ: 2 000 t surface, 2 300 t submerged
1969	5	Frigate, "Petya" class	USSR	Displ: 1 050 t
1970	2	Submarine, "F" class	USSR	Displ: 2 000 t surface, 2 300 t submerged
1971	1	Submarine tender	USSR	Displ: 790 t; ex-Soviet fleet minesweeper
(1971)	1	Frigate, "Petya" class	USSR	Displ: 1 050 t
1971–72	8	Motor torpedo boat	USSR	Similar to "Osa" class; armed with "Styx" SSMs
1972	2	Frigate, "Petya" class	USSR	Displ: 1 050 t
1972	6	Frigate, "Leander" class	UK/India	Displ: 2 450 t; being built in India; armed with "Seacat" SAMs
		Armoured fighting vehicles		
1950	(120)	Daimler and Humber AC	UK	
1953	180	M–4 Sherman	USA	Large numbers supplied before 1950

Date	Number	Item	Supplier	Comment
1956–57	210	Centurion	UK	
(1956–57)	(50)	Ferret	UK	
1957–58	150	AMX–13	France	
1964	70	PT–76	USSR	
(1965)	80	PT–76	USSR	
1967–73	500	Vijayanta	UK/India	Version of Vickers 37 produced under licence; indigenous content 68 per cent 1972
1968–71	225	T–54	Czechoslovakia	
1968–71	225	T–55	USSR	
1969–72	(120)	OT–62A	Czechoslovakia/India	Produced under licence in India
1971	(30)	OT–64	Czechoslovakia	

Register 18. Arms supplies to Nepal

Date	Number	Item	Supplier	Comment
		Aircraft		
(1962)	3	Scottish Aviation Twin Pioneer	UK	
(1963)	(1)	Il–14	USSR	Gift
1970–71	2	Short Skyvan	(UK)	
(1971)	2	Douglas C–47	Australia	
(1972)	1	Aérospatiale Alouette III	(France)	
(1972)	3	DHC–6 Twin Otter	(Canada)	
		Armoured fighting vehicles		
(1969–70)	(5)	AMX–13	Israel	

Register 19. Arms supplies to Pakistan

Date	Number	Item	Supplier	Comment
		Aircraft		
1950	10	Hawker Sea Fury FB.60 and T.61	UK	
(1950–52)	(5)	Short S.A.6 Sealand	UK	
(1950–55)	62	Bristol Freighter Mk 21/31	UK	
1951–53	36	Vickers Attacker F.1	UK	
1956	10	Lockheed T–33A	USA	
1956–58	120	NA F–86F Sabre	USA	MAP

Date	Number	Item	Supplier	Comment
(1957)	6	Lockheed RT–33A	USA	
(1957)	1	Vickers Viscount 734	UK	
1958	26	Martin B–57B Canberra	USA	MAP
(1958)	(6)	Martin RB–57 Canberra	USA	
1958–62	(75)	Cessna 0–1 Birddog	USA	
(1960–61)	(15)	Bell 47	USA	
(1960–62)	(15)	Sikorsky S–55	USA	
1962	(2)	Lockheed F–104B Star-fighter	USA	Probably refurbished
1962	12	Lockheed F–104A Star-fighter	USA	Ex-USAF; probably refurbished
(1962)	4	Grumman HU–16A Albatross	USA	
1963	4	Lockheed C–130E Hercules	USA	
1963	4	Kaman HH–43B Huskie	USA	
1963	25	Cessna T–37B	USA	
1965	4	MiG–15 UTI	China	
1965	1	Fokker Friendship	Netherlands	
1966	4	Il–28	China	
1966	40	F–6 (MiG–19)	China	
1966	90	NA F–86 Sabre	FR Germany/Iran	
1966–67	2	Lockheed C–130E Hercules	USA	
1967	1	HS Trident IE	UK	
1967	4	Lockheed C–130B Hercules	Iran	
1968	4	Sud Alouette III	France	
1968	18	Dassault Mirage III EP	France	
1968	3	Dassault Mirage III RP	France	
1968	3	Dassault Mirage III DP	France	
1968	3	Lockheed TF–104G Star-fighter	Belgium	
1968–71	12	Mi–8	USSR	U.c.: $504 000 approx; repayable over 10 years; operated by Army
1971	4	Cessna T–37	USA	
1971	(50)	F–6 (MiG–19)	China	
1971	10	Lockheed F–104 Star-fighter	Jordan	Believed to have been returned after 1971 war with India
1971	3	Northrop F–5 Freedom Fighter	Libya	Believed to have been returned
1971	2	Aérospatiale Alouette II	Saudi Arabia	Reportedly on loan
1971	10	DHC–2 Beaver	Saudi Arabia	Reportedly on loan
1972	(60)	F–6 (MiG–19)	China	
(1972)	1	Dassault Falcon	France	For VIP
1972–	(5)	Cessna/Dhamial 0–1 Birddog	USA/Pakistan	Assembled from previously acquired spares; indigenous content 60 per cent approx
1972–	10	Aérospatiale/Dhamial Alouette III	France/Pakistan	Produced under licence in Pakistan
1972–	28	Dassault Mirage V	France	20 delivered by end 1973
(1972)	2	Dassault Mirage III	France	
1974–	47	Saab MFI–17	Sweden	
...	10	Sikorsky helicopter	USA	On order

Date	Number	Item	Supplier	Comment
. . .	6	Westland Sea King	UK	On order; u.c.: $2.16 mn; for ASW
. . .	40	Northrop F–5 Freedom Fighter	Iran	To receive when Iran re-equips with F–5E. May also get NA F–86, Lockheed C–130 and helicopters
		Missiles		
(1958–64)	(400)	NWC Sidewinder	USA	To arm F–86, F–104, MiG–19 and Mirage
1965–	(500)	MBB Bo Cobra	FR Germany/ Pakistan	U.c.: $756; being built under licence in Pakistan
(1968)	(72)	Matra R–530	France	To arm Mirage; limited use due to high unit cost
		Naval vessels		
1951	1	Destroyer	UK	Displ: 1 800 t; completed 1941–42
1955	1	Coastal minesweeper	USA	Displ: 335 t; MAP transfer
1955	1	Tug	Netherlands	Dimensions: 105 x 30 x 11 ft; completed 1955
1956	1	Light cruiser, "Dido" class	UK	Displ: 5 900 t; completed 1944; refitted 1957; adapted for training 1961
1956	1	Coastal minesweeper	USA	Displ: 335 t; MAP transfer
1956–57	2	Destroyer, "Battle" class	UK	Displ: 2 325 t; completed 1946; 1 refitted in UK 1956; 1 refitted in USA under MAP
1957	2	Coastal minesweeper	USA	Displ: 335 t; MAP transfer
1958	2	Destroyer, "CH" class	USA/UK	Displ: 335 t; completed 1945; purchased by USA from UK under MAP; refitted in UK; 1 scrapped
1958	2	Destroyer, "CV" class	UK	Displ: 1 730 t; completed 1946; refitted in UK under MAP
1959	2	Coastal minesweeper	USA	Displ: 335 t; MAP transfer
1959	1	Tug	USA	Displ: 1 235 t; completed 1943; MAP transfer
(1959)	1	Water carrier	USA/Italy	Offshore procurement; built for MAP
1960	2	Tug	USA/Italy	Offshore procurement; built for MAP
1960	1	Oiler	USA/Italy	Displ: 600 t; offshore procurement; built for MAP
1962	1	Coastal minesweeper	USA	Displ: 335 t; MAP transfer
1963	1	Oiler	USA	Displ: 5 730 t; on loan under MAP
1963	1	Coastal minesweeper	USA	Displ: 335 t; MAP transfer
1964	1	Submarine, "Tench" class	USA	Displ: 1 570 t; completed 1945; ex-US; on loan
1965	4	Patrol boat, "Town" class	UK	Displ: 115 t; completed 1965
1970–71	3	Submarine, "Daphne" class	France	Displ: 700 t; new
1971–72	9	Motor gunboat, "Shanghai" class	China	Displ: 120 t full load; 4 may be converted for missile firing in Pakistan
. . .	2	Frigate, "Whitby" class	UK	Displ: 2 560 t; ex-British; on order

Date	Number	Item	Supplier	Comment
		Armoured fighting vehicles		
(1950)	(10)	Daimler AC	UK/India	
1954–55	50	M–41 Bulldog	USA	
(1954–55)	(150)	M–24 Chaffee	USA	
(1954–55)	200	M–4 Sherman	USA	
1955–60	400	M–47 and M–48 Patton	USA	
1955–65	300	M–113	USA	
(1958)	(20)	M–36	USA	
1965–66	(80)	T–59	China	
[1968	100	M–47 Patton	Italy]	Conflicting information as to whether Pakistan received
1969	150	T–54/55	USSR	
(1969–70)	(20)	PT–76	USSR	
1970–71	110	T–59	China	
1972	(100)	T–59	China	
1973	300	M–113	USA	

Register 20. Arms supplies to Sri Lanka

Date	Number	Item	Supplier	Comment
		Aircraft		
1953	9	Boulton Paul Balliol	UK	
1953	12	DH Chipmunk T.21	UK	
(1953–54)	(2)	Airspeed Oxford	UK	
1955	2	Westland Dragonfly	UK	
1955	2	Scottish Aviation Twin Pioneer C.C. Mk 2	UK	
1955–58	6	DH Dove	UK	
1958	2	Scottish Aviation Twin Pioneer C.C. Mk 2	UK	
1959	12	BAC Jet Provost T.51	UK	
1959–60	4	DH Heron	UK	
(1964)	1	Hiller UH–12 E	(USA)	
1969	3	Bell 206A Jet Ranger	USA	
1971	6	Bell 206A Jet Ranger	USA/UK	Military aid from UK
1971	6	Bell 47	USA/UK	Military aid from UK
1971	5	MiG–17	USSR	Long-term credit
1971	1	MiG–15 UTI	USSR	
1971	2	Ka–26	USSR	
1972	4	Bell 206A Jet Ranger	USA	MAP
1973	10	Cessna 150	USA	
		Naval vessels		
1955	1	Seaward defence boat, "Ford" class	UK	Displ: 120 t; ex-British
1955	4	Small patrol boat, "Seruwa" class	Italy	Displ: 13 t; u.c.: $40 000 approx
1956	2	Patrol boat, "Hansaya" class	Italy	Displ: 36 t; u.c.: $100 000 approx

Date	Number	Item	Supplier	Comment
1959	1	Escort minesweeper, "Algerine" class	UK	Displ: 1 040 t; built 1943
1959	2	Frigate, "River" class	Israel	Displ: 1 445 t; completed 1944 in Canada; sold to Israel 1950
1964	1	Hydrofoil patrol boat	(UK)	New
1966	2	Patrol boat	UK/Singapore	Displ: 15 t; new; cost of 9: $4.2 mn
1967	7	Patrol boat	UK/Singapore	Displ: 15; new
1968	12	Patrol boat	UK/Singapore	Displ: 15 t; new; assembled in Sri Lanka
1972	5	Motor gunboat, "Shanghai" class	China	Displ: 100 t
		Armoured fighting vehicles		
(1960)	(15)	Ferret	UK	
(1960)	(15)	Daimler AC	UK	
1971	20	(BTR 152) AC	USSR	
1971	(35)	Ferret	UK	
1971	18	Saladin	UK	

Middle East

Register 21. Arms supplies to Abu Dhabi

Date	Number	Item	Supplier	Comment
		Aircraft		
1968–69	3	Britten-Norman BN–2 Islander	UK	
1968–69	4	Agusta-Bell AB.206 Jet Ranger	Italy	
1969	4	DHC–4A Caribou	Canada	
1970–71	12	HS Hunter FGA.9	UK	Refurbished
1970–71	2	HS Hunter T.7	UK	
1971	1	DHC–4A Caribou	Canada	
1972	1	Britten-Norman BN–2 Islander	UK	
1972	5	Aérospatiale Alouette III	France	
1972	3	Aérospatiale/Westland SA–330 Puma	France	
1973–74	12	Dassault Mirage 5	France	Incl 2 of the reconnaissance version
1973–74	2	Dassault Mirage 5D	France	
1973	2	Aérospatiale/Westland SA–330 Puma	France	
1974	2	Short Skyvan 3 M	UK	
. . .	2	Lockheed C–130 Hercules	USA	On order; delivery 1975
		Missiles		
(1972–73)	(159)	BAC Vigilant	UK	From 2 orders
. . .	. . .	Aérospatiale Nord SS.11	France	On order; cost $17 mn

Date	Number	Item	Supplier	Comment
		Naval vessels		
1969	3	Fast patrol boat, "Kaw-kab" type	(UK)	Displ: 32 t; new
1970–71	6	Patrol craft, "Dhafeer" type	UK	Displ: 10 t; new
1973–74	10	Patrol boat	UK	
		Armoured fighting vehicles		
(1968)	(15)	Ferret	UK	
(1968)	15	Saladin	UK	
(1968)	(10)	Saracen	UK	

Register 22. Arms supplies to Bahrain

Date	Number	Item	Supplier	Comment
		Aircraft		
1965–66	2	Westland Scout Mk 1	UK	
		Armoured fighting vehicles		
1971	2	Shorland Mk 2	UK	
(1972)	(8)	Ferret	UK	
(1972)	(8)	Saladin	UK	

Register 23. Arms supplies to Dubai

Date	Number	Item	Supplier	Comment
		Aircraft		
1972	2	Bell 206A Jet Ranger	USA	
(1973)	1	Cessna 182	USA	
...	2	Bell 205	USA	On order
...	1	Bell 206B Jet Ranger	USA	On order
...	3	Aermacchi MB.326K	Italy	On order
...	1	Aermacchi MB.326L	Italy	On order
...	1	SIAI-Marchetti SF.260	Italy	On order
		Armoured fighting vehicles		
...	...	Scorpion	UK	A small number on order

Register 24. Arms supplies to Egypt

Date	Number	Item	Supplier	Comment
		Aircraft		
1950–51	(2)	Bücker Bü 181 Bestmann	FR Germany	Prior to start of local production
1950	(10)	Avro Anson	UK	
1950	20	Supermarine Spitfire F.22	UK	Reconditioned
1950–51	12	Gloster Meteor F.8	UK	
1950–51	2	Gloster Meteor T.7	UK	
(1951)	(10)	Short S.A.6 Sealand	UK	
1953	(15)	DH Vampire F.52 and T.55	UK	
1953	30	DH Vampire Mk 5 and T.55	Syria	Syria received them from Italy; may be Fiat Macchi Vampire
(1953–54)	(5)	Curtiss C–46	USA	
(1953–54)	(1)	Beech C–45	(USA)	
(1953–54)	2	Westland Dragonfly	UK	
1954–55	(12)	Gloster Meteor F.8	UK	
(1954–55)	7	Douglas C–47	USA	
(1954–55)	1	Grumman HU–16A Albatross	(USA)	
(1954–55)	(3)	Sikorsky S–51	(USA)	
(1954–55)	(5)	DH 104 Dove Mk 1	UK	
1955	15	NA T–6 Harvard 2B	Canada	
1955–56	8	Gloster Meteor NF.13	UK	
1955–56	86	MiG–15 and MiG–15 UTI	Czechoslovakia	
1955–56	39	Il–28	Czechoslovakia	
1955–56	(10)	Il–14	Czechoslovakia	
(1955–56)	(10)	An–2	USSR	
(1955–56)	(5)	Sokol Falcon M–1–D	Czechoslovakia	
(1955–56)	6	Zlin 226 Bohatir	Czechoslovakia	
1956	(3)	An–12	USSR	
1956	2	MiG–15	USSR	
1956	25	Yak–11	Czechoslovakia	
1957	10	Il–14	USSR	
1957–58	80	MiG–17	USSR	
1957–58	(30)	Il–28	USSR	29 lost in June War 1967
(1957–59)	30	Yak–18	USSR/Czechoslovakia	
1958	(3)	An–12	USSR	
(1958)	(4)	Mi–1	USSR	
(1958–61)	40	Mi–4	USSR	1 lost in June War 1967
1959	(3)	An–12	USSR	8 lost in June War 1967
1960	(3)	An–12	USSR	8 kost in June War 1967
1961	1	DH 104 Dove	UK	
1961–62	80	MiG–19	USSR	40 lost in June War 1967
1961–62	10	Tu–16	USSR	All lost in June War 1967
1962	40	MiG–21C	USSR	95 MiG–21 lost in June War 1967
(1962)	(15)	Tu–16	USSR	All lost in June War 1967
1963–64	50	MiG–21C	USSR	95 MiG–21 lost in June War 1967

Date	Number	Item	Supplier	Comment
(1965)	8	Mi–6	USSR	All lost in June War 1967
1966	20	MiG–21D	USSR	95 MiG–21 lost in June War 1967
1967	14	Su–7	USSR	
1967	50	MiG–19	USSR	
1967	100	MiG–21	USSR	
1967	20	Il–28	USSR	
1967	3	An–12	USSR	
1967–68	10	Helwan HA–200	Egypt/Spain	Licensed production began 1964; only 10 have been completed
1968	25	MiG–21	USSR	
1968	50	Su–7	USSR	
1969	(50)	MiG–21	USSR	
1969–71	(60)	Su–7	USSR	
1970–71	120	MiG–21	USSR	
1970–71	80	Mi–8	USSR	
1971	20	Mi–6	USSR	
1971–72	17	Tu–16	USSR	
1971	55	MiG–15 and MiG–17	USSR	
1972	(25)	Su–7/Su–20	USSR	Incl a few of the Su–20 swing-wing version
1972	25	MiG–21	USSR	
1972	72	MiG–21MF	USSR	Flown by Soviet pilots, reportedly turned over to Egypt
[1973	(50)	MiG–17	USSR]	War replacement; incl 35–40 "Super MiGs" longer range MiG–21. In August 1974, Pres. Sadat denied having received replacements.
[1973	(30)	MiG–19	USSR]	
[1973	(110)	MiG–21	USSR]	
[1973	(45)	Su–7	USSR]	
[1973	(25)	Mi–8	USSR]	
...	24	Westland Commando	UK	Ordered via Saudi Arabia; delivery from 1974
...	6	Westland Sea King	UK	

Missiles

Date	Number	Item	Supplier	Comment
(1961)	(159)	AS–1 "Kennel"	USSR	To arm Tu–16
1962–66	540–660	K–13 "Atoll"	USSR	To arm MiG–21
1962–67	(48)	SS–N–2 "Styx"	USSR	To arm 8 "Komar" class patrol boats
1963–65	150	SA–2	USSR	25 batteries
(1963–65)	(500)	AT–1 "Snapper"	USSR	
1967	150	SA–2	USSR	
1967–72	(480)	K–13 "Atoll"	USSR	To arm MiG–21
1968	24	"Frog 3"	USSR	
1968	20	"Samlet"	USSR	
1968	30	SS–N–2 "Styx"	USSR	To arm "Osa" class patrol boats
1970–71	(160)	SA–3	USSR	20 batteries
1970–72	(360)	SA–2	USSR	30 batteries
1971	(50)	"Frog–7"	USSR	
(1971)	25	AS–5 "Kelt"	USSR	
1972	60	SA–6	USSR	Supplied during autumn in part replacement for missiles withdrawn by USSR in summer
1972–73	(300)	AT–1 "Snapper"	USSR	
1972–73	(400)	AT–3 "Sagger"	USSR	
1973	(180)	SA–6	USSR	
1973	(500)	SA–7	USSR	

Date	Number	Item	Supplier	Comment
1973	40–60	SS–TC "Scud"	USSR	In 4 units; capable of carrying nuclear warhead. Manned by Soviet personnel
(1973)	(30)	SA–4	USSR	
		Naval vessels		
1950	1	Escort, "Hunt" class	UK	Displ: 1 000 t; completed 1940
1950	2	Corvette	UK	Displ: 672; completed 1941
(1951)	2	Motor torpedo boat	UK	Displ: 100 t
1952	3	Motor launch	UK	Displ: 65 t
(1953–54)	8	Coastal minesweeper	USA	Displ: 215 t; 2 transferred to Algeria 1962
1955	2	Destroyer, "Z" class	UK	Displ: 1 730 t; completed 1944
1956	12	Motor torpedo boat, "P 6" class	USSR	Displ: 50 t; ex-Soviet
1956	4	Fleet minesweeper, "T43" class	USSR	Displ: 420 t; ex-Soviet
1956	2	Destroyer, "Skoryi" class	USSR	Displ: 2 600; launched 1951
1956	6	Motor torpedo boat	Yugoslavia	Displ: 56 t; ex-Yugoslav
1957	4	Submarine, "W" class	USSR	Displ: 1 030 t surface, 1 180 t submerged; ex-Soviet
1957	1	Submarine, "MV" class	USSR	Displ: 350 t surface, 420 t submerged; ex-Soviet
(1957)	2	Fleet minesweeper, "T43" class	USSR	Displ: 410; ex-Soviet
(1957–58)	18	Motor torpedo boat, "P6" class	USSR	Displ: 50 t; ex-Soviet
1958	3	Submarine, "W" class	USSR	Displ: 1 030 t surface, 1 180 t submerged; ex-Soviet
1962	2	Inshore minesweeper, "T–301" class	USSR	Displ: 130 t; ex-Soviet
1962	1	Submarine, "W" class	USSR	Displ: 1 030 t surface, 1 180 t submerged; ex-Soviet
1962–67	8	Patrol boat, "SOI" type	USSR	Displ: 215 t light, 220 t full load
1962–67	8	Patrol boat, "Komar" class	USSR	Displ: 75 t; ex-Soviet
1965	18	Landing craft, "MP" class	USSR	Displ: 22 t light, 35 t loaded; ex-Soviet
1965	1	Rocker assault ship, "Polnocny" class	USSR	Displ: 900 t; new "TRV" type
1966	5	Submarine, "R" class	USSR	Replace 2 "W" class returned 1966
1966	(5)	Fleet tug	USSR	Ex-Soviet
1966	12	Patrol boat, "Osa" class	USSR	Displ: 160 t; ex-Soviet
1967	3	Motor torpedo boat, "Shershen" class	USSR	Displ: 150 t; ex-Soviet
1968–70	3	Motor torpedo boat, "Shershen" class	USSR	Displ: 150 t; ex-Soviet
1968–70	4	Patrol boat, "SOI" type	USSR	Displ: 215 t light, 220 t full load; ex-Soviet
(1969)	1	Submarine, "R" type	USSR	Displ: 1 100 t
1970–71	4	Fleet minesweeper, "Yurka" type	USSR	Displ: 500 t; ex-Soviet
(1970–71)	10	Landing craft, "Vidra" type	USSR	Displ: 300 t; ex-Soviet

Date	Number	Item	Supplier	Comment
		Armoured fighting vehicles		
(1951–52)	(25)	Charioteer	UK	
1954–55	150	M–4 Sherman	USA	10 lost in June War 1967
1954–55	32	Centurion Mk III	UK	
1954–55	151	Valentine	(UK)/Belgium	Demilitarized
(1954–55)	20	AMX–13	France	20 lost in June War 1967
(1954–55)	(20)	AMX–105A	France	
1955–56	100	BTR 152	USSR	
(1955–59)	350	BTR 40	USSR	
1956	120	T–54/55	USSR	250 lost in June War 1967
1956	150	T–34	Czechoslova-kia	280 lost in June War 1967
1956	(50)	JSU–152	USSR	
(1956–62)	150	Su–100	USSR	
1957–58	25	JS III	USSR	40 lost in June War 1967
1959	35	JS III	USSR	
(1960–64)	(250)	T–34	USSR/Cze-choslovakia	
(1962–63)	(130)	T–54	USSR/Cze-choslovakia	
(1962–66)	600	BTR 152	USSR	
1964	(150)	T–54/55	USSR	
(1965)	(30)	T–10	USSR	
(1965–66)	(100)	BTR 50	USSR	
(1966)	50	PT–76	USSR	
1967–68	300	T–54	USSR	
(1967–69)	(200)	BTR–152	USSR	
(1968)	(200)	OT–62	Czechoslova-kia	
(1968–69)	(200)	BRDM AC	USSR	
1969	250	T–54	USSR	
1969	250	T–55	USSR	
1969	100	PT–76	USSR	
1969–70	(200)	OT–64	Czechoslova-kia	
1970–71	(350)	BTR 60 P	USSR	
(1970–72)	(850)	T–54/55	USSR	
1972–73	(100)	T–62	USSR	
(1972–73)	(150)	BMP 76	USSR	
1973	(300)	T–62	USSR	
1973	(150)	T–54/55	USSR	
1973	(150)	PT–76	USSR	
1973	(300)	AC/APC	USSR	

Register 25. Arms supplies to Iran

Date	Number	Item	Supplier	Comment
		Aircraft		
(1950–51)	(6)	Beech C–45	USA	
(1952–53)	12	Piper L–18 Super Cub	USA	

Date	Number	Item	Supplier	Comment
1955	(5)	NA T–6 Texan	USA	
1955	4	DHC–2 Beaver	Canada	
1956	16	Lockheed RT–33	USA	
1956	8	Lockheed T–33A	USA	
(1956–58)	(75)	Republic F–84G	USA	
1959	2	Westland Whirlwind	UK	
1959	70	Canadair CL–13 Sabre Mk 6	Canada	
(1960)	(2)	DHC–2 Beaver	Canada	
(1961)	1	Morane Saulnier M.S.760 Paris	France	
1963	4	Lockheed C–130B Hercules	USA	MAP; later sold to Pakistan
1965	91	Northrop F–5A Freedom Fighter	USA	MAP
1965	15	Northrop F–5B Freedom Fighter	USA	
1966	10	Kaman HH–43F Huskie	USA	
1966	90	Canadair Sabre 6	FR Germany	Transferred to Pakistan
1967	16	Lockheed C–130E Hercules	USA	
1968	2	Cessna 310L	USA	
1968	6	Kaman HH–43F Huskie	USA	
1968–69	32	McDonnell-Douglas F–4 Phantom	USA	Cost of first 16: $100 mn; cost of second; $40 mn
(1968–69)	(4)	McDonnell-Douglas RF–4 Phantom	USA	
1968–70	26	Northrop F–5A Freedom Fighter	USA	
1968–70	10	Lockheed C–130 Hercules	USA	
(1968–70)	7	Northrop F–5B Freedom Fighter	USA	
1969–70	56	Agusta-Bell 205 Iroquois	Italy	For Army and Navy
1969–70	70	Augusta-Bell 206A/B Jet Ranger	Italy	For Air Force, Army and Navy and Gendarmerie
1970	12	Cessna 337 Super Skymaster	USA	
1970–71	30	Lockheed C–130 Hercules	USA	
1971	32	McDonnell-Douglas F–4 Phantom	USA	
1971	(4)	McDonnel-Douglas RF–4 Phantom	USA	
1971	16	Sud SA–321 Super Frelon	France	Cost: $28 mn
1971	11	Agusta-Bell 212	Italy	For Air Force and Navy
1971	10	Fokker-VFW F–27	Netherlands	
1971–72	10	Agusta-Sikorsky SH–3D Sea King	USA/Italy	For Navy ASW operations
1971–73	20	Meridionali/Vertol CH–47C	USA/Italy	For Air Force and Army; 4 supplied directly from USA
1972–73	3	NA Rockwell Aero Commander	USA	Cost: $2.5 mn, incl Shrike Commander
1972–73	18	Beech F33 and 690 Bonanza	USA	Cost: $1 mn, incl spares, service support and training
1973	6	NA-Rockwell Shrike Commander	USA	Cost: $2.5 mn, incl Aero Commander 690

Date	Number	Item	Supplier	Comment
1973	4	Fokker-VFW F–28	Netherlands	
1973–74	6	Boeing 707–320	USA	Cost: $60 mn, paid in oil; for flight refuelling
1973–74	6	Fokker-VFW F–27	Netherlands	
. . .	108	McDonnell-Douglas F–4 Phantom	USA	On order; delivery up to 1975
. . .	141	Northrop F–5E Tiger II	USA	On order; delivery from 1974; u.c.: $1.16 mn incl avionics
. . .	6	Lockheed P3F Orion	USA	On order; delivery from mid-1974; cost: $60 mn, incl spares, service support and training
. . .	202	Bell AH–IJ Sea Cobra	USA	On order; delivery complete 1978–79; part of $700 mn arms deal
. . .	287	Bell 214A Isfahan	USA	See above; R&D paid almost entirely by Iran
. . .	12	Beech F33 Bonanza	USA	On order; delivery 1974; cost: $900 000 incl spares, service support and training
. . .	(24)	Lockheed C–130 Hercules	USA	On order
. . .	80	Grumman F–14 Tomcat	USA	On order; cost of first 30: $930 mn
. . .	22	Meridionali/Vertol CH–47	Italy	On order
. . .	91	Agusta-Bell 206 Jet Ranger	Italy	On order
. . .	6	Agusta-Bell 212	Italy	On order; provision for carrying AS.12 missiles
. . .	4	Fokker-VFW F–27 Friendship	Netherlands	On order; delivery late-1974-mid-1975
		Missiles		
1964	100+	Raytheon MIM–23 Hawk	USA	
1966	(20)	Short Seacat	UK	
1968–69	(384)	NWC Sidewinder	USA	To arm Phantoms
1968–69	(384)	Raytheon Sparrow III	USA	To arm Phantoms
1968–69	(25) systems	Short Tigercat	UK	
1970–71	(500)	Nord SS.11	France	
1970–71	(500)	Nord SS.12	France	
1971	(384)	NWC Sidewinder	USA	To arm Phantoms
1971	(384)	Raytheon Sparrow III	USA	To arm Phantoms
1971–72	2 batt	BAC Rapier	UK	Cost: $113 mn; incl associated technical maintenance and training support costs
1971–72	(40)	Short Seacat	UK	1 triple launcher on "SAAM" class frigate; cost: $2.5 mn
1971–72	(60)	Contraves Sea Killer	Italy	1 quintuple launcher on "SAAM" class frigates
1971–73	(500)	Hughes TOW	USA	For armoured infantry, infantry and helicopter units
. . .	2500	Hughes Maverick	USA	On order; sales agreement incl participation of Iranian industry in missile projects
. . .	. . .	Hughes Phoenix	USA	On order; to arm F–14
. . .	. . .	Raytheon MIM–23 Hawk	USA	Sold in FY 1973 under Foreign Military Sales Program

Date	Number	Item	Supplier	Comment
...	...	Hughes TOW	USA	On order; to arm Phantoms
...	...	NWC Sidewinder	USA	On order; to arm Phantoms and improved model on Bell helicopters and on F–14
...	...	Raytheon Sparrow	USA	
...	...	BAC Rapier	UK	On order
...	...	Short Tigercat	UK	On order; cost: $2 mn approx.; additional missile rounds for existing system
...	...	BAC Swingfire	UK	On order; to arm British ACs
...	...	Aérospatiale MM–38 Exocet	France	On order; to arm 6 patrol boats
Naval vessels				
1955	9	Coastguard cutter, "Azar" class	Italy	Displ: 65 t; new
1956	1	Patrol vessel	USA	Displ: 85 t; completed 1955
1956	1	Seaward defence vessel	UK	Displ: 46 t; ex-British
1956	1	Oiler	Italy	Displ: 1 250 t
1957	1	Patrol vessel	USA	Displ: 85 t; completed 1957
1957	1	Landing craft, "LSIL" class	USA	Displ: 210 t; completed 1944
1959	2	Patrol vessel	USA	Displ: 85 t; completed 1959
1959	1	Landing craft, "LSIL" class	USA	Displ: 210 t; completed 1944
1959–62	4	Coastal minesweeper	USA	Displ: 320 t; launched 1958–61
1960	1	Seaward defence vessel	UK	Displ: 46 t; ex-British
1962	1	Tug	USA	Displ: 150 t; ex-US
1964	2	Corvette, "PF" class	USA	Displ: 900 t; launched 1963
1964	1	Landing craft, "LCU" class	USA	Ex-US
1964	2	Inshore Minesweeper	USA	Displ: 180 t; completed 1944
1964	1	Water tanker	USA	Displ: 1 250 t; ex-US
1964	1	Landing craft, "LSIC" class	USA	Displ: 210 t; completed 1944; on loan
1967	1	Destroyer, "Battle" class	UK	Displ: 2 325 t; completed 1946
1968	1	Corvette, "PF" class	USA	Displ: 900 t
1969	1	Corvette, "PF" class	USA	Displ: 900 t
1969–70	8	Hovercraft, "Winchester" (SR.N 6) class	UK	Displ: 10 t; new; cost: $9.8 mn, incl 2 "Wellington" class
1970	3	Patrol boat, "PGM" type	USA	Displ: 105 t; new; MAP
1970	2	Hovercraft, "Wellington" (BH.7) class	UK	Displ: 48 t; new; cost: $9.8 mn incl 8 "Winchester" class
1971	1	Repair ship	USA	Displ: 7 826 t; launched 1945
1971–72	4	Frigate, "SAAM" class	UK	Displ: 1 200 t; new; armed with Seacat SAMs and Sea Killer SSMs
1972	3	Destroyer, "Allen M. Sumner" class	USA	Displ: 2 200 t; launched 1944; 2 modernized; used for spares and training
1973-	4	Hovercraft, "Wellington" (BH.7) class	UK	On order; delivery 1973–75; cost: $13 mn approx
...	2	Store ship	UK	On order; delivery 1974; 300 ft
...	6	Missile patrol boat	France	On order; displ: 230 t; armed with Exocet SSMs
...	3	Patrol boat	FR Germany	On order; displ: 70 t

Date	Number	Item	Supplier	Comment
		Armoured fighting vehicles		
1951	15	Sherman	USA	
(1954–56)	(50)	M–24 Chaffee	USA	
(1955–57)	(100)	M–8 Greyhound	USA	
(1955–57)	(120)	M–20	USA	
(1958–62)	(400)	M–47 Patton	USA	
(1966–68)	460	M–60A1	USA	
(1966–68)	300	M–113	USA	
1967–68	270	BTR 50	USSR ⎫	Cost of Soviet APCs and trucks: $110 mn; to be paid in 8 instal-
1967–68	300	BTR 60	USSR ⎭	ments at 2-3 per cent
1971-	800	Chieftain	UK	On order; delivery 1971-75; cost: $350 mn approx, incl spares, support equipment and training
1973	(25)	M–107	USA	
1973	(25)	M–109	USA	
1973	(25)	M–110	USA	
. . .	300	Scorpion	UK	On order
. . .	300	Fox	UK	On order

Register 26. Arms supplies to Iraq

Date	Number	Item	Supplier	Comment
		Aircraft		
1951	15	DH Chipmunk T.20	UK	
(1951)	16	NA T–6 Harvard 2B	UK	Ex-RAF
(1951)	28	Hawker Fury	UK	Incl 3 trainers
1953	9	DH Vampire Mk 52	UK	
1953	3	DH Vampire T.55	UK	
1953	10	Bristol Beaufighter Mk 10	UK	
1953	6	DH Chipmunk	UK	
(1954)	4	Bristol 170 Freighter	UK	
1954	4	Westland Dragonfly	UK	
1955	15	Hunting Provost T.53	UK	
1955	14	DH Venom FB.50	UK	
(1955)	5	NA F–86 Sabre	USA	US military aid agreement of 1954
(1955)	1	DHC–2 Beaver	Canada	
1956	3	DH Vampire Mk 52	UK	
1956	3	DH Vampire T.55	UK	
1956	2	DH Heron	UK	
1957–58	15	Hawker Hunter T.6	UK	5 as gift
1958	19	MiG–15	Egypt	
1958–60	17	MiG–17	USSR	Night fighting version in 1960
1958–60	(15)	Yak–11	USSR	
(1958–60)	(15)	Il–14	USSR	5 lost in June War 1967
1959	10	Il–28	USSR	
1959	10	MiG–15 UTI	USSR	
(1959)	1	Il–28 U	USSR	

Date	Number	Item	Supplier	Comment
(1959)	(2)	An–2	USSR	
1960–62	17	MiG–19	USSR	
(1962)	10	Tu–16	USSR	1 lost in June War 1967
(1962)	4	Mi–1	USSR	
(1962–65)	8	An–12	USSR	
1963–64	12	MiG–21	USSR	
1963–64	24	HS Hunter F.59	UK	From Belgian and Dutch stocks, refurbished
1964	5	HS Hunter T.69	UK	
1964	20	BAC Jet Provost T.52	UK	
(1964)	9	Mi–4	USSR	
1964–65	12	Westland Wessex	UK	
1964–65	18	HS Hunter FGA.59	UK	
1966	4	HS Hunter FR.59	UK	
1966–67	(50)	MiG–21	USSR	13 lost in June War 1967
1967	20	Su–7	USSR	
1967	5	Il–14	USSR	Replacement
1968	1	HS 748	India	Assembled in Kanpur
(1968)	(5)	L–29 Delfin	Czechoslova-kia	
(1968–70)	30	Su–7	USSR	
1968–71	(36)	MiG–21	USSR	
(1969)	10	An–24	USSR	
1970	16	Aérospatiale Alouette III	France	
(1970–71)	(25)	Mi–4	USSR	
1971	3	Britten-Norman BN–2 Islander	UK	For photographic survey work
(1971)	12	Mi–8	USSR	
(1971)	2	Tu–124	USSR	
1973	(10)	MiG–21MF	USSR	
1973	(5)	Su–7	USSR	
1973	(5)	Mi–6	USSR	
1973	(15)	MiG–21	USSR	War replacements
1973-	. . .	L–39	Czechoslova-kia	On order; delivery from 1973
. . .	31	Aérospatiale Alouette III	France	On order
Missiles				
1962–65	30	SA–2	USSR	5 launching sites
(1963–67)	(372)	K–13 "Atoll"	USSR	To arm MiG–21
(1968–71)	(216)	K–13 "Atoll"	USSR	To arm MiG–21
1971	(12)	SA–2	USSR	
1972	(12)	SS–N–2 "Styx"	USSR	
1972–73	(24)	SA–3	USSR	
Naval vessels				
1959	2	Motor torpedo boat, "P6" class	USSR	Displ: 50 t
1960	4	Motor torpedo boat, "P6" class	USSR	Displ: 50 t
1961	6	Motor torpedo boat, "P6" class	USSR	Displ: 50 t
1962	3	Submarine chaser	USSR	Displ: 220 t; ex-Soviet
(1962)	8	Patrol boat	UK	

Date	Number	Item	Supplier	Comment
(1964)	6	Small patrol boat	USSR	
1972	2	Missile boat, ("Komar" class)	USSR	Displ: 75 t; armed with "Styx" SSMs
		Armoured fighting vehicles		
(1953–55)	(25)	Churchill	UK	
(1953–55)	20	Ferret	UK	
1954–56	(80)	Centurion	UK	
1956	10	Centurion	UK	
1956–58	40	M–24 Chaffee	USA	Under 1954 military aid agreements
1957	20	Centurion	UK	
1959	80	T–54	USSR	
1959	45	T–34	USSR	
1959–61	(25)	JS III	USSR	
1959–61	20	T–54	USSR	
1960–64	200	BTR 152	USSR	
1960–65	(80)	T–34	USSR	
1960–65	(150)	T–54	USSR	
1963	(100)	Saracen	UK	
(1966–68)	(50)	T–34	USSR	
(1968)	(50)	T–54	USSR	
(1968–70)	(45)	PT–76	USSR	
(1970)	70	Panhard AML–60/90	France	

Register 27. Arms supplies to Israel

Date	Number	Item	Supplier	Comment
		Aircraft		
(1950)	21	NA T–6 Harvard	USA	
(1950–53)	60	DH Mosquito NF.38	France	U.c.: $200; sold for scrap; overhauled in Israel
(1951)	(5)	Boeing-Sterman Kaydet PT.17	USA	
1952	40	Fokker Instructor S–11	Netherlands	
1952	4	NA F–51 Mustang	Sweden	Surplus
(1952)	(5)	Avro Anson	UK	
(1952)	(5)	Airspeed Consul	UK	
1953	(10)	Piper L–18B	USA	
1953	(10)	Piper L–21	USA	
1953	20	DH Mosquito NF.38	UK	
1953	14	Gloster Meteor F.8	UK	
1953	(5)	Gloster Meteor T.7	UK	
1953	21	NA F–51 Mustang	Sweden	Surplus
(1953)	(5)	Max Holste M.H. 1521 Broussard	France	
1954	6	Gloster Meteor NF.13	UK	
1955	15	Dassault M.D. 450 Ouragon	France	

Date	Number	Item	Supplier	Comment
1955	24	Dassault Mystère IV A	France	
1956	45	Dassault M.D. 450 Ouragon	France	10 lost in 1956
1956	36	Dassault Mystère IV A	France	
1956	8	Nord 2501 Noratlas	France	
1957–59	24	Sud Vautour 2	France	
(1958)	2	Sikorsky S–55	USA	
1959	24	Dassault Super Mystère B.2	France	
(1959)	6	Boeing C 97 Strato-freighter	USA	
(1959)	(5)	Bell 47G	USA	
(1959)	2	Hiller UH–12A	USA	
(1959–62)	(50)	Piper L–21	USA	
1960	2	Convair PBY–5 A Catalina	USA	
1960	7	Sikorsky S–58	USA	
1960	6	Nord 2501 Noratlas	France	
1960	24	Sikorsky S–58	FR Germany	Bought for Bundeswehr but diverted to Israel with US approval
1960–64	100	Potez/Bedek CM 170 Magister	France/Israel	U.c.: $200 000; built under licence
(1961)	5	Sud Alouette III	France	
1962–64	72	Dassault Mirage III–CJ	France	
1963	2	Pilatus Turbo-Porter	(Switzerland)	
1965	6	Sud SA–321 Super Frelon	France	
(1965–66)	15	Sud Alouette III	France	
(1966–67)	18	Nord 2501 Noratlas	France	
1968	48	McDonnel Douglas A–4H Skyhawk	USA	
1968	7	Sud SA–321 Super Frelon	France	
1968	25	Fouga Magister	France/FR Germany	Ex-Bundeswehr; refurbished by Sud Aviation
1968–69	25	Agusta-Bell 205 Iroquois	Italy	
1969	10	Sikorsky S–65A	USA	
1969–70	42	McDonnell Douglas A–4H Skyhawk	USA	
1969–70	10	McDonnell Douglas TA–4 Skyhawk	USA	
1969–71	80	McDonnell Douglas F–4 Phantom	USA	Incl replacements
(1970)	6	McDonnell Douglas RF–4 Phantom	USA	
(1970–71)	6	Boeing 377 Stratocruiser	USA	Ex-USAF
1971	18	McDonnell Douglas A–4H Skyhawk	USA	
1971	43	McDonnell Douglas A–4E Skyhawk	USA	Refurbished
1971–72	(6)	Lockheed C–130 Hercules	USA	
1972	(10)	Bell 206 Jet Ranger	USA	
1972–73	42	McDonnell-Douglas F–4 Phantom	USA	
1972–74	80	McDonnell-Douglas A–4N Skyhawk	USA	

Date	Number	Item	Supplier	Comment
1973	(25)	McDonnell-Douglas F–4 Phantom	USA	War replacement; from USAF
1973	(60)	McDonnell-Douglas A–4 Phantom	USA	War replacement; from US Marine Corp
1973	12	Lockheed C–130 Hercules	USA ⎫	During Oct 1973 War
1973	(6)	Sikorsky S–65	USA ⎭	
1973-	8	Boeing-Vertol CH–47	USA	
1973-	12	Sikorsky S–61	USA	
. . .	48	McDonnell Douglas F–4 Phantom	USA	On order; delivery by 1977
. . .	36	McDonnell-Douglas A–4N Skyhawk	USA	On order; delivery by 1977
		Missiles		
1956	(200)	Nord SS.10	France	
(1962–64)	(300)	Nord AS.30	France	To arm Mirage
(1962–65)	(500)	MBB Bo Cobra	FR Germany	In first phase of aid programme
1963	288	Raytheon MIM–23A Hawk	USA	$25 mn contract; 10-year loan at 3.5 per cent interest
1963	(150)	Nord.Entac	France	
(1963)	(150)	Nord SS.11	France	
1966	100+	Matra R.530	France	To arm Mirage
1968	128	Raytheon MIM–23A Hawk	USA	
1969	2	Dassault MD–660	France	Joint development; capable of carrying nuclear warhead
1969–73	(1944)	Raytheon Sparrow III	USA	To arm Phantom
1969–73	(1464)	Martin Bullpup	USA	To arm Phantom
1970–71	(300)	Shrike	USA	
1972–73	(336)	NWC Sidewinder	USA	Improved version to arm Phantom
1973	(200)	Hughes Maverick	USA ⎫	
1973	(500)	Hughes TOW	USA ⎪	
1973	(2000)	NWC Sidewinder	USA ⎬	In airlift during Oct 1973 War
1973	(500)	NWC Shrike	USA ⎪	
1973	(50)	Raytheon MIM–23 Hawk	USA ⎭	
. . .	. . .	Short Blowpipe	UK	On order; 4 launchers on each of 3 submarines
		Naval vessels		
(1950)	1	Coastguard cutter	USA	Displ: 2 150 t; built 1927
(1950)	1	Patrol vessel	USA	Displ: 295 t; ex-US
1950–51	2	Motor torpedo boat	France	Displ: 62 t
1952–53	2	Motor torpedo boat	France	Displ: 62 t
(1952–55)	4	Landing craft	USA	Displ: 1 of 22 t, 1 of 230 t, 2 of 143 t
1954–55	2	Motor torpedo boat	France	Displ: 62 t
1955	2	Patrol vessel	UK	Displ: 46 t; built 1943; ex-British
(1955)	(2)	Landing craft	UK	Displ: 143 t; ex-British
1956	2	Destroyer, "Z" class	UK	Displ: 1 710 t; completed 1944; refitted
1956–57	2	Patrol boat	FR Germany	Displ: 96 t; built 1956–57; possibly operated by customs service
1956–57	3	Motor torpedo boat	Italy	Displ: 40 t; built 1956–57; u.c.: $300 000

Date	Number	Item	Supplier	Comment
1959–60	2	Submarine, "S" class	UK	Displ: 815 t surface, 1 000 t submerged; completed 1945; refitted
1967–68	3	Submarine, "T" class	UK	Displ: 1 535 t surface, 1 740 t submerged; 2 completed in 1944, 1 in 1945; refitted
1968–69	12	Gunboat, "Saar" class	France	Displ: 220 t; new; incl 5 brought from Cherbourg after imposition of French embargo; armed with Gabriel SAMs in Israel
1968–69	4	Patrol boat	Japan	Displ: 32 t; new
1970	12	Patrol boat, "PBR" type	(USA)	Displ: 7.5 t
(1972)	6	Patrol boat, "Swift" class	USA	Displ: 22.5 t full load; ex-US
. . .	. . .	Patrol boat, "Firefish III" type	USA	On order; displ: 6 t; capable of being remote-controlled
. . .	3	Submarine	UK	Displ: 500 t; being built from FR German design to be armed with Blowpipe SAMs

Armoured fighting vehicles

Date	Number	Item	Supplier	Comment
1950–51	150	M–4 Sherman Mk 3	USA	
1950–51	(25)	Cromwell	UK	
(1950–51)	(100)	M–9	(UK)	
(1950–51)	(100)	M–5	(France)	
1954–56	150	AMX–13	France	
1955	(30)	AMX–105	France	
1955–56	(300)	M–2 and M–3	France	
1955–56	100	M–4 Sherman	France	
1957–66	250	Centurion	UK	
1961–63	(30)	AML–60/90	France	
1964–66	200+	M–48 Patton	USA/FR Germany	Ex-Bundeswehr; aid
(1965–67)	(100)	M–113	USA	
1966–67	(50)	AML–60	France	
1967–69	150	M–113	USA	
1967–69	240	Centurion	UK	
(1968–69)	(100)	M–48 Patton	USA	
1970	24	M–109	USA	Cost: $3.5 mn
(1970)	(45)	M–6 Staghound	USA	
1970–71	(130)	M–48 Patton	USA	
1970–71	(50)	M–60	USA	
(1970–71)	(50)	M–113	USA	
1970–73	(400)	Centurion	UK/Netherlands	
1972	(25)	M–107	USA	
1972–73	100	M–60	USA	
1973	(100)	M–48 Patton	USA	} War replacements
1973	(150)	M–60	USA	

Register 28. Arms supplies to Jordan

Date	Number	Item	Supplier	Comment
		Aircraft		
1950	1	Auster T.7	UK	
1950	2	Auster Autocrat	UK	
1950	5	Auster AOP.6 and 7	UK	
1950	4	DH Dove	UK	
1953	2	Auster Aiglet	UK	
1953	1	Auster T.7	UK	
1953	1	Vickers Viking	UK	Ex-BEA
1954	1	Handley Page Marathon	UK	
1954	3	MKEK4 Ugur	Turkey	Gift
1954–56	8	DH Chipmunk T.10	UK	Partly ex-RAF
1955	10	DH Vampire FB.9	UK	Ex-RAF
1955	2	DH Vampire T.55	UK	Ex-RAF
1955	3	Heliopolis Air Works Gomhuriah	Egypt	Gift
1956	3	NA T–6 Harvard 2B	UK	Ex-RAF
1956	1	Vickers Varsity	UK	Ex-RAF, specially modified for VIP transport, later presented to King Saud
1956–57	7	DH Vampire FB.52	Egypt	Gift
1958	1	Beech Twin Bonanza	USA	
1958	12	Hawker Hunter F.6	UK	US offshore procurement
1958	2	DH Heron 2D	UK	
1958	1	Westland Widgeon	UK	
1959–60	3	Airspeed Ambassador	UK	At least 2; ex-BEA
1960	1	Hawker Hunter FR.6	UK	
1960	1	DH Vampire T.55	UK	Ex-RAF
1960	2	Westland Whirlwind	UK	
1960–62	2	Hawker Hunter T.66B	UK	
1962	13	Hawker Hunter F.6	UK	18 destroyed in June War 1967
1963	4	Douglas C–47	USA	
1963	2	Handley Page Herald 400	UK	Traded for 2 ex-BEA Ambassadors
1964	3	Westland Scout	UK	
1965	2	DH Dove 8	UK	
1965	4	Sud Alouette III	France	
1966	1	Hawker Hunter T.66	UK	
1967	2	Lockheed F–104A Starfighter	USA	Delivered and withdrawn before June war 1967
1967	3	Lockheed F–104B Starfighter	USA	
1967	2	Hawker Hunter F.6	UK	Delivered before June War 1967
1967	3	Sud Alouette III	France	
1967	7	HS Hunter FGA.9	UK	U.c.: $600 000; 4 had already served in RJAF but were being over-hauled in UK in June 1967
1967	4	NA F–86F Sabre	Pakistan	Gift, interim aid after June War 1967
1967	5	HS Hunter	Saudi Arabia	
1968	4	HS Hunter FGA.9	UK	
1969	18	Lockheed F–104 Starfighter	USA	Refurbished
1969	14	HS Hunter	UK	Ex-Dutch stocks; incl 3 trainers

Date	Number	Item	Supplier	Comment
1970	18	Lockheed F–104 Starfighter	USA	Ex-Taiwan; refurbished
1970	4	HS Hunter FGA.73	UK	
1971–72	12	HS Hunter FGA.73	UK	
1972	2	Fairchild C–119K Packet	USA	Delivered out of 4 ordered; refurbished
1972–73	6	Northrop F–5B	USA	
1973	(3)	Lockheed C–130 Hercules	USA	Refurbished; ex–US
1973-	24	Northrop F–5E Tiger II	USA	On order; delivery from 1973; MAP
. . .	. . .	Bell UH–1	USA	On order; delivery held up due to lack of funds
		Missiles		
1969–70	(140)	Short Tigercat	UK	Cost: $16 mn; paid with credit from Saudi Arabia
1974	. . .	Hughes TOW	USA	Being supplied under MAP
		Armoured fighting vehicles		
(1954)	50	Charioteer 6	UK	Transferred to Lebanon in 1965
(1954–56)	50	Centurion	UK	
(1954–56)	(100)	Ferret	UK	
(1957)	(50)	M–47/48 Patton	USA	Gift
(1960–62)	(100)	Saracen	UK	
(1962–64)	(130)	Saladin	UK	
1965–66	(100)	M–47/48 Patton	USA	Gift
(1965–67)	(100)	M–113	USA	
1968	100	M–47/48 Patton	USA	
1968–69	(20)	Saracen	UK	
1968–69	(40)	Ferret	UK	
1969	100	Centurion Mk 9 and Mk 10	UK	
(1970–71)	(24)	M–52	USA	
1971–72	100	M–60	USA	
1972–74	200	M–113	USA	

Register 29. Arms supplies to Kuwait

Date	Number	Item	Supplier	Comment
		Aircraft		
(1956)	2	DH Devon	UK	To Security Department of Kuwait
(1957)	1	DH Heron	UK	To Security Department of Kuwait
(1958)	5	Auster Aiglet	UK	To Security Department of Kuwait
(1958)	3	Auster Autocrat	(UK)	To Security Department of Kuwait
1961	6	Hunting Jet Provost T.51	UK	
(1962)	2	Westland Whirlwind Series 1	UK	
1964–65	4	HS Hunter FGA.57	UK	
1964–65	2	HS Hunter T.67	UK	
1966	2	DHC–4 Caribou	Canada	

Date	Number	Item	Supplier	Comment
1968	2	HS Hunter FGA.9	UK	Ex-RAF
1968–69	12	BAC Lightning F.53	UK	
1968–69	2	BAC Lightning T.55	UK	
1968–69	6	Agusta-Bell 204B	Italy	
1969	6	BAC 167 Strikemaster	UK	
1969	3	HS Hunter T.69	UK	
1970	4	Agusta-Bell 206A Jet Ranger	Italy	
1971	2+	Lockheed C–130 Hercules	USA	
1971	6	BAC 167 Strikemaster	UK	
. . .	32	Dassault Mirage F.1	France	On order; delivery from 1974
. . .	10	Aércspatiale SA–330 Puma	France	On order
. . .	20	Aérospatiale SA–341 Gazelle	France	On order
		Missiles		
1962	350	BAC Vigilant	UK	
1968–69	(72)	HSD Firestreak or Redtop	UK	To arm Lightning
. . .	. . .	Aérospatiale SS.11	France	On order
		Naval vessels		
(1962)	(2)	Patrol launch	UK/Singapore	Length: 50 ft; new
1966–69	8	Patrol boat, "78 ft" type	UK	Displ: 40 t; new
(1970)	2	Patrol boat, "78 ft" type	UK	Displ: 40 t; new
. . .	8	Patrol boat	UK/Singapore	Length: 38 ft; being built
		Armoured fighting vehicles		
(1956)	(15)	Saracen	UK	
(1958)	(15)	Ferret	UK	
(1960)	25	Centurion	UK	
(1963–64)	(40)	Saladin	UK	
(1968–69)	(25)	Centurion Mk 9/10	UK	
(1969–70)	(50)	Saladin	UK	
1970–71	50	Vickers 37-ton	UK	Cost: $15–17.5 mn

Register 30. Arms supplies to Lebanon

Date	Number	Item	Supplier	Comment
		Aircraft		
1950	3	Percival Prentice T.1	UK	
1950	1	DH 104 Dove	UK	
1950	11	DH Chipmunk T–20/30	Canada	
1950	3	Savoia-Marchetti SM–79	Italy	
1952	6	NA T–6 Harvard 2B	UK	
1953–55	10	DH Vampire FB.52	UK	Incl some ex-RAF
1953–55	4	DH Vampire T.55	UK	
1954	3	DH Chipmunk	UK	
1954	4	NA T–6 Harvard 2B	UK	Ex-RAF

Date	Number	Item	Supplier	Comment
(1955)	1	Macchi M.B.308	Italy	
1957	6	DH Tiger Moth	Iraq	
1957–58	6	Hawker Hunter F.6	UK	Paid for by USA under offshore procurement programme
1958	6	NA T–6 Harvard 2	Iraq/Syria	
(1961)	4	Sud Alouette II	France	
1963–64	5	Sud Alouette III	France	
1965	4	Hawker Hunter FB.9	UK	Ex-RAF
1965–66	3	Hawker Hunter T.69	UK	Ex-RAF
1967	4	Potez Super Magister	France	
1967	2	Sud Alouette III	France	
1968	12	Dassault Mirage III C	France ⎫	Only 6 were operated, remainder in storage; all now offered for sale
1968	2	Dassault Mirage III B	France ⎬	
1973	4	Fouga Magister	France	Ex-French
(1973)	6	Aérospatiale Alouette	France	
1973–74	6	Agusta-Bell 212	Italy	
		Missiles		
1967–68	15	Matra R.530	France	To arm Mirage
		Naval vessels		
(1955–56)	3	Patrol boat, "Bybloss" class	France	Displ: 28 t; launched 1954–55
1958	1	Landing craft	USA	Displ: 180 t; new
(1960)	1	Patrol boat	France	Displ: 105 t; completed 1959
		Armoured fighting vehicles		
(1954)	(15)	M–6 Staghound	(UK)	
1957	42	AMX–13	France	
1958	75	M–41 Walker Bulldog	USA	MAP
(1958)	(15)	M–42	USA	
(1958)	(30)	M–59	USA	
(1960)	(15)	6–M APC	Canada	
1962–63	(50)	M–113	USA	
1965	40	Charioteer 6	Jordan	
(1965)	(15)	AEC Mk 3	UK	
(1970)	(30)	V–100 Commando	USA	
1971–72	50	(M–113) tracked APC	USA	Cost: $3 mn
1972	(15)	APC	USSR	
1972	22	AMX–13	France	Cost: $7.4 mn; 11 returned due to rust damage
1973	30	Panhard AML–VTT	France	

Register 31. Arms supplies to Oman

Date	Number	Item	Supplier	Comment
		Aircraft		
1959	4	Hunting Provost T.52	UK	
1959–60	4	Scottish Aviation Pioneer	UK	Ex-RAF
1960–61	2	Hunting Provost	UK	Replacement

Date	Number	Item	Supplier	Comment
1961	4	DHC–2 Beaver	Canada/UK	Via the British Army
1963	1	Hunting Provost	UK	Replacement
1965	1	Hunting Provost	UK	Replacement
1968	1	Douglas C–47	UK	Refurbished; commercial
1969	1	Douglas C–47	Canada	Sold after 1 year
1969–70	12	BAC 167 Strikemaster	UK	
1970	6	Short Skyvan 3M	UK	
1970	3	DHC–4 Caribou	Canada	
1970	4	Agusta-Bell 206 Jet Ranger	Italy	
1971	2	Short Skyvan 3M	UK	
1971	2	Vickers Viscount	UK/Australia	Ex-RAAF; refurbished in UK
1971	8	Agusta-Bell 205 Iroquois	Italy	
1972	2	Short Skyvan	UK	
1972	5	Agusta-Bell 205 A–1 Iroquois	Iran	
1972	2	Agusta-Bell 205 Iroquois	Saudi Arabia	
1973	1	DHC–2 Beaver	USA	Ex-civil
1973	8	BAC 167 Strikemaster	UK	
1973	2	DHC–4 Caribou	Canada	
1973	3	Vickers Viscount	Ireland	Ex-Air Lingus
...	8	Britten-Norman Defender	UK	On order; cost: $2.1 mn+
...	4	BAC 167 Strikemaster	UK	On order
...	6	Short Skyvan	UK	On order; cost $4.6 mn+
...	10	Agusta-Bell 205 Iroquois	Italy	On order
...	5	Agusta-Bell 2.4A	Italy	On order
		Naval vessels		
1971	1	Patrol boat	UK	Length: 203 ft; new
(1972)	3	Fast patrol boat, "Brooke Marine" type	UK	Displ: 135 t; new
		Armoured fighting vehicles		
(1964–65)	(15)	Ferret	UK	
(1966)	(15)	V–100 Commando	USA	
(1967)	(15)	Saladin	UK	

Register 32. Arms supplies to Qatar

Date	Number	Item	Supplier	Comment
		Aircraft		
1968	2	Westland Whirwind Series 3	UK	
1971–72	4	HS Hunter FGA.78	UK	
1971–72	2	HS Hunter T.79	UK	
		Missiles		
1970–71	(15)	Short Tigercat	UK	Cost: $1.4 mn

Date	Number	Item	Supplier	Comment
		Naval vessels		
(1971–72)	4	Fast patrol boat	UK	
		Armoured fighting vehicles		
(1968)	(10)	Ferret	UK	
(1969–70)	30	Saladin	UK	
(1970)	9	Saracen	UK	
(1971)	(10)	(Shorland Mk 2) AC	UK	

Register 33. Arms supplies to Saudi Arabia

Date	Number	Item	Supplier	Comment
		Aircraft		
1950	(2)	DH Tiger Moth	UK	RAF surplus
1950	2	Avro Anson	UK	RAF surplus
1950–52	6	Auster Aiglet	UK	
1952	6	Douglas C–47	USA	MAP
1952	10	Temco TE–1A Buckaroo	USA	MAP
1952–53	10	NA T–6 Texan	USA	MAP
(1953)	2	Convair C–131D	USA	MAP; used by Royal Flight
1953–57	(5)	NA T–28A	USA	MAP; ex-US
1955	3	Douglas B–26 Invader	USA	MAP; ex-US
1956	6	Douglas B–26 Invader	USA	MAP; ex-US
1956	12	DH Chipmunk T.10	UK	
1957	6	Fairchild C–123B Provider	USA	MAP; returned to USA 1967
1957	(5)	Beech T–34 Mentor	USA	MAP
1957	1	Westland Widgeon	UK	Used by Royal Flight
1957	4	DH Vampire FB.52	Egypt	Gift
1957	1	Vickers Varsity	Jordan	Used by Royal Flight
1957–58	12	NA F–86F Sabre	USA	MAP; ex-US
1957–58	10	Lockheed T–33A	USA	MAP; ex-US
(1959)	(2)	Cessna 180	USA	
1965	2	Sud Alouette III	France	
1966	4	Lockheed C–130E Hercules	USA	
1966	1	Cessna 310K	USA	
1966	6	Hawker Hunter FGA.9	UK }	Refurbished; supplied to Jordan 1967
1966	2	Hawker Hunter T.66	UK }	
1966	4	BAC Lighting F.52	UK	
1966	2	BAC Lighting T.54	UK	
1967	1	Lockheed C–130 Hercules	USA	
1967	2	Lockheed T–33	USA	Ex-US
1967	1	BAC Lightning F.52	UK	Replacement
1968	4	Lockheed C–130 Hercules	USA	
1968	8	Cessna 172	USA/France	Supplied by Reims Aviation via the UK
1968–69	34	BAC Lightning F.53	UK	
1968–69	6	BAC Lightning T.55	UK	

Date	Number	Item	Supplier	Comment
1968–70	16	Agusta-Bell 206A Jet Ranger	Italy	
1968–70	24	Agusta-Bell 205 Iroquois	Italy	
1969	8	NA F–86F Sabre	USA	Ex-US
1969	2	Lockheed C–140 Jet Star	USA	
1969	2	Lockheed T–33	Pakistan	Gift
1969–70	25	BAC 167 Strikemaster	UK	
1970	2	Lockheed C–130 Hercules	USA	
1970	4	Cessna 172	USA/France	Supplied by Reims Aviation
(1970)	6	Sud Alouette III	France	
1973	20	Northrop F–5B	USA	Cost: $130 mn, incl F–5E
1973	4	Lockheed C–130 Hercules	USA	Equipped for aerial tanker operations
1973	10	BAC 167 Strikemaster	UK	
1974-	30	Northrop F–5E Tiger II	USA	Being delivered; cost: $130 mn, incl F–5B
. . .	24	Westland Commando	UK ⎫	Ordered on behalf of Egypt; deliveries started 1974
. . .	6	Westland Sea King	UK ⎬	
. . .	34	Dassault Mirage IIIE	France ⎫	On order
. . .	4	Dassault Mirage IIID	France ⎭	
		Missiles		
1964	300	BAC Vigilant	UK	Cost: $1.4 mn
1966	37	BAC Thunderbird I	UK	Refurbished; from ex-British stocks; returned and replaced Hawk
1966–67	(150)	Raytheon MIM–23A Hawk	USA	Cost: $100 mn
(1968–69)	(204)	HSD Firestreak or Redtop	UK	To arm Lightning
. . .	. . .	Raytheon MIM–23B Hawk	USA	Modernization of existing system with improved missile; cost: $200–300 mn
. . .	. . .	Aérospatiale SS.11	France	On order
. . .	. . .	Matra/Thomson–CSF Crotale	France	On order
		Naval vessels		
1960	1	Patrol boat	USA	Displ: 102 t; gift
1969	3	Fast patrol boat, "Jaguar" type	FR Germany	Displ: 170 t; new
1970–72	20	Patrol boat	UK	Length: 45 ft
1971	8	Hovercraft, "Winchester" (SR.N 6) class	UK	Displ: 10 t; new
(1971–72)	20	Patrol boat	UK	Length: 20 ft
1971–73	10	Patrol boat	UK	Length: 23 ft
		Armoured fighting vehicles		
(1952–54)	(15)	M–6 Staghound	UK	
(1955–57)	(15)	M–8 Greyhound	UK	
1956	18	M–41 Walker Bulldog	USA	U.c.: $135 000; MAP
(1957–58)	(40)	M–41 Walker Bulldog	USA	
(1958–59)	(15)	M–24 Chaffee	USA	MAP
(1960–61)	55	M–47 Patton	USA	MAP
1969–70	220	Panhard AML 90	France	Cost: $95 mn
1972–73	30	AMX–30	France	
. . .	. . .	APC	USA	On order for National Guard

Register 34. Arms supplies to Sharya

Date	Number	Item	Supplier	Comment
		Armoured fighting vehicles		
1971	6	Shorland Mk 2	UK	

Register 35. Arms supplies to Southern Yemen

Date	Number	Item	Supplier	Comment
		Aircraft		
1967	6	Westland Bell 47G	UK	
1967	4	Douglas DC–3	UK/FR Germany	Ex-Bavarian Airlines; refurbished in UK
1968	4	BAC Jet Provost T.52	UK	Ex–RAF
1968	6	DHC–2 Beaver	Canada	
1969	12	MiG–17	USSR	
1969	2	MiG–15 UTI	USSR	
1969	4	BAC 167 Strikemaster	UK	
		Naval vessels		
1967	3	Inshore minesweeper, "Ham" class	UK	Displ: 120 t; ex-British
(1971–72)	15	Coastal patrol boat	UK	
		Armoured fighting vehicles		
1967	(15)	Saladin	UK	
(1967)	(15)	Ferret	UK	
1967–68	30	T–34	USSR	
(1972–73)	(20)	T–54	USSR	

Register 36. Arms supplies to Syria

Date	Number	Item	Supplier	Comment
		Aircraft		
1950	26	Fiat G.59 4B	Italy	
(1950)	(7)	Junker Ju 52/3 M	France	
1951	50	DH Vampire	Italy	May have been produced under licence in Italy; later transferred to Egypt
(1951)	(1)	Fairchild Argus	(UK)	
(1953)	(10)	DH Chipmunk	UK	
(1953)	6	Douglas C–47	France	
(1953–54)	23	Gloster Meteor F.8 and NF.13, T.7	UK	
1954	40	Supermarine Spitfire F.22	UK	Reconditioned

Date	Number	Item	Supplier	Comment
(1954)	(5)	NA T–6 Harvard	USA	Surplus; probably refurbished
(1954)	1	Beech D–18S	(USA)	
(1954)	1	DH Dragon Rapide	(UK)	
1955–56	6	MiG–15 UTI	USSR	Supplied to, and assembled in Egypt; all but 4 destroyed 1956
1955–56	25	MiG–15	USSR	See above
1957	60	MiG–17	USSR	Israel claims to have destroyed 23 MiG–15/17s
(1957)	8	Il–14	USSR	
(1957)	(10)	Yak–11	USSR	
(1957)	7	Mi–1	USSR	
(1958)	(10)	Yak–18	USSR	
(1958)	10	Mi–4	USSR	Israel destroyed 3
(1963)	7	Il–28	USSR	Israel claims to have destroyed 2
(1965)	(7)	L–29 Delfin	Czechoslova-kia	
1966	(10)	MiG–15/17	Egypt	
1967	36	MiG–21	USSR	Israel claims to have destroyed 33
1967	(20)	MiG–21	USSR	
1967	(8)	Mi–4	USSR	
1967–68	(50)	MiG–17	USSR	
1968	40	MiG–21	USSR	
1969	1	Beagle B.206	UK	For aerial survey
(1969)	(20)	Su–7	USSR	
1970–71	(10)	Su–7	USSR	
1970–71	(40)	MiG–21	USSR	
1971	9	MiG–17	USSR	
1971	22	Mi–8	USSR	
1971	2	Mi–4	USSR	
1972	(25)	MiG–21 MF	USSR	
1972	(10)	MiG–17	USSR	
1972	4	(Mi–8) helicopter	USSR	
(1972)	(20)	L–29 Delfin	Czechoslova-kia	2 squadrons
1973	(75)	MiG–21	USSR	⎫
1973	(40)	MiG–17	USSR	⎬
1973	(100)	MiG–21	USSR	⎬ War replacements
1973	(20)	Su–7	USSR	⎬
1973	(15)	Mi–8	USSR	⎭
1974	. . .	MiG–23	USSR	
1974	. . .	MiG–21	USSR	
1974	. . .	Su–7	USSR	
1974	9	Ka–25	USSR	
		Missiles		
1966	(60)	SS–N–2 "Styx"	USSR	To arm "Komar" class patrol boats
1967	(200)	K–13 "Atoll"	USSR	To arm MiG–21
(1967)	60	SA–2	USSR	Conflicting information as to whether received by Syria
1968–73	(1380)	K–13 "Atoll"	USSR	To arm MiG–21
1971	(24)	SA–2	USSR	
1972	(32)	SA–3	USSR	
1972–73	(200)	AT–1 "Snapper"	USSR	
1972–73	(300)	AT–3 "Sagger"	USSR	

Date	Number	Item	Supplier	Comment
1972–73	(500)	SA–7	USSR	
1972–73	(48)	SS–N–2 "Styx"	USSR	To arm "Osa" class patrol boats
1973	(24)	SA–2	USSR	
1973	(32)	SA–3	USSR	Incl war replacements
1973	(180)	SA–6	USSR	
1973	(30)	"Frog–7"	USSR	
1974	...	SS–IC "Scud"	USSR	
		Naval vessels		
1957	5	Motor torpedo boat	USSR	Displ: 50 t; ex-Soviet
(1959–60)	10	Motor torpedo boat	USSR	Displ: 50 t; ex-Soviet
1962	2	Fleet minesweeper, "T43" class	USSR	Displ: 500 t; ex-Soviet
1962	3	Patrol boat, "Ch" class	France	Displ: 107 t; former French submarine chaser
1963–66	6	Patrol boat, "Komar" class	USSR	Displ: 75 t
1972–73	(4)	Patrol boat, "Osa" class	USSR	Displ: 165 t
		Armoured fighting vehicles		
1956	50	Old German tank	Czechoslovakia	Reconditioned
1956	100	(BTR 152) APC	USSR	
1957	200	T–34	USSR	
(1957–58)	150	T–54	USSR	
(1959–60)	35	JS III	USSR	
(1959–60)	80	Su–100	USSR	
(1967)	(100)	BTR 152	USSR	
(1967–68)	(150)	T–54/55	USSR	

Register 37. Arms supplies to the Yemen

Date	Number	Item	Supplier	Comments
		Aircraft		
(1950)	3	Cessna AT–17 Bobcat	(USA)	Part of Imam's private fleet
(1952)	2	Aero Commander	(USA)	Part of Imam's private fleet
(1952)	3	Douglas C–47	(USA)	Part of Imam's private fleet
(1955)	2	NA T–6 Texan	Saudi Arabia	Gift; part of Imam's private fleet
1957	4	Yak–11	USSR/Czechoslovakia/Egypt	
1957	12	Il–10	USSR/Czechoslovakia/Egypt	
(1957)	(5)	MiG–15 UTI	(Czechoslovakia)	
1958	4	Il–14	USSR	

Date	Number	Item	Supplier	Comment
1958	(3)	Mi–1	USSR/Czech-oslova-kia/Egypt	
1958	26	Yak–11	USSR/Czech-oslova-kia/Egypt	
1958	24	Il–10	USSR/Czech-oslova-kia/Egypt	
1959	4	Mi–4	USSR	
(1962)	2	C–47	USA	
(1963)	3	Agusta-Bell 47J–3	Italy	
1967	12	MiG–17	USSR	
1967	12	Il–28	USSR	
		Naval vessels		
1972	17	Small patrol boat	USSR	
		Armoured fighting vehicles		
1957	30	T–34	USSR/Czech-oslova-kia/Egypt	
(1957)	(35)	BTR 152	USSR/Czech-oslova-kia/Egypt	
(1961)	(35)	BTR 40	USSR/Czech-oslova-kia/Egypt	
(1961)	50	Su–100	USSR/Czech-oslova-kia/Egypt	
1968	(50)	(T–34) Tank	USSR	

North Africa

Register 38. Arms supplies to Algeria

Date	Number	Item	Supplier	Comment
		Aircraft		
1962	6	Il–14	USSR	
1962	(10)	Mi–4	USSR	
1962	18	Heliopolis Airworks Gomhuriah	Egypt	Overhauled in Czechoslovakia 1964
1962	5	MiG–15 UTI	Egypt	
(1962)	20	MiG–15	USSR	
1963	2	Beech D–18 S	USA	
1963	4	MiG–17	Cuba	

Date	Number	Item	Supplier	Comment
(1963)	8	Il–14	USSR	
(1963–65)	30	MiG–17	USSR	
1964	8	Hughes 269A	France	US-built
1965	7	An–12	USSR	
1965	12	Il–28	USSR	
1965	4	MiG–21	USSR	
(1965)	4	Il–18	USSR	
(1965)	3	Mi–1	USSR	
1966	10	MiG–17	USSR	
1966	6	Il–28	USSR	
1966	15	MiG–21	USSR	Delivered via Egypt
1966	10	Mi–4	USSR	
1967	(17)	MiG–21	USSR	
(1967)	(6)	Il–28	USSR	
1967–68	(10)	Mi–4	USSR	
1970	28	Fouga Magister	France	Refurbished
1970	2	Sud SA–330 Puma	France	
		Missiles		
(1965–67)	(216)	K–13 "Atoll"	USSR	To arm MiG–21
1966	30	SA–2	USSR	
1967	(90)	SS–N–2 "Styx"	USSR	To arm "Komar" class patrol boat
1968–70	(24)	SS–N–2 "Styx"	USSR	To arm "Osa" class patrol boat
1969	(10)	SA–2	Egypt	
		Naval vessels		
1962	2	Coastal minesweeper	Egypt	Displ: 215 t; ex-US
1963	2	Motor torpedo boat	Egypt	Displ: 50 t
1964	6	Motor torpedo boat	USSR	Displ: 50 t; probably "P6" type
1967	2	Submarine chaser, "SOI" class	USSR	Displ: 250 t; built since 1957
1967	7	Patrol boat, "Komar" class	USSR	Displ: 75 t; armed with "Styx" SSMs
1967	1	Patrol boat, "Osa" class	USSR	Displ: 160 t; armed with "Styx" SSMs
1968–70	2	Patrol boat, "Osa" class	USSR	Displ: 160 t; armed with "Styx" SSMs
1968–71	4	Submarine chaser, "SOI" class	USSR	Displ: 250 t; ex-Soviet
(1972)	4	Motor torpedo boat	USSR	Displ: 50 t
(1973)	2	Minesweeper "T43" class	USSR	Displ: 500 t
		Armoured fighting vehicles		
1962	6	AMX–13	Morocco	
1962	10	T–34	USSR	Delivered via Morocco
(1963)	(50)	AML–60	France	
1964	100	T–34	USSR	
(1964)	50	T–54	USSR	
(1964–66)	350	BTR 152	USSR	
(1965)	(25)	Su–100	USSR	
1966	50	T–54/55	USSR	
1966	(25)	Su–100	USSR	
1966	6	JSU–152	USSR	
(1967–68)	(200)	T–54/55	USSR	

Register 39. Arms supplies to Libya

Date	Number	Item	Supplier	Comment
		Aircraft		
1959	2	Auster OAP.5	UK	Ex-RAF
1959	2	Heliopolis Air Works Gomhuriah	Egypt	
(1959)	2	Bell 47J	USA	
(1962)	3	Sud Alouette II	France	
1963	2	Lockheed T–33	USA	Gift
1964	1	Douglas C–47	USA	
1965	5	Douglas C–47	USA	
1966	1	Lockheed T–33	USA	
1968	5	Northrop F–5 Freedom Fighter	USA	
1969	5	Northrop F–5 Freedom Fighter	USA	
1969	1	Lockheed C–140 Jet Star	USA	
1970	8	Lockheed C–130 Hercules	USA	
1971	20	Fouga Magister	France	
1971	1	Dassault Falcon	France	
1971–72	4	Aérospatiale Alouette III	France	
1971–72	9	Aérospatiale SA.321 Super Frelon	France	
1971–74	58	Dassault Mirage 5	France ⎫	
1971–74	32	Dassault Mirage IIIE	France ⎬ Some were on loan to Egypt during October war of 1973	
1971–74	20	Dassault Mirage IIIB/IIIR	France ⎭	
		Missiles		
1968–69	(48)	Nord SS.12 (M)	France	To arm patrol boats
(1972)	300	BAC Vigilant	UK	
1973	(18)	Short Seacat	UK	2 triple launchers on Mk 7 frigate
1973	3 batt	Matra/Thomson-CSF Crotale	France/S. Africa	Developed in France to South African specifications with 85 per cent South African funding
1974	...	SA–2	USSR ⎫	Reportedly received total of 8 batteries
1974	...	SA–3	USSR ⎬	
1974	...	SA–6	USSR ⎭	
...	...	Matra R.550 Magic	France	On order; to arm Mirage
		Naval vessels		
(1962)	3	Fast patrol launch	(UK)	For customs and fishing
1963	2	Inshore minesweeper, "Ham" class	UK	Displ: 120 t; ex-British; lent 1963; given outright 1966
1966	1	Corvette, "Tobruk" class	UK	Displ: 440 t; completed 1966
1966	1	Maintenance repair ship	UK	Displ: 657 t; ex-British
1967	2	Coastguard vessel	UK	Displ: 100 t; new
1968–69	3	Fast patrol boat, "Susa" class	UK	Displ: 95 t; new; armed with SS.12 SSMs
1968–69	4	Coastguard vessel	UK	Displ: 100 t; new
1969	1	Logistic support ship	UK	Displ: 2 200 t; new
1969–70	4	Patrol boat, "Garian" type	UK	Displ: 100 t; new
1973	1	Frigate Mk 7	UK	Displ: 1 325 t; new; armed with Seacat SAMs

Date	Number	Item	Supplier	Comment
		Armoured fighting vehicles		
1957	(10)	Centurion	UK	
(1960–61)	(15)	Saracen	UK	
(1960–61)	(40)	Saladin	(UK)	
(1962–63)	(15)	M–113	USA	
(1966)	(15)	Ferret	UK	
(1966)	(15)	Shorland AC	UK	
1970	36	BTR–50	USSR	
(1970)	(15)	T–34	Egypt	
1970–71	(200)	T–54/55	USSR	
(1972)	(15)	BMP–76	USSR	
1972–73	170	M–113	Italy	Ex-Italian
. . .	(200)	Tank	UK or France	Order for British Chieftain from 1969; reportedly cancelled; French AMX–30 ordered instead

Register 40. Arms supplies to Morocco

Date	Number	Item	Supplier	Comment
		Aircraft		
1956	6	Morane Saulnier M.S.733 Alcyon	France	Ex-French; after extensive use in Algeria
1956	2	Morane Saulnier M.S. 760 Paris	France	
1956	1	Bell 47	France	
1956	6	Morane Saulnier M.S. 500 Criquet	France	
1956	1	Sud Alouette II	France	
1956	1	DH Heron	(France)	
1956	2	Beech Twin Bonanza	(France)	
1957	1	Max Holste M.H. 1521 Broussard	France	
1958	2	Max Holste M.H. 1521 Broussard	France	
1959	1	Sud Alouette II	France	
(1959–60)	3	Max Holste M.H. 1521 Broussard	France	
1960	4	Hawker Fury	Iraq	Gift
1961	1	Hiller UH–12E	USA	
1961	12	MiG–17	USSR	
1961	2	MiG–15 UTI	USSR	
1961	2	Il–28	USSR	
1962	3	Sud Alouette II	France	
(1962)	4	MiG–17	USSR	
(1962–63)	3	Bell 47	France	
1963	8	Fouga Magister	France	Probably gift
(1964)	50	NA T–6	USA	
(1964)	3	Sud Alouette II	France	
1966	4	Kaman HH–43F Huskie	USA	
1966	4	Northrop F–5B Freedom Fighter	USA	

69

Date	Number	Item	Supplier	Comment
1966	10	Fairchild C–119 Packet	USA	Part of $20 mn MAP
1966	4	Douglas C–47	USA	Part of $20 mn MAP
1967	12	Northrop F–5A Freedom Fighter	USA	Part of $12 mn MAP
(1967)	(6)	Douglas C–47	USA	Part of $20 mn MAP
(1967)	25	NA T–28	USA	
1968	24	Fouga Magister	FR Germany	U.c.: $166 500; total cost: $4 mn; refurbished by Sud-Aviation
1968	12	Agusta-Bell 205 Iroquois	Italy	Contract for 24 suspended after delivery of first 12
1969	5	Northrop F–5 Freedom Fighter	USA	
(1973)	5	Fairchild C–119 Packet	Canada/Italy	Ex-CAF; refurbished in Italy
. . .	6	Lockheed C–130 Hercules	USA	On order; delivery from 1974
		Naval vessels		
1960	1	Seaward patrol boat	France	Displ: 75 t
1960	1	Submarine chaser	France	Displ: 325 t; built 1942; ex-US; ex-French
1961	1	Corvette, "Chamois" class	France	Displ: 647 t; completed 1940
1964	1	Utility landing craft	France	Displ: 292 t; completed 1964
1964	1	Patrol boat, "Fougeux" class	France	Displ: 325 t; completed 1964
1965	1	Frigate	France	Displ: 1 450 t; completed 1944; ex-British
1967	1	Patrol boat	France	Displ: 125 t; completed 1967
1968	2	Patrol boat	FR Germany	
. . .	2	Patrol boat	France	On order; displ: 440 t full load
		Armoured fighting vehicles		
1956	17	AMX–13	France	
1956	17	Panhard EBR–75	France	
(1956–59)	40	M–8 Greyhound	(France)	
(1957–60)	28	AMX–13	France	
(1957–60)	19	EBR–75	France	
1962	35	T–54	USSR	
(1962)	(10)	Su–100	(USSR)	
(1963)	15	AMX–105	France	
1966	15	(M–8) AC	USA	
1966–69	(75)	AMX–13	France	
(1966–68)	50	AML–60/90	France	
1967–68	80	T–54	Czechoslova-kia	
(1968)	50	M–56	(Spain)	
(1968–70)	95	OT–64	Czechoslova-kia	

Register 41. Arms supplies to Tunisia

Date	Number	Item	Supplier	Comment
		Aircraft		
1960	9	Saab 91 Safir	Sweden	Cost: $247 000
1961	6	Saab 91 Safir	Sweden	Cost: $165 000
1963	2	Sud Alouette II	France	
1963	12	NA T–6 Texan	France	Refurbished
(1963)	3	Dassault MD 315 Flamant	France	
(1964)	6	Sud Alouette II	France	
1965	8	Aermacchi M.B. 326B	Italy	
(1968)	4	Aérospatiale Alouette III	France	
1969	12	NA F–86 Sabre	USA	
1969–70	(3)	Nord 2501 Noratlas	France	Military aid
(1971)	1+	Aermacchi Al–60	Italy	
		Missiles		
1970–71	(48)	Aérospatiale SS.12 (M)	France	To arm 2 patrol boats; military aid
. . .	. . .	Aérospatiale SS.12 (M)	France	On order; to arm 1 patrol boat
		Naval vessels		
1959	1	Corvette	France	Displ: 647 t; launched 1939
1959	1	Patrol boat	France	Displ: 75 t; ex-French; built in FR Germany
1961	1	Patrol boat	FR Germany	Displ: 75 t; new
1963	1	Patrol boat	FR Germany	Displ: 75 t; new
1967	1	Patrol boat	FR Germany	Displ: 75 t; new
1969	1	Patrol boat	France/FR Germany	Displ: 325 t; ex-French; ex–FR German; built under US offshore procurement
1969–71	8	Patrol launch	France	Displ: 38 t; military aid
1970–71	2	Patrol boat, "P48" type	France	Displ: 250 t; new; military aid; armed with SS.12 SSMs
1973	1	Destroyer, converted "Edsall" class	USA	Displ: 1 509 t; completed 1943; converted
(1973)	1	Coastal minesweeper, "Accia" class	France	Displ: 320 t; ex-US; ex-French; on loan for 1 year until completion of Corvette
. . .	1	Corvette, A69 "Aviso" type	France	On order; displ: 950 t
. . .	1	Patrol boat, "P48" type	France	On order; delivery Nov 1974; displ: 250 t; armed with SS.12 SSMs
		Armoured fighting vehicles		
1957	15	EBR–75	France	
(1958)	(10)	AMX–105	France	
(1958–60)	(20)	AMX–13	France	
1959–60	12	M–41 Walker Bulldog	USA	
(1959–60)	(10)	M–8 Greyhound	USA	
1969–70	13	AMX–13	France	Military aid
1969–70	13	AML–60	France	Military aid

Sub-Saharan Africa

Register 42. Arms supplies to Cameroon

Date	Number	Item	Supplier	Comment
		Aircraft		
1961	3	Max Holste M.H. 1521 Broussard	France	Gift at independence
1963	1	Beech Queen Air	USA	For VIP
1964(–65)	3	Dassault M.D. 315 Flamant	France	French surplus
1965–66	2	Sud Alouette II	France	
1965(–66)	(5)	Douglas C–47	France	
(1966–67)	(4)	Max Holste M.H. 1521 M Broussard	France	
(1968)	1	Dornier Do–28	FR Germany	
1970–71	3	DHC–4 Caribou	Canada	
(1972)	1	Grumman Gulfstream 2	USA	For VIP
1973	6	Fouga Magister	France	French surplus stocks; refurbished
(1973)	1	Aérospatiale SA–330 Puma	France	For VIP
		Naval vessels		
1963	1	Patrol boat	France	Displ: 40 t; launched 1943 ex-British; ex-French
1964	1	Patrol boat	France	Displ: 75 t; completed 1958; ex-French
(1967)	1	Patrol boat	France	Displ: 20 t full load; new
1970	1	Patrol boat	France	Displ: 45 t full load; new
		Armoured fighting vehicles		
(1963)	8	Ferret	UK	
(1963)	(8)	M–8 Greyhound	France	

Register 43. Arms supplies to the Central African Republic

Date	Number	Item	Supplier	Comment
		Aircraft		
1961	3	Max Holste M.H. 1521 M Broussard	France	Gift at independence
1961	1	Douglas C–47	France	Gift at independence
1961	1	Sud Alouette II	France	Gift at independence
(1963)	1	Bell 47G	USA	
1965–66	(5)	Max Holste M.H. 1521 M Broussard	France	
1965–66	2	Douglas C–47	France	
1968	1	Douglas DC–4	France	Ex-Air France; gift
1969–70	10	Aermacchi AL–60 C5	Italy	
1970	1	Dassault Falcon	France	
1971	10	Douglas A–1D Skyraider	France	
(1973)	10	Nord 2501 Noratlas	France	
(1973)	10	Sud Sikorsky S–58	France	

Register 44. Arms supplies to Chad

Date	Number	Item	Supplier	Comment
		Aircraft		
(1960)	3	Max Holste M.H. 1521 M Broussard	France	Gift at independence
(1960)	1	Sud Alouette II	France	Gift at independence
(1965)	2	Douglas C–47	France	
1971	5	Douglas A–1D Skyraider	France	Ex-Armée de l'Air
1971	10	Nord 2501 Noratlas	France	Ex-Armée de l'Air
1971	10	Alouette II	France	Ex-Armée de l'Air
1971	10	Sud-Sikorsky S–58	France	Ex-Armée de l'Air

Register 45. Arms supplies to the People's Republic of the Congo

Date	Number	Item	Supplier	Comment
		Aircraft		
(1960)	1	Douglas C–47	France	Gift at independence
(1960–61)	3	Max Holste M.H. 1521 M Broussard	France	Gift at independence
(1961)	1	Sud Alouette II	France	Gift at independence
(1969)	1	An–24	USSR	
1971	1	Il–18	USSR	Gift
1971	2	Il–14	USSR	Gift
		Naval vessels		
1962	1	Patrol boat	France	Displ: 75 t; completed 1958; returned to France 1965; re-transferred to Senegal
(1968)	4	Small patrol craft	China	
		Armoured fighting vehicles		
(1968)	(10)	BTR 152	USSR	

Register 46. Arms supplies to Dahomey

Date	Number	Item	Supplier	Comment
		Aircraft		
(1960)	2	Max Holste M.H. 1521 M Broussard	France	Gift at independence
(1960)	2	Douglas C–47	France	Gift at independence
1966	1	Aero Commander 500B	France	
(1967)	1	Sud Alouette II	France	
(1972)	1	(Reims-) Cessna 337 Skymaster	(France)	
		Armoured fighting vehicles		
(1964)	(15)	M–8 Greyhound	(France)	

Register 47. Arms supplies to Ethiopia

Date	Number	Item	Supplier	Comment
		Aircraft		
1946–52	47	Saab B–17	Sweden	
1952	8	Fairey Firefly F.1	UK	
1952	1	Fairey Firefly trainer	UK	
1953–55	17	Saab 91B Safir	Sweden	
(1954)	(5)	Avro Anson Mk 18	UK	
(1955)	2	Convair Stinson L–5	USA	
(1955)	(3)	DH Dove	UK	
(1957–58)	10	Douglas C–47	USA	
1959	5	Lockheed T–33	USA	
1960	14	NA F–86F Sabre	USA	
1960	(5)	NA T–28A	USA	
1960	14	Saab 91C Safir	Sweden	
1961	6	Convair PBY–5A Catalina	Norway	
(1961)	2	Douglàs C–54	USA	
(1962)	7	Lockheed T–33	USA	
(1964)	2	Sud Alouette II	France	
1965	1	DH Dove Mk 8	UK	
(1964–55)	5	Sud Alouette III	France	
1965	1	Il–14	USSR	
(1965)	2	Mi–8	USSR	
1965–66	12	NA T–28D	USA	
1966	12	Northrop F–5A Freedom Fighter	USA	MAP
1966	2	Northrop F–5B Freedom Fighter	USA	
(1967–68)	6	Bell UH–1H Iroquois	USA	MAP; for Army
1968	6	Agusta-Bell 204 Iroquois	Italy	
1969	4	BAC Canberra B.2	UK	Ex-RAF; refurbished
1970	5	Fairchild C–119K Packet	USA	
(1970)	5	Aérospatiale Alouette III	France	
1971	1	Reims-Cessna 337 Skymaster	FR Germany	Military aid
(1971)	2	Aérospatiale Alouette II	France	
(1971)	(3)	NA F–86 Sabre	Iran	
1972	3	Northrop F–5A Freedom Fighter	USA	
1972	(7)	Fairchild C–119K Packet	USA/Belgium	
1972	(5)	Lockheed T–33	Canada or Netherlands	
1973–74	(3)	Northrop F–5 Freedom Fighter	USA	FY 74 MAP
		Naval vessels		
1958	2	Patrol boat	USA	Displ: 101 t; ex-US
1960	2	Torpedo boat	Yugoslavia	Displ: 60 t; built 1951
1961	1	Training ship	USA	Displ: 1 766 t; completed 1944
1961	2	Patrol boat, "MGM" type	USA	Displ: 101 t
1962	1	Patrol boat, "MGM" type	USA	Displ: 101 t
1963	2	Landing craft, "LCM" type	USA	

Date	Number	Item	Supplier	Comment
1963	2	Landing craft, "LCVP" type	USA	
1966–67	4	Harbour defence craft, "Caroline" class	USA	Displ: 40 t
1971	2	Landing craft, "LCM" type	USA	
1971	1	Coastal minesweeper, "Wildervank" class	Netherlands	Displ: 373 t; completed 1956
		Armoured fighting vehicles		
1953–54	54	M–41 Walker Bulldog	USA	MAP
1953–54	39	(M–59) APC	USA	MAP
(1955)	(25)	M–24 Chaffee	USA	
(1956)	(15)	M–8 Greyhound	USA	
(1959)	(15)	M–20	USA	
(1972)	56	AML–60	France	

Register 48. Arms supplies to Gabon

Date	Number	Item	Supplies	Comment
		Aircraft		
(1961)	1	Douglas C–47	France	Gift at independence
(1961–62)	3	Max Holste M.H. 1521 Broussard	France	Gift at independence
(1962)	1	Sud Alouette II	France	
(1964)	2	Douglas C–47	France	
(1965)	1	Max Holste M.H. 1521 Broussard	France	
(1966)	2	Sud Alouette III	France	
(1968)	2	NAMC YS–11	Japan	Joint civil and military use
(1969)	1	Douglas DC–6	(USA)	Joint civil and military use
1970	1	Alouette III	France	
1970	1	Dassault Falcon 20	France	For VIP use
1970	2	Reims-Cessna 337 Skymaster	France	
(1970)	3	Nord 262 Frégate	France	Joint civil and military use
...	1	Lockheed L–100–3 Hercules	USA	On order; delivery 1975
		Naval vessels		
1961	1	Patrol boat	France	Displ: 40 t; ex-British; ex-French; returned to France 1966
1972	1	Coastguard vessel	France	Displ: 85 t; new
		Armoured fighting vehicles		
(1961)	(15)	(M–3A1) scout car	France	
(1968)	(15)	AML–60	France	

Register 49. Arms supplies to Ghana

Date	Number	Item	Supplier	Comment
		Aircraft		
1959	12	HAL HT–2 Marut	India	
1959	1	Piper Super Cub	Israel	Gift
1960	4	DH Chipmunk T.10	UK	Ex-RAF
1960	14	DHC–2 Beaver	Canada	Cost: $944 000
1961	3	An–12	USSR	Gift; never used
1961	4	Il–18	USSR	Returned to USSR
1961	8	DH Chipmunk T.10	UK	Ex-RAF
1961	1	HS Heron	UK	For VIP
1961	12	DHC–3 Otter	Canada	Cost: $1.8 mn
1961	8	DHC–4 Caribou	Canada	Cost: $5.75 mn
1962	6	Westland Whirlwind Series 3	UK	
1963	1	Mi–4	USSR	Gift
1963	2	HS Heron	UK	
1966	3	Westland Wessex Mk 53	UK	Cost: $1.3 mn, incl spares
(1966)	5	Hughes 300	USA	
1966–67	7	Aermacchi M.B. 326	Italy	
(1967)	3	Sikorsky S–55	USA	
(1967)	1	HS 125	UK	
(1969)	1	Aérospatiale Alouette III	France	
1972	2	Bell 212 Twin-Pac	USA	
1973	6	Scottish Aviation Bulldog Series 120	UK	Cost: $480 000, incl spares
1973	8	Britten-Norman BN–2 Islander	UK	Cost: $1.8 mn, incl spares
. . .	6	Short Skyvan 3M	UK	On order; delivery 1974; cost: $4.9 mn, incl spares
. . .	4	Aérospatiale Alouette III	France	On order
. . .	5	Fokker-VFW F–27 Friendship Mk 400M	Netherlands	On order; delivery 1974
. . .	1	Fokker-VFW F-27 Friendship Mk 600	Netherlands	On order; delivery 1974
		Armoured fighting vehicles		
(1959–61)	(15)	Saladin	UK	
(1959–61)	(15)	Ferret	UK	
		Naval vessels		
1959	2	Inshore minesweeper	UK	
1962	2	Seaward defence vessel, "Ford" class	UK	Displ: 120 t; new
1963	1	Training ship	UK	Displ: 600 t; built 1927
1964	1	Corvette, "Kromantse" class	UK	Displ: 440 t; new
1964	1	Coastal minesweeper, "Ton" class	UK	Displ: 360 t; ex-British
1965	1	Corvette, "Kromantse" class	UK	Displ: 440 t; new
1965	1	Maintenance repair craft	UK	Displ: 657 t; ex-British
1965	1	Fast patrol boat	FR Germany	
1967	4	Patrol boat, "P" class	USSR	Displ: 86 t; new
1968	5	Fast patrol boat	FR Germany	

Register 50. Arms supplies to Guinea

Date	Number	Item	Supplier	Comment
		Aircraft		
(1960)	4	Il–14	USSR	
(1960)	2	Il–18	USSR	
(1961)	(2)	MiG–15 UTI	USSR	
(1961)	(3)	MiG–17	USSR	
(1964)	1	Bell 47G	(USA)	
(1968–69)	(5)	MiG–17	USSR	
(1970)	4	An–14	USSR	
(1972)	(2)	Alouette (III)	France	
		Naval vessels		
1968–70	3	Motor torpedo boat, "P6" type	USSR	Displ: 66 t
1969–70	2	Patrol craft	USSR	Displ: 86 t
(1972)	1	Motor torpedo boat, "P6" type	USSR	Displ: 66 t
1973	4	Patrol boat, "Shanghai" class	China	Displ: 100 t full load
		Armoured fighting vehicles		
1959	12	T–34	Czechoslovakia	
1959	10	BTR 152	Czechoslovakia	
(1969)	(10)	BTR–40	USSR	
(1971)	(10)	BRDM	USSR	

Register 51. Arms supplies to the Ivory Coast

Date	Number	Item	Supplier	Comment
		Aircraft		
1961–62	4	Max Holste M.H. 1521 M Broussard	France	Gift
1961–62	3	Douglas C–47	France	Gift
1967	1	Aero Commander 500	(USA)	
1967	1	Beech 18	(USA)	
1967	2	Sud Alouette III	France	
1967	2	Sud Alouette II	France	
1968	2	Dassault Fan Jet Falcon	France	
(1968)	3	Reims-Cessna 150	France	
(1969)	1	Sud Alouette III	France	
1970	1	Aérospatiale SA–330 Puma	France	
1971	3	Reims-Cessna 337C Skymaster	France	
1971	2	Fokker-VFW F–27 Friendship	(Netherlands)	
. . .	3	Aérospatiale SA–330 Puma	France	On order

Date	Number	Item	Supplier	Comment
		Naval vessels		
1961	1	Submarine chaser	France	Displ: 110 t; ex-US; ex-French
1963	1	Patrol boat, "VC" type	France	Displ: 75 t; completed 1958
1968	1	Patrol boat	France	Displ: 235 t; new
		Armoured fighting vehicles		
(1963)	(15)	(M–8) AC	France	
(1966)	10	AMX–13	France	
(1968)	17	AML–60	France	

Register 52. Arms supplies to Kenya

Date	Number	Item	Supplier	Comment
		Aircraft		
1963	6	DH Chipmunk T.21	UK	Ex-RAF
1964–65	7	DHC–2 Beaver	UK/Canada	Financed by British loan
1965	4	DHC–4 Caribou	UK/Canada	Financed by British loan
(1967)	3	Sud Alouette II	France	
(1967)	4	DHC–2 Beaver	Canada	
(1968)	1	Aero Commander 680	USA	
(1970)	2	Hughes 269	USA	
1971	6	BAC 167 Strikemaster	UK	
1972	5	Scottish Aviation Bulldog Series 100	UK	
1972	2	DHC–4 Caribou	Canada	
(1973)	1+	Piper Navajo	(USA)	
		Naval vessels		
1964	1	Seaward defence vessel, "Ford" class	UK	Displ: 120 t; ex-British; sold 1971
1966	3	Patrol boat	UK	Displ: 96 t; new; cost: $2.1 mn
		Armoured fighting vehicles		
(1964)	20	Ferret	UK	
(1968)	(15)	Saracen	UK	
(1969)	(10)	Saladin	UK	
(1970–71)	(15)	AML–60/90	France	

Register 53. Arms supplies to Liberia

Date	Number	Item	Supplier	Comment
		Aircraft		
(1964)	2	Douglas C–47	USA	Operated by Army

Date	Number	Item	Supplier	Comment
		Naval vessels		
1957	2	Patrol boat	USA	Displ: 11.5 t; gift
(1966)	(2)	Landing craft	(USA)	Displ: (20 t)
1967	1	Motor gunboat	USA	Displ: 100 t; new; MAP
		Armoured fighting vehicles		
(1959)	(15)	M–3 Al White	USA	

Register 54. Arms supplies to Malagasy

Date	Number	Item	Supplier	Comment
		Aircraft		
1961	2	Max Holste M.H. 1521 Broussard	France	Gift
1961	2	Douglas C–47	France	Gift
(1961)	1	Bell 47G	France	
(1961)	1	Sud Alouette III	France	
1963	1	Dassault M.D. 312 Flamant	France	Gift
(1964)	1	Dassault M.D. 312 Flamant	France	
1965	3	Max Holste M.H. 1521 Broussard	France	
1965	1	Douglas C–47	France	
(1966)	1	Sud Alouette III	France	
(1967)	2	Max Holste M.H. 1521 Broussard	France	
(1969)	1	Sud Alouette II	France	
		Naval vessels		
1961	1	Patrol boat, "YMS" type	France	Displ: 280 t; ex-French coastal minesweeper
1963	1	Patrol boat, "VC" type	France	Displ: 75 t; launched 1958; returned to France 1967
1963	5	Patrol boat	FR Germany	Displ: (46) t; part of $6 mn aid programme; used by Maritime Police
1965	1	Patrol boat, "YMS" type	France	Displ: 280 t; built 1942; ex-US; ex-French
1966–67	1	Patrol boat	France	Displ: 1 040 t; built 1959; former trawler, converted to coastguard and training ship 1966–67
1967	1	Patrol boat	France	Displ: 235 t light; new
. . .	1	Transport ship	Mexico	On order; displ: 810 t
		Armoured fighting vehicles		
(1963)	(15)	M–8 Greyhound	France	

Register 55. Arms supplies to Malawi

Date	Number	Item	Supplier	Comment
		Naval vessels		
. . .	3	Gunboat	UK	On order
		Armoured fighting vehicles		
1972	9	Ferret	S. Africa	

Register 56. Arms supplies to Mali

Date	Number	Item	Supplier	Comment
		Aircraft		
1962	2	Douglas C–47	USA	Gift
(1962)	2	Mi–4	USSR	
(1962)	(2)	Yak–18	USSR	
(1963)	1	MiG–15 UTI	USSR	
(1963)	(3)	Yak–12 M	Poland	
(1963–65)	5	MiG–15	USSR	
1970–71	(3)	MiG–17 SB	USSR	Aid
		Armoured fighting vehicles		
(1961)	(15)	BTR 40	USSR	
(1963)	10	T–34	USSR	

Register 57. Arms supplies to Mauritius

Date	Number	Item	Supplier	Comment
		Armoured fighting vehicles		
1971	4	Shorland Mk 2	UK	

Register 58. Arms supplies to Mauritania

Date	Number	Item	Supplier	Comment
		Aircraft		
1960	2	Max Holste M.H. 1521 Broussard	France	Gift
1960	1	Douglas C–47	France	Gift
(1967)	2	Douglas C–47	France	
(1968)	2	Max Holste M.H. 1521 Broussard	France	
1969	1	Il–18	USSR	

Date	Number	Item	Supplier	Comment
		Naval vessels		
1966	1	Patrol boat	France	Displ: 75 t; completed 1957
1969	2	Patrol boat	France	Displ: 75 t
		Armoured fighting vehicles		
(1960–61)	(15)	(M–8) AC	France	
(1968–69)	(15)	AML–60	France	

Register 59. Arms supplies to Niger

Date	Number	Item	Supplier	Comment
		Aircraft		
1960	3	Max Holste M.H. 1521 M Broussard	France	Gift
1960	1	Douglas C–47	France	Gift
(1968)	1	Dassault M.D. 312 Flamant	France	
(1969)	1	Max Holste M.H. 1521 M Broussard	France	
1970–71	4	Nord 2501 Noratlas	FR Germany	Ex-Luftwaffe; refurbished
1971	2	Reims-Cessna 337 Skymaster	France	
1971	2	Douglas DC–6B	FR Germany	Ex-Luftwaffe
(1971)	1	Aero Commander 500	(FR Germany)	
(1971–72	3	Douglas C–47	France	
		Naval vessels		
1966	2	River gunboat	FR Germany	
		Armoured fighting vehicles		
(1960)	(8)	M–8 Greyhound	France	
(1960)	(8)	M–20	France	

Register 60. Arms supplies to Nigeria

Date	Number	Item	Supplier	Comment
		Aircraft		
1963	3	DHC–3 Otter	Canada	
1963	2	Nord 2501 Noraltas	FR Germany	10 originally agreed upon but only 2 delivered; sold back
1963	14	Piaggio P. 149D	FR Germany	26 originally ordered but only 14 delivered
(1963)	1	Westland Gnome Whirlwind	UK	Bought from Bristow Helicopters

Date	Number	Item	Supplier	Comment
1964	1	DH Heron	UK	Cost: $210 000
1964	20	Dornier Do–27	FR Germany	30 originally ordered but only 20 delivered
[1965	5	Fouga Magister	FR Germany]	Conflicting reports
1967	10	MiG–17	USSR/Czechoslovakia	
1967	8	Westland Whirlwind 2	Austria	
1967	12	L–29 Delfin	Czechoslovakia	U.c.: $205 000
1967	6	MiG–15 UTI	(Poland)	
1967	2	BAC Jet Provost	Sudan	Gift
1968	1	Il–28	(USSR)	
1968	1	Il–28	Algeria	
1968	2	Il–28	Egypt	
1968	31	MiG–17	USSR/Egypt/Algeria	
1969	1	Il–28	USSR	
[1969	4-5	Su–7	USSR/Egypt]	Unconfirmed reports
[1969	(2)	MiG–19P	USSR/Egypt]	Unconfirmed reports
1969	5	Douglas DC–3	Belgium	Purchased from Sabena
1969	1	Piper Aztec D	(Belgium)	
1971	1	Douglas DC–6	(USA)	
1972	1	Fairchild Hiller FH–1100	(USA)	
1972	6	Fokker-VFW F–27 Friendship	Netherlands	
1973	3	Piper Navajo	USA/Switzerland	Cost: $1 mn, incl spares; sold by Piper International, Geneva
1973-	20	Scottish Aviation Bulldog Series 120	UK	On order; delivery from late-1973; cost: $1.85 mn, incl spares, support equipment and training
1973	1	Fokker-VFW F–28	Netherlands	For VIP
...	3	Piper Navajo	USA	On order; cost $1 mn, incl spares
...	4	Dornier Do–28 Sky servant	FR Germany	On order
...	4	MBB Bo 105	FR Germany	On order
Naval vessels				
1959	1	Survey craft	UK	Displ: 544 t gross; built 1954
1959	1	Survey craft	UK	Displ: 114 t gross; built 1955
1959	1	Survey craft	UK	Displ: 79 t gross; built 1959
1959	1	Escort minesweeper	UK	Displ: 1 000 t; completed 1944; ex-British
1959	1	Landing craft	UK	Displ: 350 t; ex-British
1959	2	Minesweeping launch	UK	Displ: 85 t; ex-British
1959	1	Seaward defence launch	UK	Displ: 46 t; ex-British
(1959)	1	Presidential yacht	(UK)	Displ: 280 t; transferred to inland waterways 1966
1962	1	Seaward defence boat, "Ford" class	UK	Displ: 120 t; completed 1961
(1963)	1	Patrol boat	Netherlands	Displ: 320 t; launched 1942; gift
1965	1	Anti-aircraft and anti-submarine frigate	Netherlands	Displ: 1 724 t; completed 1965; cost: $9 809 000
1966	3	Seaward defence vessel, "Ford" class	UK	Displ: 120 t; ex-British

Date	Number	Item	Supplier	Comment
1967–68	2	Seaward defence vessel, "Ford" class	UK	Displ: 120 t
1972	2	Corvette	UK	Displ: 500 t; new; cost: $9.6 mn
. . .	2	Fast patrol boat	UK	On order; displ: 105 t; cost: $3.3 mn
		Armoured fighting vehicles		
1960–68	(40)	Ferret	UK	
1966–70	(50)	Saladin	UK	
1968	(15)	Saracen	UK	
1968	13	Panhard AML–60/90	France	

Biafra[a]

Date	Number	Item	Supplier	Comment
		Aircraft		
1967	2	Douglas B–26 Invader	(France)	
1967	2	Douglas B–26 Invader	Portugal	To replace B–26
1968	4	Sud Alouette II and III	(France)	In addition to 3 seized from Aero Contractors Company
(1969)	2	Gloster Meteor	. .	Never reached Biafra
1969	19	MFI–9B Militrainer	Sweden	U.c.: $11 700 in first batch; fitted with rockets
1969	6	NA T–6	. .	Fitted with machine-guns
1969	2	Douglas C–47	. .	Ex-Luftwaffe; equipped with bomb racks in addition to other transports seized, mostly from Nigerian Airways

[a] Does not include items which were hijacked or otherwise seized.

Register 61. Arms supplies to Rhodesia (incl the Central African Federation)

Date	Number	Item	Supplier	Comment
		Aircraft		
1951	11	Supermarine Spitfire F.22	UK	Reconditioned
1951–54	8	Supermarine Spitfire F.22	UK	
1953–55	32	DH Vampire FB.9 and T.11	UK	
1954	13	Hunting Provost T.53	UK	
1956	8	Douglas C–47	UK	Ex-RAF; 4 went to Zambia 1964
(1957)	(4)	Canadair DC–4M North Star	(Canada)	
1959	4	Canadair Argonaut	UK	Ex-BOAC
1959	30	English Electric Canberra B.2	UK	1 Canberra squadron returned to UK after break-up of federation in 1963; has 15
1959	3	English Electric Canberra T.4	UK	
(1961)	1	Beech Baron	(USA)	
1962	5	Sud Alouette III	France	

Date	Number	Item	Supplier	Comment
1962–63	12	Hawker Hunter FGA.9	UK	Ex-RAF; bought at favourable rates; modernized
1963	3	Sud Alouette III	France	
1967	6–7	Piaggio P.166	Italy	
1967	4	Sud Alouette III	S.Africa	
[1967	12	Aermacchi-Lockheed AL60	S.Africa]	Rumour denied in Italy
[(1971)	7	Aerfer-Aermacchi AM.3C	Italy/S. Africa]	Rumour denied in Italy
1971	7	Aermacchi-Lockheed AL60	(S.Africa)	
(1973)	(2)	Aérospatiale SA–330 Puma	(S. Africa)	
		Armoured fighting vehicles		
(1960)	30	Ferret	UK	
(1972)	(30)	AML–60	S. Africa	

Register 62. Arms supplies to Rwanda

Date	Number	Item	Supplier	Comment
		Aircraft		
(1963)	1	Sud Alouette II	(Belgium)	
(1964)	1	Dornier Do–27	FR Germany	
(1965)	1	Helio H–395 Super Courier	USA	
1972	3	Aerfer Aermacchi AM.3C	Italy	
(1973)	(2)	Aérospatiale Alouette III	France	
. . .	6	Aermacchi MB.326 6B	Italy	On order
		Armoured fighting vehicles		
(1962)	(5)	AML–60/90	(Belgium)	

Register 63. Arms supplies to Senegal

Date	Number	Item	Supplier	Comment
		Aircraft		
1960–61	2	Douglas C–47	France	Gift
1960–61	4	Max Holste M.H. 1521M Broussard	France	Gift
1960–61	2	Bell 47G	France	Gift
(1963)	1	Piper Aztec	(USA)	
(1964)	2	Douglas C–47	France	
(1967)	1	Sud Alouette II	France	
1971	1	Reims-Cessna 337 Skymaster	France	

Date	Number	Item	Supplier	Comment
		Naval vessels		
1961	1	Patrol boat	France	Displ: 110 t; ex-US; ex-French
1963	1	Patrol boat, "VC" type	France	Displ: 75 t; completed 1958
1965	1	Patrol boat, "VC" type	France	Displ: 75 t; completed 1958; returned to France from People's Republic of Congo
1971	1	Patrol boat	France	Displ: 235 t; new
. . .	12	Patrol boat, "Vosper 45" type	UK/ Singapore	On order from Vosper Thornycroft, Singapore
		Armoured fighting vehicles		
(1961)	(15)	M–8 Greyhound	France	
(1969)	(15)	AML–60	France	

Register 64. Arms supplies to Sierra Leone

Date	Number	Item	Supplier	Comment
		Aircraft		
1973	2	Hughes 300	USA/Sweden	Supplied by Saab
1973-	4	Saab-Scania MFI–15	Sweden	

Register 65. Arms supplies to Somalia

Date	Number	Item	Supplier	Comment
		Aircraft		
1960	8	NA F–51D Mustang	Italy	Transferred from Italian-controlled Cuerpo Aeronautica della Somalia
1960	(3)	Douglas C–47	Italy	Transferred from Italian-controlled Cuerpo Aeronautica della Somalia
(1960)	(4)	Beech C–45	Italy	Transferred from Italian-controlled Cuerpo Aeronautica della Somalia
1961	2	Heliopolis Air Works Gomhuriah	Egypt	
1962	8	Piaggio P.148	Italy	Gift
1962	2	Agusta-Bell 47G–2	Italy	Sold to "Guardia di finanza" anti-smugglers corps
1963	6	MiG–15 UTI	USSR	
1965	3	MiG–15	USSR	
(1965)	20	Yak–11	USSR	
1965–66	12	MiG–17	USSR	
(1966)	(3)	MiG–15	USSR	
(1966)	3	An–2	USSR	
(1967)	(2)	Il–28	USSR	

Date	Number	Item	Supplier	Comment
1968	1	An–24	USSR	
1973	(6)	MiG–15	USSR	
1973	(18)	MiG–17	USSR	
1973	(3)	Il–28	USSR	
1973	(3)	Mi–4	USSR	
1973	(5)	Mi–8	USSR	
1973	(2)	An–24	USSR	
1973	(2)	An–26	USSR	
1973	(2)	Il–18	USSR	
(1974)	(6)	MiG–19	USSR	
1974	...	MiG–21	USSR	
		Naval vessels		
1966	2	Patrol boat, "Poluchati" class	USSR	Displ: 100 t
1968	2	Patrol boat, "Poluchati" class	USSR	Displ: 100 t
(1970)	4	Motor torpedo boat, "P4" class	USSR	Displ: 25 t normal max; ex-Soviet
(1971–72)	2	Patrol boat, "Poluchati" class	USSR	Displ: 100 t
1973	(2)	Motor torpedo boat, "P6" class	USSR	Displ: 50 t
		Armoured fighting vehicles		
1960	(20)	AC	Egypt	
(1961)	(15)	Ferret	UK	
1962	5	(Comet) medium tank	UK	Obsolete
1965	65	BTR–152	USSR	
1965–67	150	T–34	USSR	Obsolete
(1968)	(15)	V–100 Commando	USA	
(1972–73)	(200)	BTR–152	USSR	
(1972–73)	(60)	BTR–40	USSR	
1973	(30)	BTR–50	USSR	
1973–74	100	T–54	USSR	

Register 66. Arms supplies to the Sudan

Date	Number	Item	Supplier	Comment
		Aircraft		
1957	4	Hunting Provost T.53	UK	Purchased 1956; used for training in UK for 1 year; 2 crashed
1957	4	Heliopolis Air Works Gomhuriah Mk 2	Egypt	Gift
1958	2	Hunting Provost T.53	UK	To replace crashed Provosts
(1959)	1	Hunting Pembroke C–54	UK	
1960	2	Hunting Pembroke C–55	UK	
1961	4	Hunting Jet Provost T.51	UK	
1962	2	Douglas C–47	(USA)	2 DC–3s converted from civil use 1962

Date	Number	Item	Supplier	Comment
1962	4	Hunting Jet Provost T.52	UK	
1963	(2)	Hunting Jet Provost T.52	UK	
1964	3	Dornier Do–27	FR Germany	
1964	4	Fokker F–27M Troopship	Netherlands	
1968	8	Pilatus Turbo-Porter	Switzerland	
1969	5	BAC 145 Jet Provost	UK	
1970	16	MiG–21	USSR	Part of $112 mn arms deal
1970	6	An–12	USSR	
1970	5	An–24	USSR	
1970	10	Mi–8	USSR	
(1970)	(3)	Mi–4	USSR	
1972	8	F–4/MiG–17	China	Gift; with complete set of parts; agreement 1970
		Missiles		
1971	(1 batt)	SA–2	USSR	
		Naval vessels		
1962	4	Patrol boat	Yugoslavia	Displ: 100 t; built 1961–62
1969	2	Patrol boat	Yugoslavia	Displ: 190 t; ex-Yugoslav
1969	2	Landing craft	Yugoslavia	Displ: 410 t; ex-Yugoslav
1969	1	Survey ship	Yugoslavia	
1969	1	Water carrier	Yugoslavia	
1969	1	Oiler	Yugoslavia	Displ: 420 t; ex-Yugoslav; refurbished
		Armoured fighting vehicles		
(1958–59)	20	T–34/85	Egypt	
(1958–60)	60	Ferret	UK	
1960	5	AC	USSR	
1960	25	(BTR 152) APC	USSR	
1961–63	3	Ferret	UK	
1961–63	9	Saladin	UK	
(1961–63)	30	M–4 Sherman	(USA)	
(1962–65)	97	Saladin	FR Germany	Agreement 1961
(1964–65)	(50)	Saracen	UK	
(1965–66)	(45)	V–100 Commando	USA	
(1969)	(25)	BTR–152	USSR	
1969–70	(100)	T–54/55	USSR	
(1969–70)	(50)	BTR 50	USSR	
(1970)	(60)	OT–64	Czechoslovakia	
1972	(10)	T–59	China	
(1972)	20	T–62	China	

Register 67. Arms supplies to Tanzania

Date	Number	Item	Supplier	Comment
		Aircraft		
1965	5	DHC–4 Caribou	Canada	Aid
1965	8	Piaggio P.149	FR Germany	Aid

Date	Number	Item	Supplier	Comment
(1965)	2	Dornier Do–28	FR Germany	Aid
1966	6	DHC–2 Beaver	Canada	Aid
1966	8	DHC–3 Otter	Canada	Aid
(1967)	1	An–2	(USSR)	
1971	8	DHC–4 Caribou	Canada	
1971	(5)	Soko Galeb	Yugoslavia	
(1972)	5	Piper Cherokee 140	USA	
1973	12	F–4/MiG–17	China	Pilots have been trained in China; air base built with Chinese aid
1973	2	Bell 47G–3B–2	Italy	
1973	2	Agusta Bell 206–A Jet Ranger	Italy	
1973-	12	F–6/MiG–19	China	
. . .	1	HS 748	UK	For VIP
		Naval vessels		
1964	2	Coastguard boat	FR Germany	Displ: 50 t; gift
1964	4	Patrol boat	FR Germany	Displ: 112 t; on loan; later transferred to Kenya
1966	4	Patrol boat	China	Displ: 7 t
1970–71	6	Patrol boat, "Shanghai" class	China	Displ: 100 t full load
		Armoured fighting vehicles		
1964	(15)	BTR 40	USSR	
(1966)	15	BTR 152	USSR	
(1967)	14	T–62	China	
1971	20	T–59	China	

Register 68. Arms supplies to Togo

Date	Number	Item	Supplier	Comment
		Aircraft		
1960	2	Max Holste M.H. 1521M Broussard	France	Gift
1960	1	Douglas C–47	France	Gift
1970	1	Sud Alouette II	France	
1971	2	Reims-Cessna 337 Skymaster	France	
		Naval vessels		
(1960)	1	River gunboat	(France)	Length: 95 ft
(1965)	3	Patrol boat	(France)	Length: 100 ft
		Armoured fighting vehicles		
(1960)	(15)	AC	France	

Register 69. Arms supplies to Uganda

Date	Number	Item	Supplier	Comment
		Aircraft		
1964	10	Piaggio 149D	FR Germany	
1964	2	Potez-IAI Magister	Israel	
1965	2	Westland Scout	UK	Police Air Wing
(1965–68)	10	Potez-AIA Magister	Israel	
1966	1	Douglas C–47	USA	
1966	3	Cessna 180	USA	Police Air Wing
1966	3	Piper Aztec	(USA)	Incl 1 with Police Air Wing
1966	5	MiG–17	USSR/Cze-choslovakia	Ex-Czechoslovak Air Force
1966	2	MiG–15 UTI	USSR/Cze-choslovakia	Ex-Czechoslovak Air Force
1966	1	DHC–4 Caribou	Canada	Police Air Wing
1966	9	L–29 Delfin	Czechoslova-kia	
1966–67	8	Piper L–18 Super Cub	Israel	
(1968–69)	4	Bell 206 Jet Ranger	USA	Police Air Wing
(1968–69)	(5)	Douglas C–47	Israel	Surplus
1970	1	DHC–6 Twin Otter	Canada	Police Air Wing
1971	2	Bell 205 A–1 Iroquois	USA	Police Air Wing
1971	4	Bell 212 Twin-Pac	USA	Police Air Wing
1971	1	IAI Commodor Jet	Israel	
1973	7	(Mi–4) helicopter	USSR	
1973	6	Agusta-Bell 205 Iroquois	Italy	
1973	2	Agusta-Bell 206A Jet Ranger	Italy	
1973	8	(Northrop F–5) fighter bomber	(Libya)	Gift from a "friendly country"
		Missiles		
1973-	...	Nord SS.11	France	To arm Savien AC
		Armoured fighting vehicles		
(1965)	15	Ferret	UK	
1967–68	36	OT–64	(Czechoslova-kia)	
(1968–70)	(10)	BTR–40	USSR	
(1968–70)	(10)	BTR–152	USSR	
1970	12	M–4 Sherman	Israel	
1973	58	(PT–76) light tank	USSR	
1973	62	(BTR–40) AC	USSR	
1973-	80	Savien AC	France	Armed with SS.11 ATMs; financed by Libya

Register 70. Arms supplies to Upper Volta

Date	Number	Item	Supplier	Comment
		Aircraft		
1964	1	Douglas C–47	France	Gift
1965	2	Max Holste M.H. 1521 Broussard	France	Gift

Date	Number	Item	Supplier	Comment
(1966)	1	Max Holste M.H. 1521 Broussard	France	
(1969)	1	Douglas C–47	France	
(1970)	1	Aero Commander 500	France	
(1971)	1	Reims-Cessna 337 Skymaster	France	
		Armoured fighting vehicles		
(1960)	(15)	AC	(France)	

Register 71. Arms supplies to Zaïre

Date	Number	Item	Supplier	Comment
Zaïre				
		Aircraft		
1960	15	Il–14	USSR	Returned after 1 month
1961	2	NA T–6 Harvard	Belgium	Purchased from Belgian Cogea company; intended for Katanga, but diverted
1961	2	Piper PA–20 Pacer	(Belgium)	
1961	1	DH Tigermoth	(Belgium)	
1961	1	Douglas C–54	(Belgium)	
1962	2	Douglas DC–4	UK	Purchased from Trans-World Airlines
1962	3	DH Dove	Belgium	Ex-Belgian; obtained from base in Rwanda Urundi
1962	1	Sikorsky S–55	Belgium	
1962	1	Dornier Do–27	FR Germany	Gift
1962	3	Douglas C–47	Iran	Purchased from Persian company
(1962)	2	DH Heron	(Belgium)	
1963	5	Douglas C–47	USA	MAP
1963	6	Vertol H–21 Shawnee	USA	
1963	6	Fouga Magister	France	9 were originally ordered for Katanga; 6 were released for Congo (K)
1963	2	NA T–6 Harvard	Belgium	
1963	2	Dornier Do–27	FR Germany	Gift
(1963)	3	Douglas C–54	(USA)	
(1963)	6	Curtiss C–46	USA	
(1963)	3	Beech 18	USA	
(1963)	2	Beech C–45	USA	
(1963)	4	BAC Pembroke	UK	
1964	6	NA T–28D	USA	MAP
1964	5	Douglas C–47	USA	
1964	4	Lockheed C–130E Hercules	USA	Flown by US pilots; part of Stanleyville episode; returned to USA
1964	9	On Mark B–26K Counter Invader	USA	MAP
1964	12	NA T–6G Harvard	Italy	Part of military aid agreement; surplus

Date	Number	Item	Supplier	Comment
(1964)	2	Auster	(USA)	
(1964)	3	DH Dove	(Belgium)	
1964–65	(20)	NA T–6	USA	
1965	12	Piaggio P.148	Italy	Part of military aid agreement
(1965)	7	Bell 47	USA	
(1965)	5	Sud Alouette II	France	
(1965)	2	Douglas C–47	Italy	Part of military aid agreement
1966	10	NA T–28D	USA	MAP
1966	8	Sud Alouette III	France	
1966	2	DHC–4 Caribou	Canada	Gift
1966	1	Dornier Do–28	FR Germany	
1967	3	Lockheed C–130E Hercules	USA	On loan for 1 year
1969–70	17	Aermacchi M.B. 326	Italy	
1970	12	Siai-Marchetti SF 260	Italy	
1971	7	Aérospatiale SA–330 Puma	France	
(1971)	3	Lockheed C–130 Hercules	USA	For paratroop lifting
(1972)	7	Aérospatiale Alouette III	France	
(1973)	12	Siai-Marchetti SF.260	Italy	
...	...	Lockheed C–130 Hercules	USA	On order; delivery from 1975
...	17	Dassault Mirage 5	France	On order; option for further 17
...	23	Aérospatiale SA–330 Puma	France	On order
...	...	DHC–5 Buffalo	Canada	On order
		Naval vessels		
(1961)	(1)	River boat	(Belgium)	Length: 260 ft; refitted in 1967
1964	2	Patrol boat	USA	Length: 50 ft
1964	4	Speed boat	(USA)	Length: 21 ft
		Armoured fighting vehicles		
1960	(15)	M–3A1	Belgium	
1960	(15)	M–8 Greyhound	Belgium	
(1963–64)	30	Ferret	UK	
(1964)	10	M–4 Sherman	(Israel)	
1969–71	60	AML–60/90	France	

Katanga

Date	Number	Item	Supplier	Comment
		Aircraft		
1960	6	DH Dove	Belgium	Ex-Force Publique
1960	1	Sud Alouette II	Belgium	Ex-Force Publique
1960	1	Sikorsky S–55	Belgium	Ex-Force Publique
1960	1	Piper L–18C	Belgium	
1961	3	Fouga Magister	(France)	
1961	1	DH Heron	Belgium	
1961	8	NA T–6 Harvard	Belgium	
1961	5	Dornier Do–28	FR Germany	
1961	5	Piper PA–20A Pacer	S. Africa	Probably returned to S. Africa
(1961)	2	Douglas C–47	(USA)	
1962	11	NA T–6 Harvard	Belgium	
1962	2	DH Vampire T.11	(Belgium)	
1962	1	Douglas DC–3 (C–47)	Belgium	

Register 72. Arms supplies to Zambia

Date	Number	Item	Supplier	Comment
		Aircraft		
1964	4	Douglas C–47	Rhodesia	Received after break-up of federation
1964	2	Hunting Pembroke C–1	Rhodesia	Received after break-up of federation
(1964)	4	Fokker Friendship	Netherlands	
1965	2	HS Chipmunk	UK	
1965	4	DHC–4 Caribou	Canada	
1965	6	DHC–2 Beaver	Canada	
1966	1	HS 748	UK	
1969	5	Agusta-Bell 205 Iroquois	Italy	
1971	1	HS 748	UK	
1971	6	Aermacchi M.B. 326	Italy	
1971	4	Soko Jastreb	Yugoslavia	
1971	2	Soko Galeb	Yugoslavia	
(1971)	1	DHC–4 Caribou	Canada	
(1971)	1	Agusta-Bell 212	Italy	
1971–72	8	Siai-Marchetti SF.260	Italy	
1973-	25	Agusta-Bell 205 Iroquois	Italy	Being delivered
...	6	Aermacchi M.B.326	Italy	
		Missiles		
1971	10 systems	BAC Rapier	UK	Cost: $15 mn
		Naval vessels		
1966	1	Tank landing craft, LCT (8) type	UK	Displ: 657t; ex-British
		Armoured fighting vehicles		
1964	(15)	Ferret	UK	

South Africa

Register 73. Arms supplies to South Africa

Date	Number	Item	Supplier	Comment
		Aircraft		
(1950)	(5)	Lockheed P–2V–5 Neptune	USA	
1952–54	30	DH Vampire FB.5	UK	
1952–54	20	DH Vampire T.55	UK	
1955	4	Sikorsky S–51	USA	
(1955)	(20)	Douglas C–47	USA	
(1955)	9	DH Devon C–Mk 1	UK	
(1955)	(5)	Auster AOP.9	UK	
(1955)	2	DH 114 Heron	UK	

Date	Number	Item	Supplier	Comment
1956	36	Canadair CL–13 B Sabre Mk 6	Canada	
(1956)	3	Sikorsky S–55	USA	
1957	8	Avro Shackleton MR–3	UK	
1957	1	Canadair CL–13 B Sabre Mk 6	Canada	
1958	1	Canadair CL–13 B Sabre Mk 6	Canada	
(1958)	2	Sikorsky S–55	USA	
(1958)	2	Dornier Do–27B	FR Germany	
1959	2	Canadair CL–13 B Sabre Mk 6	Canada	
(1959)	1	Vickers Viscount	UK	
1960	1	Canadair CL–13 B Sabre Mk 6	Canada	
1961	1	Canadair CL–13 B Sabre Mk 6	Canada	
1962	25	Cessna 185	USA	
1962	6	English Electric Canberra B.12	UK	
1962	7	Sud Alouette II	France	
1963	7	Lockheed C–130B Hercules	USA	
1963	16	Dassault Mirage III CZ	France	Armed with Matra R. 530 AAMs
1964	6	Westland Wasp AS.1	UK	
1964	3	Dassault Mirage III BZ	France	
1965	1	Cessna 320 Skyknight	USA	
1965	6	BAC Canberra B(1) 58	UK	Refurbished
1965	16	HS Buccaneer S.2	UK	
1965–66	54	Sud Alouette III	France	
1965–66	20	Dassault Mirage III EZ	France	Armed with AS.20 and AS.30 ASMs
1966	12	Cessna 185	USA	
1966	5	Douglas C–54	(USA)	
1966	4	Westland Wasp AS.1	UK	
1966	4	Dassault Mirage III RZ	France	
1966–67	16	Sud SA–321 Super Frelon	France	
1967	6	Lockheed C–130E Hercules	USA	Report
1967	(20)	Aermacchi-Lockheed AL 60	Italy	
1967	16	Aermacchi M.B. 326	Italy	Complete
1967	10	Aermacchi M.B. 326	Italy	In major component form
1968	40	Atlas-Macchi M.B. 326 Impala	Italy/S. Africa	In subassemblies
1967–73	150	Atlas-Macchi M.B. 326 Impala	Italy/S. Africa	Produced under licence
1968	3	Dassault Mirage III DZ	France	
1968	16	Sud Alouette III	France	
1969	9	Piaggio P. 166	Italy	
1969–70	3	HS 125	UK	
1969–70	9	Transall C.160	France	
1970	3	Aérospatiale Alouette III	France	
1970–71	20	Sud SA–330 Puma	France	
1971	3	HS 125	UK	To replace earlier 3 lost in accident

Date	Number	Item	Supplier	Comment
1971	1	Dassault Mirage III	France	Replacement
1973	(7)	Dassault Mirage III	France	Supplementary deliveries incl 4 of reconnaissance version
1973–74	9	Piaggio P.166	Italy	
1973-	40	Aerfer-Aermacchi AM.3C	Italy	U.c.: $120 000 fully equipped
1973–74	6	Westland Wasp	UK	Ordered 1971; under Simonstown Agreement; export licence for last of 7 revoked
. . .	48	Dassault Mirage F1	France/S. Africa	To be produced partly under licence in S. Africa; 16 imported complete from France from France
. . .	36	Dassault Mirage III	France/S. Africa	To be produced under licence in S. Africa
. . .	50	Aermacchi M.B. 326 K	Italy/S. Africa	Partial assembly in S. Africa; 6 imported completed from Italy in 1974

Missiles

Date	Number	Item	Supplier	Comment
(1956)	200	NWC Sidewinder	USA	To arm Sabre
1963	(96)	Matra R.530	France	To arm Mirage IIIC
1965–66	(60)	Nord AS 20/30	France	To arm Mirage IIIE
1971–73	3 batt	Matra/Thomson–CSF Cactus	France	Specifications drawn up by and 85 per cent R&D paid by S. Africa
1974	555	Short Tigercat	Jordan	
. . .	. . .	Matra R.550 Magic	France	Reportedly on order for Mirage

Naval vessels

Date	Number	Item	Supplier	Comment
1950	1	Destroyer, "W" class	UK	Displ: 2 165 t; launched 1943; modernized 1964–66
1952	1	Destroyer, "W" class	UK	Displ: 2 165 t; launched 1943; modernized 1964–66
1954	1	Seaward defence vessel, "Ford" class	UK	Displ: 120 t; new
1955	1	Seaward defence vessel, "Ford" class	UK	Displ: 120 t; new
1955–59	10	Coastal minesweeper, "Ton" class	UK	Displ: 360 t; launched 1955–59
1956	1	Anti-submarine frigate	UK	Displ: 2 160 t; "type 15"; launched 1943 as "W" class; ex-British; converted 1951; refitted 1956
1958–59	3	Seaward defence vessel, "Ford" class	UK	Displ: 120 t; launched 1958–59
1963	2	Frigate, "Whitby" class	UK	Displ: 2 144 t; launched 1960:–61
1964	1	Frigate, "Whitby" class	UK	Displ: 2 144 t; launched 1963
1965	1	Tanker	Denmark	Displ: 12 500 t
1970–72	3	Submarine, "Daphne" class	France	Displ: 850 t; surface, 1 040 t submerged; new; cost: $37.8 mn
1971	1	Survey ship, "Hecla" class	UK	Displ: 1 930 t; new
. . .	1	Submarine "Daphne" class	France	Displ: 850 t; being built for Africa

Date	Number	Item	Supplier	Comment
...	6	Corvette, "Joao Continho" class	Portugal	Displ: 1 250 t; on order; hulls to be built in Portugal, fitting in S. Africa
		Armoured fighting vehicles		
(1950)	(40)	Comet	UK	
1955–59	(168)	Centurion	UK	100 sold to Switzerland 1960–61
(1956–60)	(250)	Saracen	UK	
(1957–58)	(50)	M–3A1 White	USA	
(1961–72)	(800)	AML–60/90	France/S. Africa	Produced under licence in S. Africa
1962	(32)	Centurion	Israel	
(1963–64)	(60)	Ferret	UK	
1974	41	Centurion	Jordan	

Central America

Register 74. Arms supplies to Cuba

Date	Number	Item	Supplier	Comment
		Aircraft		
(1949–50)	6	Douglas C–47	USA	
(1951–53)	(3)	Beech C–45	USA	
(1952–53)	(3)	Curtiss C–46	USA	
1953–56	18	Douglas B–26 Invader	USA	
(1954–55)	(5)	NA T–28	USA	
(1955)	4	Lockheed T–33	USA	
(1956)	3	Bell 47G	USA	
(1956–57)	(3)	Piper Tri Pacer	USA	
1957	3	DHC–2 Beaver	(Canada)	
(1957)	7	Bell 47J	USA	
(1957)	1	Bell 47H	USA	
(1957)	2	Hiller UH–12A	USA	
(1957–58)	(3)	Convair PBY–5A Catalina	USA	
1958	2	Westland Whirlwind	UK	
1958	17	Hawker Sea Fury	UK	
1960–61	20	Il–14	USSR	
1960–61	24	Mi–4	USSR	
1960–62	20	An–2	USSR	
1961	(5)	MiG–15	Czechoslovakia	Cuban T.S.: $226 000
(1961)	30	MiG–17	USSR	
1961–62	(15)	Zlin 226 Bohatir	Czechoslovakia	
1962	42	MiG–21	USSR	Cuban T.S.: $2.4 mn
1962	33	Il–28	USSR	Were returned to the USSR
(1962)	30	MiG–15 UTI	USSR	

Date	Number	Item	Supplier	Comment
(1962)	(10)	An–24	USSR	
1962–63	40	MiG–17	USSR	
(1962–63)	40	MiG–19	USSR	Cuban T.S.: $675 000
1963	25	MiG–15	Czechoslova-kia	Cuban T.S.: $558 000
(1963)	20	Mi–1	USSR	
1965–66	3	MiG–21	USSR	
1971	5	MiG–21	USSR	
1972	(10)	MiG–21MB	USSR	
1973	(20)	MiG–21MF	USSR	
		Missiles		
1961–62	500	SA–2	USSR	At 24 missile sites
1961–62	40	"Frog"	USSR	At 4 or 5 missile sites
1961–62	(50)	"Samlet"	USSR	
1961–62	(100)	AT–1 "Snapper"	USSR	
1962	(240)	K–13 "Atoll"	USSR	To arm MiG–21
(1962)	20	"Salish"	USSR	
1962–66	(100)	SS–N–2 "Styx"	USSR	For use with "Komar" class patrol boats
(1971–72)	(90)	K–13 "Atoll"	USSR	To arm MiG–21
1972	(24)	SS–N–2 "Styx"	USSR	4 launchers in 2 pairs on "Osa" class patrol boats
		Naval vessels		
1950	1	Lighthouse tender	UK	Displ: 815 t; built 1906
1953	2	Escort patrol vessel	USA	Displ: 640 t; completed 1942 and 1944; ex-US
1956	7	Auxiliary patrol craft	USA	Displ: 45 t
(1957)	3	Auxiliary patrol craft	USA	Displ: 45 t
1962	12	Patrol boat, "Komar" class	USSR	Displ: 75 t; ex-Soviet
1962	6	Submarine chaser "Kronstadt" class	USSR	Displ: 300 t; ex-Soviet
1962–64	12	Motor torpedo boat, "P4" class	USSR	Displ: 50 t; ex-Soviet
1963	12	Motor torpedo boat, "P6" class	USSR	Displ: 75 t; ex-Soviet
1964	6	Patrol boat, "SOI" type	USSR	Displ: 215 t; ex-Soviet
(1965)	4	Patrol boat, "Komar" class	USSR	Displ: 75 t; ex-Soviet armed with "Styx" SSMs
1966	2	Patrol boat, "Komar" class	USSR	Displ: 75 t; ex-Soviet armed with "Styx" SSMs
1967	6	Patrol vessel, "SOI" type	USSR	Displ: 215 t; ex-Soviet
1972	2	Patrol boat, "Osa" class	USSR	Displ: 165 t; ex-Soviet armed with "Styx" SSMs
		Armoured fighting vehicles		
(1957)	(25)	AC	UK	
1959	88	Blinded vehicle	USA	Probably M–6 Staghound, M3 A1 White and M–3 half tracks
(1959–60)	(100)	T–34	USSR	
1960	60	(BTR 40) APC	USSR	
(1960–61)	(75)	T–54/55	USSR	
(1960–64)	100	Su–100	USSR	

Date	Number	Item	Supplier	Comment
1961–64	(150)	(BTR 60, BTR 152) APC	USSR	
1962	60	JS II	USSR	
(1962–63)	(100)	T–34	USSR	
(1963)	(75)	T–54/55	USSR	
(1966)	(30)	BRDM	USSR	
(1969)	(40)	PT–76	USSR	

Register 75. Arms supplies to the Dominican Republic

Date	Number	Item	Supplier	Comment
		Aircraft		
(1951–52)	11	Republic F–47 Thunder-bolt	USA	
(1951–52)	6	Beech C–45	USA	
1952	7	DH Vampire F.1	Sweden	
1952	42	NA F–51 Mustang	Sweden	Cost: $1.3 mn
(1952–53)	6	Curtiss C–46	USA	
(1952–53)	(5)	Beech T–11	USA	
(1955)	1	DHC–2 Beaver	USA	
(1955)	2	Convair PBY–5A Catalina	USA	
1955–56	25	DH Vampire FB.50	Sweden	
(1956–57)	2	Sikorsky S–55	USA	
(1959)	3	Cessna 170	USA	
(1959)	6	Douglas C–47	USA	
(1960)	7	Douglas B–26 Invader	USA	US surplus stocks
(1961–62)	2	Bell 47	USA	
(1962)	2	DHC–2 Beaver	Canada	
(1963–64)	2	Sud Alouette II	France	
(1965–66)	(3)	Hiller UH–12	USA	
1967	1	Aero Commander 500	USA	
(1969)	1	Sud Alouette III	France	
1971	7	Hughes OH–6A	USA	
		Naval vessels		
1950	1	Tug	USA	Displ: 40 t
(1950)	2	Patrol vessel	USA	Displ: 280 t; completed 1942–43
1952	1	Tug	USA	Displ: 40 t
1957	1	Coastguard vessel	USA	Displ: 60 t
1960	1	Medium landing ship	USA	Displ: 743 t; completed 1945
1960	1	Motor launch	(USA)	Length: 53 ft; completed 1960
1964	2	Oiler	USA	Displ: 1 400 t full load; ex-US
1965	2	Patrol vessel	USA	Displ: 280 t; ex-US minesweeper
1966	1	Coastguard vessel	USA	Displ: 107 t; completed 1966
1967–68	2	Coastguard vessel	USA	Displ: 60 t
1972	1	Fleet ocean tug	USA	Displ: 1 235 t; launched 1942; FY 1973 ship lease
1972	1	Auxiliary tug, "Maricopa" class	USA	Displ: 534 t; launched 1945
1972	1	Brooke Marine launch	UK	Displ: 15 t

Date	Number	Item	Supplier	Comment
		Armoured fighting vehicles		
(1950)	(5)	M–3 Stuart	USA	
(1955)	(15)	Scout car	(USA)	
(1958)	20	AMX–13	France	
(1960)	(15)	AC	(USA)	

Register 76. Arms supplies to Guatemala

Date	Number	Item	Supplier	Comment
		Aircraft		
(1955)	12	NA F–51D Mustang	USA	
1960	10	Douglas B–26 Invader	USA	
(1961)	(3)	Cessna 180	USA	
(1963)	(2)	Cessna 182	USA	
(1963)	3	Sikorsky S–55	USA	
(1964)	(3)	Hiller UH–12	USA	
(1965)	8	Lockheed T–33	USA	
(1965)	1	Aero Commander 680	USA	
(1966)	3	Douglas C–47	USA	
(1968)	1	Douglas C–54	USA	
1971	6	Cessna A–37	USA	
1971	6	Bell UH–1 Iroquois	USA	
1973	8	Cessna A–37B	USA	
		Naval vessels		
1959	1	Patrol boat	Sweden	Displ: 310 t; launched 1933; ex-Swedish minesweeper; cost: $130 000
(1960)	4	Small patrol boat	USA	Displ: 20 t; ex-US
1964	1	Aircraft rescue boat	USA	Length: 63 ft
		Armoured fighting vehicles		
(1950)	(15)	M–2 and M–3A1 White	USA	
(1950)	10	M–3 Stuart	USA	
(1955)	10	M–4 Sherman	USA	
(1972–73)	(15)	M–113	USA	
...	8	AMX–13	France	On order; delivery 1974; ex-Austrian; refurbished

Register 77. Arms supplies to Haiti

Date	Number	Item	Supplier	Comment
		Aircraft		
(1952–53)	6	NA F–51D Mustang	USA	
(1955)	1	Cessna C–78	USA	

Date	Number	Item	Supplier	Comment
(1955)	2	Beech C–45	USA	
(1956)	1	Boeing 307 Stratoliner	USA	
(1957)	3	Douglas C–47	USA	
(1961)	2	NA T–28A	USA	
1971–72	4	(Bell 206 Jet Ranger)	USA	
		Naval vessels		
1955	1	Coastguard patrol boat	USA	Displ: 160 t; ex-US buoy tender
1956	2	Coastguard patrol boat	USA	Displ: 100 t; ex-US
1957	1	Tank landing ship	USA	Displ: 134 t; ex-US
1960	1	Coastguard patrol boat	USA	Displ: 650 t; on loan
		Armoured fighting vehicles		
(1950)	9	M–5 Stuart	USA	
(1955–56)	(15)	M–2	USA	
1971	(5)	M–113	USA	

Register 78. Arms supplies to Honduras

Date	Number	Item	Supplier	Comment
		Aircraft		
(1950–51)	(3)	Republic F–47D Thunderbolt	USA	Took part in 135th Honduran revolution
(1952–53)	(8)	NA F–51D Mustang	USA	
(1957)	(2)	Douglas C–47	USA	
1958	1	Fairchild C–119 Packet	USA	
1958	1	Curtiss C–46	USA	
1958	1	Douglas C–54	USA	
1958	8	Chance Vought F–4U Corsair	USA	
1958	(4)	Convair PBY–2 Pirateer	USA	
(1958)	1	Sikorsky S–52	USA	
1959	1	Douglas C–54	USA	
1959	4	Chance Vought F–4U Corsair	USA	
(1959)	(2)	Douglas C–47	USA	
(1959)	2	Cessna 180	USA	
(1960)	3	Lockheed T–33	USA	
(1961)	2	Cessna 185	USA	
(1964)	3	Sikorsky S–55	USA	
1969	4	NA/Fiat F–86K Sabre	Venezuela	Ex-FR German; cost: $1.5 mn
1971	4	NA F–51 Mustang	(USA)	
1971	2	Douglas B–26 Invader	(USA)	
1973	5	Cessna T–41 A	USA	
		Naval vessels		
(1963)	3	Coastal patrol craft	(USA)	Small coastguard cutters

Date	Number	Item	Supplier	Comment
		Armoured fighting vehicles		
(1951)	(15)	M–6 Staghound	USA	
(1951–52)	(15)	M–3A1 White	USA	
(1954–55)	(10)	M–24 Chaffee	USA	

Register 79. Arms supplies to Jamaica

Date	Number	Item	Supplier	Comment
		Aircraft		
1963	4	Cessna 185 Skywagon	USA	
1963	1	Bell 47G	UK	Ex-British Army
1964	1	Bell 47G	(UK)	
1967	1	DHC–6 Twin Otter	Canada	
1971	1	Bell 206A Jet Ranger	USA	
1974	1	Britten-Norman BN–2 Islander	UK	Cost: $600 000
		Naval vessels		
1964	3	Patrol boat	USA	Displ: 33 t; completed 1941; returned to USA 1966–67
1966	1	Patrol boat	USA	Displ: 60 t
1967	2	Patrol boat	USA	Displ: 60 t; MAP
1974-	3	Patrol boat	USA	Displ: 104 t; being built; delivery from 1974
		Armoured fighting vehicles		
(1965)	(15)	Ferret	UK	

Register 80. Arms supplies to Mexico

Date	Number	Item	Supplier	Comment
		Aircraft		
(1950)	45	NA T–6	USA	
1952–53	5	Convair PBY–5A Catalina	USA	
(1960)	15	DH Vampire F.3	Canada	Ex-RCAF
(1960)	2	DH Vampire T.55	Canada	
1960–61	30	NA T–28	USA	Ex-USAF
(1960–61)	19	Bell 47G	USA	
1961	15	Lockheed T–33A	USA	
1961	(5)	DH Vampire F.3	Canada	Ex-RCAF
(1961)	2	Douglas C–118A	USA	
(1961)	1	Douglas DC–7	USA	
(1962)	10	Beech T–34 Mentor	USA	
(1962)	15	Beech T–11	USA	
(1962)	(5)	Hiller UH–12E	USA	

Date	Number	Item	Supplier	Comment
(1963)	4	Bell 47J	USA	
(1964)	(5)	Cessna 180	USA	
(1964)	18	Lockheed 60	USA/Mexico	Produced under licence from Lockheed in Mexico
(1964–65)	8	Sud Alouette III	France	
(1964–65)	7	Sud Alouette II	France	
(1965)	5	Douglas C–54	USA	
(1966)	1	Fokker-VFW F–27 Friendship	Netherlands	
1967	12	Boeing-Stearman PT–13 Kaydet	USA	Refurbished
(1968)	(3)	Lockheed T–33	(Netherlands)	To balance attrition
1970	20	Beech Musketeer Sport	USA	
1970	(1)	Cessna 150	USA	For Navy
1971	1	Lockheed C–140 Jet Star	USA	
1971	1	Bell 212 Twin-Pac	USA	For VIP
1971	3	Britten-Norman BN–2 Islander	USA/UK	Through US distribution
1971	1	HS 125	(UK)	For VIP
1973	5	Bell 205 Iroquois	USA	
1973	5	Bell 206A Jet Ranger	USA	
(1973–74)	5	IAI Arava	Israel	On order; cost: $15 mn; some production and overhaul may take place in Mexico
. . .	20	Beech F33C	USA	On order; delivery 1974; cost: $1.3 mn

Naval vessels

Date	Number	Item	Supplier	Comment
1952	9	Patrol boat, "PC" type	USA	Displ: 280 t; built 1943–44
(1952)	6	Landing craft	USA	Length: 119 ft
1962	20	Escort minesweeper	USA	Displ: 650 t; completed 1943–44
1963	1	Ocean tug	USA	Displ: 534 t; MAP loan
1964	4	Frigate, "Rudderow" class	USA	Displ: 1 400 t; completed 1945
1964	1	Oiler, "Yog" class	USA	Displ: 440 t; built 1943
1964	1	Oiler, "Yog" class	USA	Displ: 534 t; built 1943
1970	2	Destroyer, "Fletcher" class	USA	Displ: 2 100 t; completed 1943
1971	1	Rescue ship	USA	Displ: 1 653 t; ex-US landing ship
1971	5	Tug	USA	Ex-US
1972	1	Dry dock	USA	FY 1973 ship lease; small auxiliary floating dry dock
1972	1	Rescue ship	USA	Displ: 1 653 t; ex-US landing ship
1972–73	19	Minesweeper, "AUK" class	USA	Displ: 890 t; FY 1973 ship sales; cost: $28 000; 9 to be used for spares
1973	1	Minesweeper, "Admirable" class	USA	Displ: 650 t; completed 1943–44; FY 1973 ship sale; to be used for spares

Armoured fighting vehicles

Date	Number	Item	Supplier	Comment
(1950–51)	(25)	M–3 and M–5 Stuart	USA	
(1950–51)	(50)	M–3A1 White	USA	
(1955–56)	(25)	M–4 Sherman	(USA)	

Date	Number	Item	Supplier	Comment
(1956)	(50)	M–8 Greyhound	USA	
(1960–61)	(15)	Humber Mk IV	UK	
1963–64	(15)	MAC–1	USA	
1964	(15)	HW–K11	FR Germany	

Register 81. Arms supplies to Nicaragua

Date	Number	Item	Supplier	Comment
		Aircraft		
(1950)	4	Beech C–45	USA	
(1953)	3	Douglas C–47	USA	
1954	26	NA F–51 Mustang	Sweden	Cost: $400 000
(1962)	10	Cessna 180	USA	
(1964)	3	Piper Super Cub	USA	
(1965)	1	Hughes 300	USA	
1966	6	NA T–28	USA	
1966	6	Lockheed T–33	USA	
1966	6	Douglas B–26 Invader	USA	
1971	4	Hughes OH–6A	USA	
(1973–74)	14	IAI Arava	Israel	
		Armoured fighting vehicles		
(1958–59)	(15)	AC	USA	

Register 82. Arms supplies to Panama

Date	Number	Item	Supplier	Comment
		Aircraft		
1969	4	Cessna 185 Skywagon	USA	
1969	2	Douglas C–47	USA	
(1970)	3	Fairchild Hiller FH–1100	USA	
(1970)	1	DHC–6 Twin Otter	Canada	
1971	1	Douglas DC–6	USA	
(1971)	2	Douglas C–47	USA	
(1971)	2	Bell UH–IH Iroquois	USA	
(1971)	1	Cessna 180	USA	
		Naval vessels		
1971	2	Patrol boat, "Vosper" type	UK	Displ: 96 t; new; cost: $1.65 mn

Register 83. Arms supplies to Salvador

Date	Number	Item	Supplier	Comment
		Aircraft		
1954	3	Beech T–34 Mentor	USA	
(1959)	6	Chance Vought F–4U–5 Corsair	USA	
1965	5	Cessna (0–1 Birddog)	USA	Unspecified type
1968	6	Cavalier F–51 Mustang	USA	Cost: $300 000; refurbished
1968	1	Canadair DC–4M	USA	
1969	1	Fairchild-Hiller FH–1100	USA	
1969	6	Cavalier F–51 Mustang	(USA)	Replacements
(1970)	3	Douglas B–26 Invader	(USA)	
(1971)	2	Douglas C–54	(USA)	
. . .	25	(IAI Arava)	Israel	On order
		Naval vessels		
1959	2	Patrol boat	UK	Displ: 46 t
		Armoured fighting vehicles		
. . .	12	AMX–13	France	On order; delivery 1974; ex-Austrian, refurbished

South America

Register 84. Arms supplies to Argentina

Date	Number	Item	Supplier	Comment
		Aircraft		
1950	(20)	Fiat G.46	Italy	Last of order of 70
1950	1	Fiat G.59	Italy	
(1950–53)	12	Douglas C–54	USA	
(1952)	(5)	Piper L 4/PA 11	USA	
1954	15	Sikorsky S–51	USA	
1955	6	Grumman S–2A Tracker	USA	
1956	10	Chance Vought F–4U–5/5N Corsair	USA	
1956	3	Sud Djinn	France	Credit of $285 000 for Djinn & Broussards
(1956)	(10)	Martin PMB–5A Mariner	USA	
(1956)	(5)	NA T–6 Texan	USA	
(1956)	3	Convair PBY–5A Catalina	USA	
1957	6	Lockheed P–2E Neptune	UK	Ex-RAF
(1957)	58	NA T–28A	USA	
(1957)	12	Grumman F–9F Panther	USA	
(1957)	10	Max Holste M.H. 1521C Broussard	France	Credit of $285 000 for Djinn & Broussards

Date	Number	Item	Supplier	Comment
(1958)	15	Beech T–34 Mentor	USA	Prior to start of licence production
(1958)	11	Piper L–21	USA	
(1958–60)	52	Chance Vought F–4U–5/5N Corsair	USA	
(1959)	(5)	NA T–6G	USA	
1960	28	NA F–86F Sabre	USA	MAP
1960	3	Beech C–45H	USA	
(1960)	(5)	Hiller UH–12E	USA	
(1960)	5	Sikorsky S–55	USA	
1960–61	34	FMA/Beech T–34 Mentor	USA/Argentina	Built under licence
1960–61	24	FMA/Morane Saulnier M.S. 760A Paris	France/Argentina	Assembled in Argentina; agreement 1956 for 48 worth $7.1 mn
(1960–64)	30	Bell 47	USA	
(1961)	(12)	Sikorsky S–55	USA	
1962	3	Grumman HU–16A Albatross	USA	
1962	2	Grumman TF–9J Cougar	USA	
1962	2	Sud Alouette II	France	
(1962)	4	Sikorsky S–58	USA	
(1962)	5	Piper Apache	USA	
1962–63	24	FMA/Morane Saulnier M.S. 760A Paris	France/Argentina	Second batch assembled in Argentina; agreement 1956 for 48 worth $7.1 mn
1962–65	41	FMA/Beech T–34 Mentor	USA/Argentina	Built under licence
1964	6	Piper Aztec C	USA	
(1964)	8	DHC–2 Beaver	(Canada)	
1965	1	Sikorsky S–58	USA	
1965	2	DHC–3 Otter	Canada	
1966	2	Douglas C–47	USA	MAP
1966	12	Douglas A–4B Skyhawk	USA	MAP; value of 25: $8.7 mn; incl spares
1966	15	Bell 47J	USA	MAP
1966	1	HS 748 Series 2	UK	
1966	45	Sud T–28 Fennec	France	U.c.: $6 000
1966–67	6	Lockheed P–2H Neptune	USA	For Navy; to replace P–2E
1967	13	Douglas A–4B Skyhawk	USA	Second batch; MAP; value of 25: $8.7 mn; incl spares
1967	2	Douglas C–118	USA	MAP
1967–69	30	FMA/Cessna 182	USA/Argentina	Produced under licence in Argentina; licence agreement: 500 to be produced over 5 years; most resold to Cessna
1968	7	Fairchild Hiller FH–1100	USA	For Army
1968	3	Lockheed C–130 Hercules	USA	
1968	14	Aero Commander	USA	Cost: $1.5 mn
1968	2	Fokker-VFW F–27 Mk 2	Netherlands	On loan; purchased in 1969
1968–69	9	DHC–6 Twin Otter	Canada	Cost: $5 mn approx, incl spares
1968–70	15	Bell UH–1 Iroquois	USA	8 for Air Force; 7 for Army
1969	5	Piper Turbo Navajo	USA	
1969	6	Aermacchi M.B. 326K	Italy	Cost: $3.5 mn; for Navy
1969	8	Fokker-VFW F–27 Mk 400	Netherlands	Cost: $14.4 mn; on credit
1969–70	14	Hughes OH–6/500	USA	Military and civil versions

Date	Number	Item	Supplier	Comment
1969–70	6	Alouette III	France	For Navy
1970	25	Douglas A–4 Skyhawk	USA	
(1970)	7	Bell 206A Jet Ranger	USA	Cost: $625 000
1970–71	10	BAC Canberra B.62	UK	Ex-RAF; refurbished
1970–71	2	BAC Canberra T.64	UK	
1971	1	Fairchild Turbo Porter	USA	For Navy
1971	5	Short Skyvan 3M	UK	For Navy
1971	1	HS 125	UK	For Navy
1971	2	Fokker-VFW F–27 Mk 600	Netherlands	
1971	1	Fokker-VFW F–28	Netherlands	
(1971)	12	Cessna 185	USA	For Army
(1971)	1	Beech 100 King Air	USA	For Army
(1971)	1	Douglas DC–6	USA	
1972	16	Douglas A–4B Skyhawk	USA	For use on aircraft carrier
1972	1	Lockheed C–130 Hercules	USA	
1972	4	Sikorsky S–61 D–4	USA	For Navy
1972	2	Dassault Mirage IIIB	France	
1972	6	Aermacchi M.B. 326 GB	Italy	
1972–73	12	Dassault Mirage IIIE	France	
1973	5	Aérospatiale SA–315 Lama	France	
. . .	6	Hughes 500M	USA	On order for Navy
. . .	3	Lockheed L–188 Electra	USA	On order for Navy; from airline surplus; being refurbished; delivery to be completed by 1975
. . .	120	Hughes OH–6	USA/Argentina	To be produced under licence; initial indigenous content 22 per cent to rise to maximum 50 per cent
. . .	5	Fokker-VFW F–28	Netherlands	On order; for use with Air Force operated airline

		Missiles		
(1965)	(40)	Short Seacat	UK	
1969	(36)	Nord AS.11 and AS.12	France	To arm M.B. 326
1969–70	(60)	MBB Bo 810 Cobra 2000	FR Germany	To arm Daimler-Benz Unimog vehicles
1970	(10)	Tigercat	UK	
1972–73	(60)	Matra R.530	France	To arm Mirage
. . .	. . .	HSD Sea Dart	UK	On order; 1 twin launcher on each Type 42 frigate
. . .	30	Nord AS–12	France	On order; to arm Alouette III
. . .	20	Nord SS–11	France	On order; to arm Alouette III

		Naval vessels		
1950	1	Oiler	UK	Displ: 14 352 t; completed 1950
1950	3	Transport ship	Canada	Displ: 3 100 t; completed 1950

Date	Number	Item	Supplier	Comment
1951	2	Cruiser, "Brooklyn" class	USA	Displ: 10 000 t approx; completed 1939; original value $37 mn; bought for $7.8 mn
1951	3	Transport	Italy	Displ: 3 825 t; completed 1950
1954	1	Icebreaker	USA	Displ: 4 854 t; completed 1954
1958	1	Aircraft carrier	UK	Displ: 14 000 t; completed 1946; modernized 1952–53 and 1955–56
1960	2	Submarine, "Balao" class	USA	Displ: 1 520 t standard, 2 425 t submerged; completed 1944–45; modernized 1959–60; loan agreement
1960	1	Salvage vessel	UK	Displ: 1 600 t; completed 1942; ex-British
1961	3	Destroyer, "Fletcher" class	USA	Displ: 2 100 t; completed 1943
1961	2	Patrol vessel	USA	Displ: 1 235 t; completed 1942; ex-US tugs
1965	2	Patrol vessel	USA	Displ: 1 863 t full load; launched 1943; tug type; on lease
1968	6	Coastal minesweeper, "Ton" class	UK	Displ: 360 t; ex-British – modernized in UK 1968
1968	1	Aircraft carrier	Netherlands	Displ: 15 892 t; completed 1945; ex-British; ex-Dutch
(1969)	6	Tug	USA	Displ: 70 t; ex-US
1970	1	Dock landing ship	USA	Displ: 5 480 t; completed 1943
1971	2	Submarine, "Balao" class	USA	Displ: 1 870 t; completed 1945
1971	2	Destroyer, "Fletcher" class	USA	Displ: 2 100 t; completed 1943
1972	2	Destroyer, "Allen M Sumner" class	USA	Displ: 2 200 t; completed 1944; FY 1973 ship sale; u.c.: $229 500
1972	2	Auxiliary tug, "Maricopa" class	USA	Displ: 689 t; launched 1944-45
1973	1	Destroyer, "Gearing" class	USA	Displ: 2 425 t; completed 1945; FY 1973 ship sale; cost: $229 500
. . .	2	Guided missile destroyer, type 42	UK	Displ: 3 500 t; on order; 1 to be assembled in Argentina, armed with Sea Dart SAMs and helicopters
. . .	2	Submarine, type 205	FR Germany	Displ: 1 000 t; being built
. . .	2	Patrol boat	FR Germany	Displ: 240 t; being built

		Armoured fighting vehicles		
(1952–53)	(75)	M–3	USA	
1966	5	M–41 Walker Bulldog	USA	Delivered out of an order for 50
(1967–69)	(75)	M–113	USA	
(1969–73)	24	AMX–155	France	
1969–71	60	AMX–13	France/ Argentina	30 assembled locally
(1969–71)	24	AML–VTT	France	
(1970–73)	72	Mowag Roland	Switzerland/Argentina	Produced under licence in two versions

Register 85. Arms supplies to Bolivia

Date	Number	Item	Supplier	Comment
		Aircraft		
(1952–53)	8	Boeing B–17	(USA)	
(1955–56)	6	Fairchild PT–19	(USA)	
1958	(5)	Boeing-Stearman PT–17 Kaydet	Argentina	
1960	4	NA F–51D Mustang	Uruguay	
(1960)	1	Douglas C–54	(USA)	For VIP
(1964)	20	NA T–6	USA	
(1965)	6	Cessna T–41	USA	
1966	5	Cessna 185	USA	
1966	3	NA T–28	USA	
(1967)	1	NA T–28	USA	
(1967)	(3)	Hiller OH–23	USA	
1968	10	NA F–51 Mustang	USA	MAP; refurbished
1968	12	Hughes 500M	USA	U.c.: $75 800; for COIN
(1968)	2	NA T–28	USA	
(1968)	2	Cessna 185	USA	
1972	9	EMB–326 GB Xavante	Brazil	Option on further 9
1972	6	Convair CV–440	Spain	
1973	3+N	NA F–86F Sabre	USA	MAP
1973	8	Cessna 185 Skywagon	USA	MAP
1973	2	Cessna Turbo Centurion	USA	MAP
1973	1	Beech King Air	USA	MAP
1973	1	Cessna 414	USA	MAP
1973–74	13	Canadair T–33 A/N	Canada	Refurbished; cost: $4 mn, incl spares
1973–74	8	Fokker Instructor S–11	Brazil	
1974	18	Aerotec T–23 Uirapuru	Brazil	MAP
		Armoured fighting vehicles		
(1967)	(15)	V–100 Commando	USA	
(1970)	(15)	M–113	USA	

Register 86. Arms supplies to Brazil

Date	Number	Item	Supplier	Comment
		Aircraft		
1950–57	(50)	NA T–6	USA	
1953–54	62	Gloster Meteor F.8	UK	
1953–54	10	Gloster Meteor T.7	UK	
1955	25	Republic F–47D Thunderbolt	USA	
1956	12	Fairchild C–119 Packet	USA	
1956–60	30	Lockheed AT–33	USA	
1957	12	Sikorsky S–55	USA	
1957	24	Douglas B–26 B/C Invader	USA	

Date	Number	Item	Supplier	Comment
1957	2	Kawasaki-Bell KH–4	Japan	
(1957)	4	Lockheed VC–60 Lodestar	USA	
1957–59	95	Fokker Instructor S–11	Netherlands/Brazil	Produced under licence in Brazil
1958	14	Lockheed P–2V–7 Neptune	UK	Ex-RAF
1958	2	Westland Widgeon	UK	For Navy
1959	15	Douglas C–47	USA	
1960	12	Bell 47G–2	USA	
1960	14	Grumman HU–16A Albatross	USA	
1960	20	Lockheed F–80C Shooting Star	USA	
1960	3	Westland Whirlwind	UK	For Navy
1960	30	Morane Saulnier M.S. 760 Paris	France	
(1960–62)	70	Fokker Instructor S–12	Netherlands/Brazil	Produced under licence in Brazil
1961	6	Sikorsky S–58	USA	
(1961)	(10)	Lockheed L–1049 Super Constellation	USA	
(1961)	(10)	Bell 47J	USA	
1961–62	13	Grumman Tracker S–2A	USA	
1962	6	Fairchild C–119 Packet	USA	
1962	2	BAC Viscount	UK	
(1962)	11	Douglas C–54	USA	
(1962)	12	Cessna 0–1 Birddog	USA	
(1962–63)	(10)	Convair PBY–5 Catalina	USA	
1963	6	NA T–28	USA	
1963	(5)	Beech H–18	USA	
1963	6	HS–748 Mk 2	UK	
1963	6	Pilatus P–3	Switzerland	Cost: $176 000
(1963)	(6)	Fairchild C–119 Packet	USA	
(1963)	(38)	Beech E–18	USA	
1964	12	Beech Super H–18	USA	
1964	2	Beech H–18	USA	
1964	1	Douglas EC–47	USA	
1964	12	Sud T–28 Fennec	France	
(1964)	6	Hughes 269A	USA	For Navy
1965	6	Lockheed T–33A	USA	
1965	3	Lockheed C–130E Hercules	USA	
1965	3	Westland Wasp AS.1	UK	For Navy
1966	2	Lockheed C–130E Hercules	USA	
1966	20	Hughes 200	USA	
1966	3	Westland Whirlwind 3B	UK	For Navy
1967	5	Lockheed T–33A	USA	
1967	6	Bell UH–ID Iroquois	USA	
1967	4	NAMC YS–11	Japan	
1967–68	40	Cessna T–37	USA	
1968	6	Fairchild-Hiller FH–1100	USA	
1968	2	BAC–111	UK	Cost: $2.4 mn
1968	12	DHC–5 Buffalo	Canada	U.c.: $1.7 mn

Date	Number	Item	Supplier	Comment
(1968)	11	Hughes 500	USA	For Navy
(1968)	6	Bell SH–1D Iroquois	USA	
(1968)	8	Cessna 0–1 Birddog	USA	
1968–69	24	Lockheed AT–33	USA	MAP; armed version
1968–69	7	Bell 206A Jet Ranger	USA	
1968–69	5	Lockheed C–130 Hercules	USA	
1968–69	6	HS.125	UK	U.c.: $856 900
1968–69	7	Potez Super Magister	France	In exchange for 23 M.S. 760
1969	6	Bell UH–1D Iroquois	USA	
1969	2	Westland Whirlwind Series 3	UK	For Navy
1969–70	4	Sikorsky S–61B	USA	For Navy
1970	12	DHC–5 Buffalo	Canada	
1972	25	Cessna T73	USA	
1972–73	4	HS.125	UK	
1972–73	12	Dassault Mirage IIIE	France	
1972–73	4	Dassault Mirage IIIB	France	
1972-	112	EMBRAER/Aermacchi M.B.326 GB	Italy/Brazil	Produced under licence in Brazil; 54 received by spring 1974; production rate 2/month
1973	(3)	Silvercraft SH–4	Italy	Imported, prior to start of licensed production
1973-	22	Bell UH–1H Iroquois	USA	
1973-	8	Sikorsky S–58	USA	To support oil drilling operations
1974	18	Bell 206B Jet Ranger	USA	For Navy
1974	6	HS.748	UK	On order; cost: $12.5 mn
...	36	Northrop F–5E Tiger II	USA }	On order; cost: $80 mn approx; agreement may involve future coproduction
...	6	Northrop F–5B	USA }	
...	2	Sikorsky S–61	USA	On order for ASW operations
...	1	HS.125	UK	On order

Missiles

Date	Number	Item	Supplier	Comment
1966	(50)	Short Seacat	UK	
1972–73	(72)	Matra R.530	France	To arm Mirage
1972–73	4 systems	Aérospatiale/MBB Roland	France/FR Germany	Partial assembly in Brazil
...	...	Short Seacat	UK	On order; 2 triple launchers on each of 6 Vosper Mk 10 frigates
...	20	Aérospatiale MM–38 Exocet	France	On order; 2 twin launchers on each of 2 general-purpose Vosper Mk 10 frigates
...	...	GAF Ikara	Australia	On order; 1 launcher on each of 4 ASW Vosper Mk 10 frigates

Naval vessels

Date	Number	Item	Supplier	Comment
(1950)	2	Oiler	USA	Displ: 2 228 t; completed 1944-45; ex-US tankers
1951	1	Cruiser, "St Louis" class	USA	Displ: 10 000 t; completed 1938
1951	1	Crusier, "Brooklyn" class	USA	Displ: 9 700 t; completed 1938
1953	6	Tug	Netherlands	Displ: 130 t; completed 1953

Date	Number	Item	Supplier	Comment
1954	3	Tug	USA	Displ: 534 t; launched 1954
1954	2	Transport, "Pereira" class	Japan	Displ: 4 800 t; completed 1954
1955	10	Corvette	Netherlands	Displ: 911 t; launched 1954-55
1956–57	2	Transport, "Pereira" class	Japan	Displ: 4 800 t; completed 1956-57
1957	2	Submarine, "Gato" class	USA	Displ: 1 525 t standard; completed 1943
1958	2	Survey ship, "Frigate" type	Japan	Displ: 1 763 standard; completed 1958
1959	2	Destroyer, "Fletcher" class	USA	Displ: 2 100 t; completed 1942-43; on extended 5-year loan
1960	2	Coastal minesweeper	USA	Displ: 270 t; completed 1942-43
1961	2	Destroyer, "Fletcher" class	USA	Displ: 2 000 t; completed 1943-44
1961	1	Aircraft carrier "Minas Gerais"	UK	Displ: 15 890 t; completed 1945; reconstructed in Netherlands 1957-60; delivered 1961; cost $9 mn, reconstruction cost: $27 mn
1962	1	Repair ship	USA	Displ: 1 625 t; completed 1945; MAP loan
1963	2	Submarine, "Balao" class	USA	Displ: 1 526 t standard; completed 1943-44
1967	1	Destroyer, "Fletcher" class	USA	Displ: 2 100 t; completed 1944
1968	1	Destroyer, "Fletcher" class	USA	Displ: 2 100 t; built 1943
1968	1	Repair ship	USA	Displ: 5 200 t; ex-US
1968	1	Oiler	(Japan/Brazil)	Displ: 10 500 t dead weight; built by Ishikawajuma Do Brazil Estalei-sos
1971	1	Tank landing ship	USA	Displ: 1 653 t; ex-US; on loan
1971–72	4	Fast minesweeper, "Schütze" class	FR Germany	Displ: 230 t; new; 6 more projected
1972	3	Submarine "Guppy II" type	USA	Displ: 1 870 t; completed 1944, 1946 and 1949; FY 1973 ship sale; u.c.: $153 000
1972	1	Destroyer, "Allen M Sumner" class	USA	Displ: 2 200 t; completed 1944; FY 1973 ship sale; cost: $229 500
1972	1	Destroyer, "Fletcher" class	USA	Displ: 2 100 t; completed 1945; FY 1973 ship sale; cost: $153 000
1972	1	Tank landing ship, "Suffolk Country" class	USA	Displ: 4 164 t light, 8 000 t full load; launched 1956; FY 1973 ship lease
1972–73	2	Submarine "Oberon" class	UK	Displ: 1 610 t
1973	1	Submarine "Guppy II" type	USA	Displ: 1 870 t; completed WW II; modernized 1948-51
1973	1	Destroyer "Allen M Sumner" class	USA	Displ: 2 100 t; ex-US; modernized
...	1	Submarine, "Oberon" class	UK	On order; displ: 1 610 t; delivery expected in 1974
...	6	Frigate, Vosper Mk 10, "Nitheroi" class	UK	On order; delivery 1976-79; cost: $283 mn; versions: 2 general-purpose and 2 ASW to be built in UK; 2 ASW to be built in Brazil; armed with Seacat, Exocet and Ikara missiles

Date	Number	Item	Supplier	Comment
		Armoured fighting vehicles		
(1950–52)	(50)	M–8 Greyhound	USA	
(1951)	(15)	M–2	USA	
(1952)	(50)	M–3 Stuart	USA	
(1955–56)	(50)	M–4 Sherman	USA	
1960–61	(50)	M–41 Walker Bulldog	USA	
1960–61	(10)	M–59	USA	
(1965)	(20)	M–47 Patton	USA	
1966	55	M–41 Walker Bulldog	USA	
(1966)	(40)	M–113	USA	
(1971–72)	(24)	M–108	USA	
1972–73	4	Tank	France/FR Germany	Armed with Roland SAM; AMX-30 from France or Marder from FR Germany

Register 87. Arms supplies to Chile

Date	Number	Item	Supplier	Comment
		Aircraft		
1952	17	Republic F–47 Thunderbolt	USA	
1952	8	DHC–2 Beaver	(Canada)	
(1952)	2	Beech T–11	USA	
(1952–53)	(5)	Beech Twin Bonanza	USA	
(1952–53)	20	Beech C–45	USA	
1953	36	Beech T–34 Mentor	USA	
(1954)	32	Douglas B–26 Invader	USA	
(1954)	6	Sikorsky S–55	USA	
1955	6	Beech D–18S	USA	
1955	5	DH Vampire T.55	UK	
(1955–56)	(10)	Cessna 180	USA	
1956	5	Beech Twin Bonanza	USA	
1956	10	Beech T–34 Mentor	USA	
(1956)	(10)	Douglas C–47	USA	
1957	5	DHC–3 Otter	Canada	
(1957)	11	Bell 47	USA	
(1957)	3	Douglas C–54	USA	
(1959)	4	Cessna 0–1 Birddog	USA	
(1959)	20	Lockheed F–80C Shooting Star	USA	
1960	20	Beech T–34 Mentor	USA	
(1960)	(4)	Douglas C–47	USA	
1961	6	Grumman HU–16B Albatross	USA	
1961	4	Hiller UH–12E	USA	
1961	4	DHC–3 Otter	(Canada)	
(1961)	(15)	Sikorsky S–58	USA	
(1961)	(3)	Lockheed T–33A	USA	

Date	Number	Item	Supplier	Comment
(1962)	6	Cessna T–37B	USA	MAP
(1962)	2	Bell 47G	USA	For Navy
1964	8	Lockheed T–33A	USA	
1964	2	Cessna T–37B	USA	MAP
1965	(11)	Douglas C–47	USA	
1965	2	Douglas DC–6B	USA	
1966	3	Douglas DC–6B	USA	
1966	2	Beech T–34 Mentor	USA	
1966	6	Hiller UH–12E	USA	MAP
1966	2	Bell UH–1D Iroquois	USA	MAP
1966	3	DHC–6 Twin Otter	Canada	
(1966)	(2)	Cessna T–37B	USA	
1967	5	DHC–6 Twin Otter	Canada	
(1967)	2	Piper Cherokee	USA	
1968	1	HS–748	UK	Cost: $1.08 mn
1969	18	HS Hunter FGA.9	UK ⎫	Refurbished; cost: $9.6 mn; credit
1969	3	HS Hunter T.7	UK ⎬	for 7 years
1970	1	Piper PA–31 Turbo Navajo	USA ⎭	
1970	4	Bell 206A Jet Ranger	USA	For Navy
1970	9	Beech 99A	USA	Cost: $7.1 mn; incl spares
(1970)	1	HS Hunter T.7	UK	
(1970–71)	9	HS Hunter FGA.71	UK	
1971	1	Lockheed C–130 Hercules	USA	
1972	3	Lockheed C–130 Hercules	USA	
1973	8	HS Hunter FGA.71	UK	
1973	6	HS Sea Vampire T.22	UK	Ex-British Royal Navy; refurbished
1973	3	Corvair PBY–5A Catalina	France	Ex-French, after use in the Pacific
1973-	10	Aérospatiale SA–330 Puma	France	For Army
(1974)	8	Cessna T–37 B	USA	Ex-USAF

		Missiles		
1964	20	Short Seacat	UK	
1971–72	...	Aérospatiale MM–38 Exocet	France	Fitted on 2 "Almirante" class destroyers
...	...	Short Seacat	UK	1 quadruple launcher on 2 "Leander" class frigates
...	...	Aérospatiale MM–38 Exocet	France	On order; 4 launchers on 2 "Leander" class frigates
...	300	Aérospatiale A.S.11 and AS.12	France	On order; cost: $3 mn approx; for use with helicopters

		Naval vessels		
1951	2	Cruiser, "Brooklyn" class	USA	Displ: 9 700 t; completed 1938; cost: $37 mn
1953	1	Training ship	Spain	Displ: 3 040 t; completed 1952
1956	1	Oiler	France	Displ: 9 000 t; completed 1956
1959	1	Transport	Netherlands	Displ: 2 000 t; completed 1959
1960	2	Survey ship	USA	Displ: 1 235 t; completed 1943
1960	1	Landing craft	USA	Displ: 743 t; completed 1945

Date	Number	Item	Supplier	Comment
1960	3	Tank landing craft	USA	Displ: 143 t light; 329 t full load; launched 1944
1960	1	Destroyer, "Almirante" class	UK	Displ: 2 730 t; completed 1960
(1960)	3	Patrol vessel	USA	Displ: 534 t; completed as ocean tugs 1942-45
1961	2	Submarine, "Balao" class	USA	Displ: 1 526 t; completed 1944; 1 overhauled 1966
1962	1	Destroyer, "Almirante" class	UK	Displ: 2 730 t; completed 1960
1963	1	Auxiliary repair dry dock	USA	Displ: 5 200 t; ex-US; on loan
1963	2	Destroyer, "Fletcher" class	USA	Displ: 2 100 t; completed 1943 and 1944
1963	1	Helicopter support ship	USA	Displ: 1 625 t; completed 1945
1964	1	Landing craft	USA	Displ: 290 t light; 750 t full load; new
1965	2	Motor torpedo boat	Spain	Displ: 134 t; completed 1965
1966	2	Motor torpedo boat	Spain	Displ: 134 t; completed 1966
1967	4	Escort destroyer	USA	Displ: 1 400 t; ex-US
1967	1	Transport	Denmark	Displ: 2 660 t registered completed 1953
1967	1	Oiler	Denmark	Displ: 17 300 t; completed 1967
1968	1	Landing craft	USA	Displ: 290 t light, 750 t full load; new
1971	1	Patrol boat	USA	Displ: 1 235 t; launched 1943; former ocean tug
1972	1	Landing ship	USA	Displ: 1 625 t light, 4 050 t full load; FY 1973 ship sale; cost: $75 000
1972	1	Gasoline tanker	USA	Displ: 1 850 t light, 4 570 t full load; completed 1944; FY 1973 ship lease
1972	1	Fleet ocean tug	USA	Displ: 1 235 t
1972	1	Cruiser	Sweden	Displ: 8 200 t; completed 1947; expected lifetime 10-20 years more
1974	2	Frigate, "Leander" class	UK	Displ: 2 450 t; cost: $72 mn incl "Oberon" class submarines; armed with Seacat SAMs; not **affected by the British arms embargo**
. . .	2	Submarine, "Oberon" class	UK	Displ: 1 610 t; on order; cost: $72 mn incl "Leander" class frigates not affected by the British arms embargo

Armoured fighting vehicles

(1951–52)	30	M–4 Sherman	USA	
(1952)	(10)	M–3 Stuart	USA	
(1955)	(15)	M–3A1 White	USA	
1964	30	M–41 Bulldog	USA	
1966–67	20	(Mowag Roland) blinded vehicles	Switzerland	Swiss T.S.: cost: $568 000

Register 88. Arms supplies to Colombia

Date	Number	Item	Supplier	Comment
		Aircraft		
1950–51	13	DHC–2 Beaver	Canada	
1954	6	Canadair T–33	USA/Canada	US reimbursable assistance pro-gramme
(1955)	3	Douglas C–54	USA	
(1955)	(12)	Beech T–34 Mentor	USA	
1956	6	Canadair CL–13 Sabre Mk 6	Canada	
1956	4	DHC–3 Otter	Canada	
(1957–58)	11	Bell 47G	USA	
(1958)	(1)	Aero Commander 560	USA	
(1959)	(6)	NA F–86F Sabre	USA	
(1959)	8	Douglas B–26/RB–26	USA	MAP
(1959)	6	Bell 47 D1	USA	
(1960)	2	Bell 47J	USA	
1961	6	Kaman HH–43 Huskie	USA	
1961	3	Hiller UH–12E	USA	
1962	3	Bell UH–1B Iroquois	USA	
1963	6	Pilatus Porter P–6	Switzerland	
(1963)	(1)	Hiller UH–12E	USA	
1964	2	Douglas C–54	USA	Surplus
1964	3	Douglas C–47	USA	Surplus
(1966)	6	Hughes 300	USA	
(1967)	2	Douglas C–54	USA	
1968	2	Lockheed C–130E Hercules	USA	
(1968)	3	Bell UH–1B Iroquois	USA	
1968–69	12	Hughes OH–6A	USA	
1969	30	Cessna T–41D	USA	
1969	10	Cessna T–37C	USA	
1969	4	Douglas C–54	Brazil	
1971	1	Bell 212 Twin-Pac	USA	
1971	1	Fokker-VFW F–28	Netherlands	
1972–73	14	Dassault Mirage 5	France	
1972–73	2	Dassault Mirage 5D	France	
1972–73	2	Dassault Mirage 5R	France	
1973	4	HS.748	UK	For transport in remote areas
		Naval vessels		
1952	1	Oiler	USA	Displ: 5 984 t full load; ex-US
1952–53	2	Frigate, "Tocama" class	USA	Displ: 1 430 t; completed 1944
1954	1	Tender	Sweden	Displ: 560 t; completed 1954
1956	2	Coastguard vessel	FR Germany	Displ: 146 t; new
(1956)	1	Small transport	USA	Ex-US freight ship
(1956)	1	Small transport	Netherlands	Displ: 633 t
1958	2	Destroyer, "Holland" class	Sweden	Displ: 2 650 t; completed 1958
1959	1	Oiler	FR Germany	Displ: 22 682 t gross; built 1952
1961	1	Destroyer, "Fletcher" class	USA	Displ: 2 100 t; completed 1943
1963	1	Tug	USA	Displ: 1 235 t; built 1942
1964	3	Coastguard vessel	FR Germany	Displ: 123.5 t; new
1965	1	Oiler	USA	Displ: 5 984 t full load; ex-US

Date	Number	Item	Supplier	Comment
1965	1	Destroyer transport	USA	Displ: 1 400 t; completed 1945
1966	1	Oiler	Spain	Displ: 9 214 t; new
1966	1	Oiler	Sweden	Displ: 22 096 t gross; completed 1950
1968–69	3	Destroyer transport	USA	Displ: 1 400 t; completed 1943-44
1969	1	Survey ship	USA	Displ: 640 t; completed 1944
1971	2	Tug	USA	Displ: 534 t; launched 1943-45
1972	1	Destroyer, "Allen M Sumner" class	USA	Displ: 2 200 t; completed 1944; FY 1973 ship sale; cost: $229 500
1972	1	Escort ship. "Courtney" class	USA	Displ: 1 450 t; completed 1957; FY 1973 ship sale; cost: $122 400
1972	2	Midget submarine	Italy	Displ: 70 t; new
...	2	Submarine, type 209	FR Germany	On order; displ: 1 000 t
		Armoured fighting vehicles		
(1950)	(5)	M–3	USA	
(1950)	(5)	M–3 Stuart	USA	
(1950)	(5)	M–8 Greyhound	USA	

Register 89. Arms supplies to Ecuador

Date	Number	Item	Supplier	Comment
		Aircraft		
1954–55	6	BAC Canberra B.6	UK	
1954–55	12	Gloster Meteor FR.9	UK	
(1959)	12	Lockheed F–80C Shooting Star	USA	
1960	3	Bell 47	USA	Reimbursable MAP
(1960)	(5)	Lockheed T–33A	USA	
(1962)	(5)	Beech T–34 Mentor	USA	
1965	1	Douglas DC–3	USA	
1965	2	Douglas DC–6B	USA	
1965	8	Cessna T–41A	USA	
1965	9	NA T–28	USA	
1965	(5)	Cessna 180	USA	
1965	1	Beech Queen Air	USA	
1968	1	Cessna 177 Cardinal	USA	
(1968)	1	Cessna 320 Executive Skyknight	USA	
1970	12	Cessna T–41D	USA	
1970	1	Douglas DC–6B	Chile	
(1970)	1	Fairchild-Hiller FH–1100	USA	
1970–71	3	HS 748 Series 2A	UK	
1971	2	Fairchild Turbo-Porter	USA	
1971	1	Short Skyvan 3M	UK	
1971	1	Douglas DC–6B	Portugal	
1972	8	BAC 167 Strikemaster	UK	
1973	4	BAC 167 Strikemaster	UK	

Date	Number	Item	Supplier	Comment
1974	24	Cessna 150 Aerobat	USA	
...	4	BAC 167 Strikemaster	UK	On order; cost: $4.8 mn
...	6	Aérospatiale Alouette III	France	On order
...	4	Aérospatiale SA–315 Lama	France	On order; cost: $2.5 mn
...	12	SEPECAT Jaguar	UK/France	On order; u.c.: $7 mn; incl 2 trainers
		Naval vessels		
1954–55	6	Patrol boat	FR Germany	Displ: 45 t; new
1955	2	Frigate, "Hunt" class	UK	Displ: 1 000 t; completed 1940-41
1958	2	Medium landing ship	USA	Displ: 743 t beaching, 1 095 t full load; completed 1945
1960	2	Escort patrol boat	USA	Displ: 640 t; completed 1943-44
1960	1	Tug	USA	Displ: 1 235 t; launched 1945
1963	1	Supply ship	USA	Displ: 630 t; ex-US
1963	1	Water carrier	USA	Displ: 415 t light, 1 235 t full load; built 1945
1964	1	Tug	USA	Displ: 295 t; built 1952
1965	1	Survey ship	USA	Displ: 560 t; launched 1941; on loan under MAP
1965	2	Gunboat	USA	Displ: 101 t; ex-US; MAP
1967	1	Escort destroyer	USA	Displ: 1 400 t; launched 1943; MAP
1971–72	3	Patrol craft	FR Germany	Displ: 119 t; new
		Armoured fighting vehicles		
(1957)	30	M–3 Stuart	USA	
(1965–66)	(21)	M–41 Walker Bulldog	USA	
(1966)	(15)	M–113	USA	MAP
1971	27	AML–60/90	France	
1971	10	UR–416	FR Germany	
1971–72	41	AMX–13	France	

Register 90. Arms supplies to Guyana

Date	Number	Item	Supplier	Comment
		Aircraft		
1968	2	Helio H–295 Courier	(USA)	
1971	2	Britten Norman BN–2 Islander	UK	
		Naval vessels		
...	3	Patrol craft	UK	On order; length: 110 ft
		Armoured fighting vehicles		
(1970)	4	APC	(UK)	

Register 91. Arms supplies to Paraguay

Date	Number	Item	Supplier	Comment
		Aircraft		
(1950)	(3)	Piper L–4 Cub	USA	
1960	14	NA T–6	Brazil	Gift
1960	5	Fairchild PT–19	Brazil	Gift
(1961)	2	Bell 47	USA	
1962	3	Convair CV–240	Argentina	
1962	1	Morane-Saulnier M.S. 760 Paris	Brazil	Gift
(1962)	2	Douglas C–54	USA	
(1962)	3	Hiller UH–12E	USA	
1964	4	Douglas C–47	USA	MAP
1964	1	DH Dove	Argentina	Gift
(1965)	(3)	Cessna 185	USA	MAP
1967	5	Douglas C–47	USA	MAP
1967	1	Grumman Goose	Argentina	
1968	1	DHC–6 Twin Otter	Canada	
1972	12	Bell 47	USA	
1972	1	DHC–3 Otter	Argentina	
...	20	Aerotec T–23 Uirapuru	Brazil	On order
		Naval vessels		
1963	1	Small tug	USA	Length: 63.2 ft; ex-US
1964–65	3	Minesweeper	Argentina	Displ: 450 t; completed 1936-37
1967	1	Tug	USA	Length: 66.2 ft; MAP
1970	2	Ferry	USA	On lease
		Armoured fighting vehicles		
1956	2	Nahuel DL–43	Argentina	
(1960)	(10)	M–4 Sherman	(USA)	

Register 92. Arms supplies to Peru

Date	Number	Item	Supplier	Comment
		Aircraft		
(1950)	6	DHC–2 Beaver	Canada	
(1953)	2	Hiller UH–12B	USA	
1955	8	Douglas B–26C Invader	USA	MAP
1955	20	NA F–86F Sabre	USA	MAP
1955	9	Lockheed T–33A	USA	MAP
1956	16	Hawker Hunter F.52	UK	Ex-RAF
1956	9	English Electric Canberra B(1)8	UK	
(1956)	1	Sud Alouette II	France	
1956–57	5	Piaggio P. 136L	Italy	
(1957)	4	Bell 47	USA	
(1958)	5	Helio H–295 Courier	USA	

Date	Number	Item	Supplier	Comment
(1958)	4	Douglas C–54	USA	
(1958)	12	Lockheed C–60 Lodestar	USA	
1959	1	Hawker Hunter T.62	UK	
(1959)	4	Beech C–45	USA	
(1959)	10	Lockheed F–80C Shooting Star	USA	
(1960)	6	Bell 47G	USA	
(1960)	9	Cessna 185 Skywagon	USA	
(1960)	5	Alouette II	France	
1960–62	5	Sud Alouette III	France	
1961	3	Lockheed C–130 Hercules	USA	
1961	15	Cessna T–37B	USA	
(1961)	(1)	Douglas DC–6	USA	
1962	2	Bell 47G	USA	
1962	(5)	Morane Saulnier M.S. 760A	France	
(1962)	6	Beech T–34 Mentor	USA	
(1962)	2	Cessna 320 Skynight	(USA)	
1963	11	Cessna T–37B	USA	
1964	4	Douglas C–47	USA	
1964	5	Grumman HU–16B Albatross	USA	
1965	9	Bell UH–1D Iroquois	USA	
1965	3	DHC–2 Beaver	Canada	
(1965)	26	Cessna T–41A	USA	
1966	2	BAC Canberra T.4	UK	Refurbished
1966	6	BAC Canberra B.2	UK	
(1966)	18	Beech Queen Air 65–80	USA	
1967	1	Fairchild-Hiller Turbo Porter	USA	
1967	4	NAMC YS–11	Japan	
(1967)	3	Beech Queen Air 65–80	USA	
1968	1	Douglas C–54	USA	
1968	3	DHC–6 Twin Otter Series 100	Canada	
1968–70	12	Dassault Mirage 5	France	Cost; $36 mn; incl spares and technical support
1968–70	2	Dassault Mirage 5D	France	
(1969)	5	Douglas DC–6	(USA)	
1970	3	Mi–8	USSR	Donated during earthquake crisis
1970	6	BAC Canberra B.2	UK	Cost: $4.8 mn; possibly ex-Rhodesian; refurbished
1970–71	6	Lockheed C–130 Hercules	USA	
1971	16	DHC–5 Buffalo	Canada	Cost: $60 mn, incl spares
1971	8	DHC–6 Twin Otter Series 300	Canada	Cost: $4.8 mn
(1971)	2	Bell 212 Twin-Pac	USA	
1972	(5)	Beech T–42 Baron	USA	
1973	13	Bell UH–1 Iroquois	USA	For oil-seeking
1973	3	Mi–8	USSR	Gift
1973	8	Aérospatiale Alouette III	France	For oil-seeking
1973	3	Fokker-VFW F–28 Fellowship	Netherlands	
1973–74	14	Bell 212 Twin-Pac	USA	Cost: $11.5 mn, incl spares and technical support

Date	Number	Item	Supplier	Comment
...	(24)	Cessna A–37	USA	On order
...	8	BAC Canberra B(1) Mk 8	UK	On order; ex-RAF; refurbished
...	8	Dassault Mirage 5	France	On order
...	6	Pilatus Turbo Porter	Switzerland	On order
...	2	GAF Nomad	Australia	On order; for Army
		Missiles		
1973	20	Aérospatiale MM–38 Exocet	France	
		Naval vessels		
1951	1	Landing ship	USA/UK	Displ: 1 625 t; built 1943 in USA; sold to Peru by British firm
1951	2	River gunboat	UK	Displ: 365 t; completed 1951
1952	3	Destroyer escort, "Bostwich" class	USA	Displ: 1 240 t; completed 1943; reconditioned and modernized; MAP
1954	2	Submarine, "Abateo" class	USA	Displ: 825 t submerged; completed 1954
1955	1	Oiler, "Sechura" class	UK	Displ: 8 700 t; completed 1955
1955	1	Oiler, "Talara" class	Denmark	Displ: 7 000 t; completed 1955
1957	2	Submarine, "Abate" class	USA	Displ: 825 t standard, 1 400 t submerged; completed 1957
1957	1	Landing ship	USA	Displ: 1 653 t; completed 1943; ex-US
1958	1	Oiler, "Sechura" class	UK	Displ: 8 700 t; completed 1958
1959	2	Medium landing ship, "Lomas" class	USA	Displ: 513 t; completed 1945; ex-US
1959	1	Cruiser, "Almirante" class	UK	Displ: 8 800 t; completed 1943; ex-US; reconstructed 1951-53
1960	1	Destroyer, "Fletcher" class	USA	Displ: 2 120 t; completed 1943; MAP
1960	2	Corvette	USA	Displ: 890 t; completed 1945; ex-US; MAP
1960	1	Cruiser, "Almirante" class	UK	Displ: 8 281 t; completed 1942; ex-British; refitted 1955-56
1960	4	Patrol boat, "Rio" class	Italy	Displ: 37 t; completed 1960; u.c.: $120 000 approx
1961	1	Tug	USA	Displ: 534 t; completed 1944; MAP
1961	1	Destroyer, "Fletcher" class	USA	Displ: 2 120 t; completed 1943; MAP
1961	1	Tug	USA	Displ: 1 235 t; completed 1943
1963	1	Transport	USA	Displ: 6 194 t; completed 1941; MAP
1963	1	Water carrier	USA	Displ: 1 235 t; ex-US; on loan
1965	6	Patrol boat, "Vosper" class	UK	Displ: 100 t; completed 1965
1966	1	Gunboat	USA	Displ: 130 t; new; MAP
1972	1	Gunboat	USA	Displ: 130 t
1973	2	Destroyer, "Ferre" class	UK	Displ: 2 800 t; completed 1953-54; refurbished
1973	1	Cruiser	Netherlands	Displ: 9 529 t; laid down 1939, launched 1944, completed 1953; cost: $7.5 mn approx
...	2	Submarine	FR Germany	On order; displ: 1 000 t

Date	Number	Item	Supplier	Comment
		Armoured fighting vehicles		
(1950–51)	(10)	M–3 Stuart	USA	
1954	40	AMX–13	France	
(1957–58)	60	M–4 Sherman	USA	
(1958–59)	50	M–3A1 White	USA	
1969–70	78	AMX–13	France	
(1971)	116	UR–416	FR Germany	
(1972)	112	UR–416	FR Germany	
1973	22	T–55	USSR	

Register 93. Arms supplies to Trinidad and Tobago

Date	Number	Item	Supplier	Comment
		Naval vessels		
1965	2	Patrol boat, "Vosper" type	UK	Displ: 96 t; new
1972	2	Patrol boat, (later) "Vosper" type	UK	Displ: 100 t; new

Register 94. Arms supplies to Uruguay

Date	Number	Item	Supplier	Comment
		Aircraft		
1950	12	NA B–25 Mitchell	USA	
(1950)	(7)	NA F–51 Mustang	USA	
(1951)	3	Beech C–45	USA	
1952	1	DHC–2 Beaver	Canada	
(1953)	3	DHC–1 Chipmunk	(Canada)	
1955	3	Lockheed T–33	USA	
1956	3	Lockheed F–80C Shooting Star	USA	
(1956)	2	Martin PBM–5 Mariner	USA	
(1956)	3	Piper Cub	USA	
(1958)	2	Bell 47G	USA	
(1958)	3	Beech SNB–5	USA	
1960	11	Lockheed F–80C Shooting Star	USA	
(1960)	3	Lockheed T–33	USA	
(1960)	2	Piper Super Cub	USA	
(1961)	1	Bell 47	USA	For Navy
(1961)	1	Lockheed Constellation	USA	
(1962)	1	Sikorsky S.58	USA	
1963	2	Cessna 182	USA	
1964	4	Hiller UH–12	USA	

Date	Number	Item	Supplier	Comment
1965	3	Grumman S–2A Tracker	USA	
1965	5	Cessna U–17 Skywagon	USA	
1966	3	Cessna U–17 Skywagon	USA	
1966	1	Beech T–34 Mentor	USA	
(1967)	6	Lockheed AT–33	USA	MAP
1970	2	Fokker-VFW F–27 Friendship	Netherlands	
1971	2	Fairchild-Hiller FH–227 Friendship	USA	
1973	1	Fairchild-Hiller FH–227	USA	
1973–74	2	Bell UH–1H Iroquois	USA	
1973–74	2	Beech Queen Air	USA	
		Naval vessels		
1951	2	Frigate, "Bostwich" class	USA	Displ: 1 240 t; completed 1943
1951	1	Training ship, "Castle" class	Canada	Displ: 1 010 t; completed 1944; ex-British; ex-Canadian corvette
1959	1	Patrol boat	FR Germany	Displ: 70 t; new
1962	1	Oiler	Japan	Displ: 17 920 t gross; new
1965	1	Tug	USA	MAP
1966	1	Escort vessel	USA	Displ: 890 t; completed 1942; on loan
1968	1	Patrol boat	USA	Displ: 60 t; new
1969	1	Coastal minesweeper	USA	Displ: 370 t; ex-French;ex-US
1969	1	Salvage vessel	USA	Displ: 560 t; ex-US
1970	1	Patrol boat	USA	Displ: 700 t; ex-French; ex-US
(1971)	1	Oiler	Spain	Measurement: 19 350 t; new
1972	1	Escort ship, "Dealy" class	USA	Displ: 1 450 t; commisioned 1954; FY 1973 ship sale; cost: $122 400
1972	2	Mechanized landing craft	USA	Displ: 55 t full load; FY 1973 ship lease
		Armoured fighting vehicles		
(1957)	10	M–3 Al White	USA	
(1960)	(10)	M–24 Chaffee	USA	
(1965)	18	M-113	USA	

Register 95. Arms supplies to Venezuela

Date	Number	Item	Supplier	Comment
		Aircraft		
1950	(19)	DH Vampire FB.5	UK	
(1951–52)	2	Sikorsky S–51	USA	
1953	6	English Electric Canberra B.2	UK	Refurbished
(1953)	(15)	Douglas C–47	USA	
(1954)	(5)	Lockheed T–33A	USA	
(1954)	3	Beech D 185	USA	
1955	(3)	DH Vampire T.55	UK	

Date	Number	Item	Supplier	Comment
1955	(10)	DH Venom FB.4	UK	
1955	(5)	DH Sea Venom	UK	
1955–56	22	NA F–86F Sabre	USA	MAP
(1956)	(5)	Douglas C–54	USA	
1957	2	English Electric Canberra T.4	UK	
1957–58	8	English Electric Canberra B(1)8	UK	
1958	18	Fairchild C–123B Provider	USA	
1958	5	DH Vampire FB.5	UK	
1958–59	34	Beech T–34 Mentor	USA	
(1958–59)	3	Bell 47G	USA	
(1958–59)	4	Sikorsky S–55	USA	
(1961–62)	6	Beech Queen Air 65	USA	
(1962–63)	(7)	Grumman HU–16A Albatross	USA	
1963	15	Hunting Jet Provost T.4	UK	
(1963–64)	3	Bell 47J	USA	
(1964)	6	Sikorsky S–55	USA	
1965	12	BAC Canberra B.2	UK	Ex-RAF; refurbished
1965	2	BAC Canberra PR.2	UK	
1966	1	HS–748	UK	Cost; $1.4 mn
1966	74	NA/Fiat F–86K	FR Germany	Cost: $10 mn approx; 47 used for spare parts
1966–67	20	Sud Alouette II and III	France	
(1969–72)	12	Bell UH–1D Iroquois	USA	
1971	4	Lockheed C–130 Hercules	USA	
1971	12	Cessna 182 Skylane	USA	
1972	16	NA Rockwell OV–10 Bronco	USA	
1972	16	Canadair CF–5A	Canada ⎫	Cost: $35 mn
1972	4	Canadair CF–5D	Canada ⎬	
1973	12	NA Rockwell T–2 Buckeye	USA	
1973	1	Cessna Citation	USA	
1973–74	7	Dassault Mirage IIIE	France	
1973–74	6	Dassault Mirage 5	France	
1973–74	2	Dassault Mirage IIID	France	

Missiles

Date	Number	Item	Supplier	Comment
1969	(10)	Short Seacat	UK	Cost: $2.4 mn
1972	100	NWC Sidewinder	USA	To arm CF-5
. . .	40	Matra/OTO Melara Otomat	France/Italy	On order; delivery 1974; to arm 3 Vosper patrol boats and some Italian-built corvettes

Naval vessels

Date	Number	Item	Supplier	Comment
1953–54	2	Destroyer	UK	Displ: 2 600 t; completed 1953-54; refitted 1959; modernized 1960; cost: $14 mn
1954–56	8	Coastguard vessel, "Rio" class	France	Displ: 38 t; built 1954-56

Date	Number	Item	Supplier	Comment
1956	1	Destroyer	UK	Displ: 2 600 t; completed 1956; refitted 1964-65
1956	3	Fast frigate, "Almirante" class	Italy	Displ: 1 300 t; completed 1956; modernized in Italy 1961-62 for AA and ASW
1957	3	Fast frigate, "Almirante" class	Italy	Displ: 1 300 t; completed 1956; modernized in Italy 1961-62 for AA and ASW
1958	6	Medium landing ship	USA	Displ: 743 t; built 1945; MAP purchase; only 4 commissioned
1960	1	Submarine, "Balao" class	USA	Displ: 1 526 t standard; completed 1943
1960	12	Patrol craft	USA	Displ: 280 t; ex-US; sub chasers
1961	1	Survey ship, "Puerto" class	USA	Displ: 650 t; completed 1945; converted in USA to hydrographic survey ship and buoy tender
1962	1	Repair ship	USA	Displ: 1 625 t light, 4 100 t full load; laid down 1945; on loan
1962	1	Tug	USA	Displ: 1 235 t; completed 1944; on loan
1963	3	Survey ship, "Puerto" class	USA	Displ: 650 t; completed 1945; MAP lease
(1963)	1	Medium harbour tug	USA	On loan
1965	1	Tug	USA	Ex-US; large harbour tug
(1965)	1	Submarine, "Balao" class	USA	Displ: 1 526 t; transfer approved 1965
(1966)	1	Medium harbour tug	USA	On loan
1972	1	Submarine, "Guppy II" type	USA	Displ: 1 870 t; completed 1945; cost: $150 000
1972	1	Destroyer, "Allen M Sumner" class	USA	Displ: 2 200 t; commissioned 1945; FY 1973 ship sale; cost: $229 500
1973	1	Submarine, "Guppy II" type	USA	Displ: 1 870 t; completed WWII; modernized 1948-51
. . .	6	Fast patrol boat, "Vosper Thornycroft" 121 ft class	UK	On order; delivery 1974; displ: 150 t approx; at least 3 to be armed with Otomat SSMs
. . .	2	Submarine	FR Germany	Displ: 2 200 t; on order; delivery 1974-75
. . .	6-8	Corvette	Italy	Displ: 1 000 t; some may be armed with Otomat SSMs

		Armoured fighting vehicles		
(1950)	(10)	M–3 Stuart	USA	
(1951)	(15)	M–2 and M–9	USA	
1954	(20)	M–18	USA	
1954	(15)	M–8 Greyhound	USA	
1954	(20)	AMX–13	France	
(1968)	(15)	Shorland	UK	
1972–73	142	AMX–30	France	Cost: $60 mn
1972–73	20	AMX–155	France	

Europe

Register 96. Arms supplies to Greece

Date	Number	Item	Supplier	Comment
		Aircraft		
(1950–53)	50	Douglas C–47	USA	
(1951–52)	(20)	Lockheed T–33	USA	
(1952–53)	(20)	NA T–6	USA	
(1953–54)	150	Republic F–84F	USA	MAP
(1953–54)	25	Republic RF–84 F	USA	MAP
(1954–55)	(20)	Canadair T–33 A–N	Canada	
(1954–56)	82	Canadair CL–13 Sabre Mk 2 and Mk 4	Canada	
1956–57	23	Canadair CL–13 Sabre Mk 4	UK	Ex-RAF
(1957)	(4)	Sikorsky S–55	USA	
(1958–59)	50	NA F–86D Sabre	USA	MAP
(1960)	(50)	NA F–100D Super Sabre	USA	
1964	1	Grumman Gulfstream	UK	From Grumman European service and repair centre in UK
1964	69	Republic F–84F	FR Germany	NATO aid; surplus
1964–65	36	Canadair F–104G Star-fighter	Canada	Refurbished
1965	20	Cessna T–37B	USA	
1965–67	40	Northrop F–5 Freedom Fighter	USA	MAP
1966	10	Sikorsky S–55	USA	
1966	10	Fairchild C–119G Packet	USA	
1967	8	Sud Alouette II	France	U.c.: $109 000
1967	17	Republic F–84F	FR Germany	NATO aid; surplus, for spares
1967	6	Republic RF–84F	FR Germany	NATO aid; surplus
1967–68	10	Bell 47G	USA	U.c.: $50 000
1968–69	12	Northrop F–5A Freedom Fighter	USA	
1968–69	9	Northrop F–5B	USA	
1969	5	Lockheed F–104 Star-fighter	USA	
1969	2	Bell 47G	USA	
1969	2	NA Rockwell Courser Commander	USA	
1969	18	Convair F–102 Delta Dagger	USA	US surplus stocks
1969	6	Agusta-Bell 205A	Italy	
1969	8	Grumman HU–16B Albatross	Norway	From Norwegian Air Force; for ASW
1970	40	Nord 2501 Noratlas	FR Germany	Ex-Luftwaffe
(1970–71)	20	Cessna T–41	USA	
1971	6	Republic F–84	Netherlands	NATO aid; refurbished
(1971)	16	Northrop RF–5A	USA	
1972	3	Lockheed T–33	Netherlands	NATO aid
. . .	36	McDonnell-Douglas F–4	USA	On order; delivery 1974–76; cost: $150 mn
. . .	40	Dassault Mirage F–1	France	On order
. . .	2	Canadair CL–215	Canada	On order

Date	Number	Item	Supplier	Comment
		Missiles		
(1955–59)	(900)	NWC Sidewinder	USA/ FR Germany	Built under licence in Germany; Greek subcontractor
(1958–59)	(24)	Usamicon MGR–1 Honest John	USA	2 battalions
(1959–60)	(40)	Western Electric Nike Ajax	USA	
(1959–60)	(40)	Western Electric Nike Hercules	USA	
1965	(75)	Raytheon MIM–23 Hawk	USA	1 battalion
1967	(400)	MBB Bo 810 Cobra 2000	FR Germany	NATO aid
1972	50	Aérospatiale MM–38 Exocet	France	To arm gunboats
		Naval vessels		
1950	13	Assault landing craft	UK	Displ: 81.5 t; on loan 1950-59
1951	2	Destroyer, "Gleaves" class	USA	Displ: 1 630 t; completed 1940-41
1951	4	Destroyer escort, "Bostwich" class	USA	Displ: 1 240 t; 1 completed in 1943, 3 in 1944
1953	2	Minelayer	USA	Displ: 720 t; launched 1944-45
1953	1	Dock landing ship	USA	Displ: 4 790 t; launched 1943
1955	1	Oiler	USA	Capacity 700 t; ex-US
1957–58	2	Submarine, "Gato" class	USA	Displ: 1 525 t standard, completed 1943; MAP loan
1957–58	2	Patrol vessel	USA	Displ: 257 t; completed 1944; ex-US
1958	6	Medium landing ship	USA	Displ: 743 t beaching, 1 095 t full load; ex-US
1959	3	Destroyer, "Fletcher" class	USA	Displ: 2 100 t; completed 1942-43
1959	7	Coastal patrol vessel	USA	Displ: 251 t; ex-US
1959	2	Landing craft	USA	Displ: 143 t; ex-US
1959	1	Oiler	USA	Displ: 850 t; completed 1944; MAP
(1959–61)	13	Minor landing craft	USA	LSM type
(1959–63)	34	Minor landing craft	USA	LCVP type
1960	1	Destroyer, "Fletcher" class	USA	Displ: 2 100 t; completed 1943
1960	3	Tank landing ship	USA	Displ: 1 653 t; ex-US
1960	1	Repair ship	USA	Displ: 3 800 t; completed 1943
1960	1	Boom defence vessel	USA/FR Germany	Displ: 680 t; built 1959 under off-shore procurement
1961	3	Landing craft	USA	Displ: 143 t; ex-US
1962	2	Destroyer, "Fletcher" class	USA	Displ: 2 100 t; completed 1943; MAP
1962	3	Landing craft	USA	Displ: 143 t; ex-US
1964	1	Tank landing ship	USA	Displ: 1 653 t; ex-US; MAP
1964	1	Tank landing ship	UK	Displ: 2 256 t; launched 1943
1964–65	6	Coastal minesweeper	USA	Displ: 320 t; completed 1964-65; MAP
1965	2	Submarine, "Balao" class	USA	Displ: 1 526 t standard; completed 1944; 1964 MAP loan
1967	6	Fast patrol boat	Norway	Displ: 69 t; completed 1967
1968	2	Minesweeper	USA	Displ: 320 t; MAP

Date	Number	Item	Supplier	Comment
1968	1	Vosper torpedo boat	FR Germany	Displ: 95 t; built in UK 1962; NATO aid
1968	1	Vosper torpedo boat	FR Germany	Displ: 75 t; built in UK 1962; NATO aid
1969	5	Coastal minesweeper	Belgium	Displ: 330 t light; ex-Belgian
1969	5	Torpedo boat	FR Germany	Displ: 190 t; completed 1951-56
1969–70	2	Coastal minesweeper	USA	Displ: 320 t; new
1971	1	Destroyer, "Gearing" class	USA	Displ: 2 425 t; completed 1944
1971	1	Tank landing ship	USA	Displ: 1 653 t; ex-US
1971	1	Dock landing ship	USA	Displ: 4 790 t light; completed 1945
1971	1	General support ship	USA	Displ: 1 750 t; completed 1944
1971–72	2	Destroyer, "Allen M Sumner" class	USA	Displ: 2 200 t; completed 1944
1972	2	Submarine, "Guppy II A, I A" type	USA	Displ: 1 840 t; completed 1944; cost of 1: $153 000
1972	1	Destroyer, "Gearing" class	USA	Displ: 2 425 t; commissioned 1945; FY 1973 ship sale; cost: $229 500
1972	1	Gasoline tanker	USA	Displ: 1 850 t light, 4 570 t full load; completed 1944; FY 1973 ship lease
1972	1	Medium harbour tug	USA	FY 1973 ship lease
1972	4	Minesweeping launch	USA	Displ: 10 t
1972	4	Fast gunboat	France	Displ: 220 t; new; armed with Exocet SSMs
1972–73	4	Submarine	FR Germany	Displ: 1 000 t; new
		Armoured fighting vehicles		
(1952)	(50)	M–24 Chaffee	USA	
(1952)	(100)	M–26 Pershing	USA	
(1954–56)	(300)	M–47 Patton	USA	
(1955–56)	(80)	M–41 Walker Bulldog	USA	
(1955–56)	(200)	M–59	USA	
(1959–64)	(300)	M–48 Patton	USA	
(1963)	(30)	M–113	USA	
(1965–67)	(200)	M–113	USA	
(1967)	(30)	M–47 Patton	FR Germany	NATO aid; for spares
(1968–70)	(12)	M–44	FR Germany	NATO aid
(1968–70)	(12)	M–52	FR Germany	NATO aid
(1969)	(12)	M–107	USA	
1971	55	AMX–30	France	
1973	(12)	M–110	USA	
...	130	AMX–30	France	On order
...	100+	APC	France	On order

Register 97. Arms supplies to Turkey

Date	Number	Item	Supplier	Comment
		Aircraft		
(1951)	36	Lockheed T–33 A–N	USA	
1952	24	Beech T–34 Mentor	Canada	MAP

Date	Number	Item	Supplier	Comment
1952–53	(130)	Republic F–84F	USA	
(1953)	(8)	Beech C–45	USA	
1954–56	82	Canadair CL 13 Sabre Mk 2 and Mk 4	Canada	
(1956)	3	Douglas C–54	USA	
(1956)	(30)	Republic RF–84F	USA	
1956–57	25	Canadair CL–13 Sabre Mk4	UK	Ex-RAF
(1957–59)	200	Piper L–18 Super Cub	USA	
1958	260	NA F–100C Super Sabre	USA	MAP
(1958)	(30)	Lockheed RT–33A	USA	
(1959)	50	NA F–86D Sabre	USA	MAP
(1960)	(25)	NA F–100F Super Sabre	USA	
(1961)	23	Cessna T–37	(USA)	Might be from Canada
1962–63	(65)	NA F–86K Sabre	Netherlands	Overhauled by Fiat in Italy
1963	38	Canadair F–104G Star-fighter	Canada	MAP offshore procurement
1964	5	Lockheed C–130E Hercules	USA	
1964	42	Republic F–84F	FR Germany	NATO aid; surplus
1965	40	Northrop F–5 Freedom Fighter	USA	
1965	5	Lockheed C–130E Hercules	USA	
1966	18	Cessna U–17A	USA	
1966	15	Dornier Do–27	FR Germany	NATO aid
1966	5	Dornier Do–28 B–1	FR Germany	NATO aid
1966	(20)	Agusta-Bell 47	Italy	
1966	13	Agusta-Bell 204B	Italy	
1966–68	75	Northrop F–5 Freedom Fighter	USA	
1967	42	Republic F–84F	FR Germany	NATO aid; surplus
(1967)	7	Agusta-Bell 204B	Italy	
(1967)	8	Grumman S–2 Tracker	Netherlands	
1967–68	(5)	Bell 47G	USA	
1968	3	Dornier Do–27	FR Germany	NATO aid; surplus
1968	18	Lockheed T–33	FR Germany	NATO aid; surplus
1968–69	36	Convair F–102A Delta Dagger	USA	Ex-USAF; MAP
1968–69	3	Convair TF–102	USA	
1968–69	(35)	Agusta-Bell 206A Jet Ranger	Italy	For Army
1969	40	NA F–100C Super Sabre	USA	
1969	15	Siat 223 Flamingo	FR Germany/ Spain	Built in Spain
(1969)	25	Northrop F–5 Freedom Fighter	USA	
1971	5	Beech T–42 Baron	USA	MAP; value: $550 000
1971	12	Lockheed T–33	FR Germany	Ex-Luftwaffe
1971	2	Dornier Do–28	FR Germany	U.c.: $184 000
1971–72	12	Grumman S–2 Tracker	USA	
1971–72	2	Grumman TS–2	USA	
1971–72	20	Transall C–160	FR Germany	
1972	19	Cessna T–41	USA	MAP
1972	3	Agusta-Bell 205 Iroquois	USA	

Date	Number	Item	Supplier	Comment
1972	9	Lockheed T–33	USA/Nether-lands/Canada	NATO aid
1972	(5)	Republic RF–84F	France	
1972	7	Lockheed F–104 Star-fighter	Spain	
(1972)	4	Cessna 206	USA	For Army
(1972)	2	Britten-Norman BN–2 Islander	UK	
. . .	40	McDonnel-Douglas F–4 Phantom	USA	On order; delivery by 1976
. . .	42	Northrop F–5E Tiger II	USA	On order; incl assembly and licensed production

Missiles

Date	Number	Item	Supplier	Comment
(1955)	75	Western Electric Nike Ajax	USA	
(1958)	(600)	NWC Sidewinder	USA	
(1959)	(75)	Western Electric Nike Hercules	USA	
(1960)	(24)	Usamicon MGR–1 Honest John	USA	
1964	(300)	MBB Bo 810 Cobra 2000	FR Germany	
(1966)	300	Martin Bullpup	USA/Europe	Built under licence to European consortium
1967–73	(500)	MBB Bo 810 Cobra 2000	Turkey/FR Germany	Produced under licence in Turkey
(1968)	(100)	Nord SS.11	France	
. . .	. . .	Hughes TOW	USA	On order
. . .	. . .	Aérospatiale MM–38 Exocet	France	On order; to arm patrol boats

Naval vessels

Date	Number	Item	Supplier	Comment
1950	2	Submarine, "Gur" class	USA	Displ: 1 526 t; launched 1943-45
1950	1	Submarine rescue ship	USA	Displ: 1 294 t; launched 1946; adapted 1947
1952	5	Coastal minelayer	USA	Displ: 1 294 t; launched 1945 as LSM; converted 1952; NATO aid
1952	1	Repair ship	USA	Displ: 1 625 t; launched 1944
1953	4	Motor launch	USA	Displ: 63 t; ex-US
1954	2	Submarine, "Gur" class	USA	Displ: 1 526 t; launched 1943-45; on loan
1957	4	Destroyer, "Milne" class	UK	Displ: 2 115 t; completed 1941-42; refitted 1959; ex-British
1957	9	Coastal escort, "Batia" class	Canada	Displ: 672 t; completed 1940-42; ex-Bangor class
1958	1	Submarine, "Gur" class	USA	Displ: 1 526 t; launched 1943-45
1958	1	Coastal minelayer	USA	Displ: 540 t; completed 1958; MAP
1958	4	Coastal minesweeper	Canada	Displ: 390 t; ex-Canadian
1958–59	4	Coastal minesweeper	USA	Displ: 320 t; ex-US
1959–60	2	Torpedo boat, "Nasty" class	FR Germany	Displ: 70 t; completed 1959-60; war reparations

Date	Number	Item	Supplier	Comment
1960	2	Submarine, "Gur" class	USA	Displ: 1 526 t; launched 1943-45
1960–61	9	Motor launch	FR Germany	Displ: 70 t; built 1960-61
1961	1	Boom defence vessel	USA	Displ: 680 t; launched 1960; procured by USA from FR Germany
1964	3	Patrol boat, "Akhisar" class	USA	Displ: 280 t
1964	1	Boom defence vessel	France	Displ: 732 t; built 1938
1965	2	Patrol boat, "Akhisar" class	USA	Displ: 280 t
1965	4	Coastal minesweeper	USA	Displ: 320 t; ex-US
1965	1	Minelayer	Denmark	Displ: 1 880 t; launched 1964
1966–67	6	Motor torpedo boat, "Jaguar" class	FR Germany	Displ: 160 t; built 1966-67; NATO aid
1967	2	Destroyer, "Fletcher" class	USA	Displ: 2 050 t; launched 1943
1967	1	Coastal minesweeper	USA	Displ: 320 t; ex-US
1967	2	Inshore minesweeper	USA	Displ: 120 t; ex-US
(1968)	1	Motor torpedo boat, "Jaguar" class	FR Germany	Displ: 160 t; NATO aid
1969	3	Destroyer, "Fletcher" class	USA	Displ: 2 050 t; completed 1943-44
1969	1	Submarine depot ship	USA	Displ: 8 100 t; completed 1944
(1969)	2	Torpedo boat, "Nasty" class	FR Germany	Displ: 70 t; NATO aid
1970	1	Boom defence vessel	USA	Displ: 780 t; completed 1952; ex-Dutch
1970	3	Coastal minesweeper, "MSC" type	(USA)	Displ: 320 t; ex-French, ex-British
1970–71	4	Submarine, "Guppy II A" type	USA	Displ: 1 850 t; completed 1944
1971	2	Destroyer, "Gearing" class	USA	Displ: 2 425 t; completed 1945-46: modernized
1971–72	7	Gunboat	USA	New
1972	1	Submarine, "Guppy II A" type	USA	Displ: 1 850 t; completed 1944-45
1972	1	Submarine, "Guppy I A" type	USA	Displ: 1 850 t; completed 1944; modernized 1951
1972	1	Destroyer, "Gearing" class	USA	Displ: 2 425 t; commissioned 1947; FY 1973 ship sale; cost: $229 500
1972	2	Destroyer, "Allen M Sumner" class	USA	Displ: 2 250 t; completed 1944-45; 1 modernized early 1960s, 1 in 1972
1972	1	Fleet ocean tug	USA	Displ: 1 235 t; launched 1942; FY 1973 ship lease
1972	1	Barracks craft	USA	Displ: 2 660 t full load approx; completed 1944-45; FY 1973 ship lease
1972	1	Supply ship	FR Germany	Measurement; 2 101 gross t; ex-FR German
1972	2	Minelayer	FR Germany	Displ: 1 653 t; former US landing ship
1973	2	Fast patrol boat, "Ashville 1968" class	USA	Displ: 225 t; commissioned 1969
...	4	Submarine	FR Germany	On order; displ: 1 000 t; at least 1 as NATO aid

Date	Number	Item	Supplier	Comment
		Armoured fighting vehicles		
(1950)	(25)	M–36	USA	
(1952)	(100)	M–26 Pershing	USA	
(1950–52)	(50)	M–24 Chaffee	USA	
(1955–58)	(540)	M–47 Patton	USA	
(1957–58)	(100)	M–41 Walker Bulldog	USA	
(1957–58)	(400)	M–59	USA	
(1961–64)	(140)	M–48 Patton	USA	
(1963)	(100)	M–113	USA	
1964	481	M–113	Italy	
1968–70	(24)	M–44 and M–52	FR Germany	NATO aid
1969–70	69	M–74	FR Germany	NATO aid; surplus
(1969–70)	79	M–48 Patton	FR Germany	NATO aid; surplus
1972–73	250	M–48 Patton	USA	MAP

Appendix 1

The glossary of weapons

The glossary of weapons is intended as a reference to more detailed but concise information about the major arms listed in the Country Registers. The weapons are listed alphabetically under the categories *aircraft, missiles* and *armoured fighting vehicles.* (For *naval vessels,* see their descriptions in the Country Registers.)

The information given includes: the firm which produces the weapon (for aircraft and missiles) as well as the designation by which the weapon is referred to; the country in which the firm is located; a brief description of the type of aircraft, missile or tank; the year in which the weapon first entered production or, if that date is unknown, the first known date with a note of explanation; and finally, comments providing such particulars as what other versions of the weapon appear in the registers, whether a firm produces under licence from another country, and so on.

The information in these brief descriptions was taken mainly from the series of *Jane's;* most of the information about the armoured fighting vehicles was taken from von Senger and Etterlin, *Taschenbuch der Panzer.*

Firm: Designation	Country	Description	Date[a]	Comments
Aircraft				
Aerfer-Aermacchi AM.3C	Italy	general purpose monoplane	1970	
Aermacchi M.B. 308	Italy	cabin monoplane	around 1950	
Aermacchi M.B. 326	Italy	armed jet trainer	1958	Versions: B, GB, K
Aermacchi-Lockheed AL 60	Italy	cabin monoplane	1961	Produced under licence from USA; version: C5
Aero				*See* North America Rockwell
Aérospatiale SA–315 Lama	France	helicopter	1969[d]	Produced under licence in India as Cheetah
Aérospatiale SA–341 Gazelle	France	helicopter	1971	Version H for military export
Aérospatiale (Fouga/ Potez/Sud) CM 170 Magister	France	trainer	1954	
Aérospatiale (Nord) 262 Frégate	France	light transport	1962[f]	
Aérospatiale (Nord) 2501 Noratlas	France	transport	1950[f]	
Aérospatiale (Potez/Sud) CM 170 Super Magister	France	trainer	1962	
Aérospatiale (Sud) Alouette II	France	helicopter	1955	

Firm: Designation	Country	Description	Date[a]	Comments
Aérospatiale (Sud) Alouette III	France	helicopter	1959	
Aérospatiale (Sud) Djinn	France	helicopter	1955	
Aérospatiale (Sud) Horizon	France	cabin monoplane	1962	
Aérospatiale (Sud) SA–321 Super Frelon	France	helicopter	1963	
Aérospatiale (Sud) T–28 Fennec	USA/France	trainer	. . .	NA T–28 produced under licence in France
Aérospatiale (Sud) Vautour 2	France	fighter/fighter bomber	1952	Versions: A, N
Aérospatiale/Westland SA–330 Puma	UK/France	helicopter	1965[f]	
Aerotec T–23 Uirapuru	Brazil	trainer	1968	

Aero Engine Services Ltd.

Firm: Designation	Country	Description	Date[a]	Comments
AESL CT4 Airtrainer	New Zealand	trainer	1972[d]	
AESL Airtourer	New Zealand	monoplane	1962	Versions: 150, T.8
Agusta-Bell 47	Italy	helicopter	1954[b]	Produced under licence from USA; versions: G-2, J-3
Agusta-Bell 204 Iroquois	Italy	helicopter	1961 (B)	Versions: A and B produced under licence from USA
Agusta-Bell 205 Iroquois	Italy	helicopter	1965	Bell 205A-1 produced under licence from USA
Agusta-Bell 206A Jet Ranger	Italy	helicopter	1966	Produced under licence from USA
Agusta-Bell 212 Twin Pac	Italy	helicopter	. . .	Produced under licence from USA
Agusta-Sikorsky SH–3 Sea King	Italy	helicopter	1967	Produced under licence from USA
Airspeed Ambassador	UK	transport	. . .	
Airspeed Consul	UK	transport	. . .	
Airspeed Oxford	UK	trainer	1938[c]	
An–2	USSR	light transport	1947[d]	
An–12	USSR	heavy transport	1958	
An–14	USSR	light transport	1965	
An–24	USSR	transport	1962	
An–26	USSR	transport	1969[e]	Version of An–24
Armstrong Whitworth Seahawk	UK	naval fighter	1954	Versions: Mk 100, Mk 101
Auster AOP.6	UK	monoplane		
Auster AOP.7	UK	monoplane	late 1940s	Version: T. Mk 7 trainer
Auster AOP.9	UK	monoplane	1954	
Auster Aiglet	UK	trainer	early 1950s	
Auster Autocrat	UK	cabin monoplane	late 1940s	
Avro 696 Shackleton	UK	maritime reconnaissance (bomber)	1955 (Mk3)	
Avro Anson	UK	trainer	1933	Version: Mk 18

132

Firm: Designation	Country	Description	Date[a]	Comments
British Aircraft Corporation				
BAC 111	UK	transport	1965	
BAC 145	UK	trainer	1967[e]	Developed version of Hunting Jet Provost
BAC 167 Strikemaster	UK	trainer	1968	Developed version of Hunting Jet Provost
BAC Lightning	UK	supersonic all-weather interceptor	1959	Versions: F.2, F.52, F.53; trainer: T.4, T.54, T.55
BAC (English Electric) Canberra	UK	long-range bomber	1951	Versions: B.2, B.6, B(1)8, B(1)12, B(1)58, B.15, B.16, B.62; reconnaissance: PR.2, PR.57; trainer: T.4, T.64
BAC (Hunting) Jet Provost	UK	trainer	1959	Versions: T.Mk4, T.51, T.52
BAC (Hunting) Pembroke	UK	monoplane	around 1952	Versions: C–1, C–54, C–55
BAC (Hunting) Provost	UK	trainer	1950	Versions: T.51, Mk 3, T.52, T.55
BAC (Vickers/Supermarine) Attacker F.1	UK	fighter	1951[e]	
BAC (Vickers) Varsity	UK	transport	late 1940s	
BAC (Vickers) Viking	UK	transport	late 1940s	
BAC (Vickers) Viscount	UK	transport	late 1940s	Versions: 723, 730, 734
Beagle B.125 Bulldog	UK	trainer	1969[f]	Versions: Series 100, Series 120
Beagle B.206	UK	light transport	1964	
Beagle-Auster T.7				*See* Auster AOP.7
Beech 18	USA	light transport	1937	Continuous production since 1937; versions: D–18S, E–18, H–18, Super H–18
Beech 99	USA	light transport	1968[g]	Version: A
Beech C–45	USA	light transport	WW II	Version: H
Beech SNB–5	USA	trainer	. . .	
Beech T–11	USA	trainer	WW II	
Beech T–34 Mentor	USA	trainer	1948	
Beech T–42 Baron	USA	cabin monoplane	1963	
Beech Bonanza	USA	cabin monoplane	late 1940s	Version: F33
Beech King Air	USA	transport	1968[g]	Versions: 90, 99, 100; date refers to B99
Beech Musketeer	USA	cabin monoplane	1962	Version: Sport
Beech Queen Air 65	USA	transport	1959	
Beech Queen Air 80	USA	transport	1961	Development of model 65
Beech Twin Bonanza	USA	cabin monoplane	early 1950s	
Bell 47 (HH–13)	USA	helicopter	1946	Continuous production since 1946; versions: D, D–1, G, G–2, G–3B, G–3B–2, H, J
Bell 204 (UH–1) Iroquois	USA	helicopter	1959[g]	Version: 204B (UH–1B)
Bell 205 (UH–1) Iroquois	USA	helicopter	1959[g]	Versions: 205A, A–1, UH–1D, H

133

Firm: Designation	Country	Description	Date[a]	Comments
Bell 206A Jet Ranger	USA	helicopter	1966	Versions: A, A–1, B
Bell 209 (AH–1J)	USA	helicopter	1970	
Bell 212 Twin-Pac	USA	helicopter	1970	
Bell 214	USA	helicopter	1970[f]	Development of UH–1H
Bell 214A Isfahan	USA	helicopter	1972	Development on Iranian specifications
Blackburn				*See* Hawker Siddeley
Boeing Stratofreighter C–97	USA	transport	1949	
Boeing 299 Fortress (B 17)	USA	bomber	1939	
Boeing 307 Stratoliner	USA	transport	WW II	
Boeing 377 Stratocruiser	USA			Civil version of C–97 above
Boeing 707	USA	transport	1955	
Boeing 720	USA	transport	1960	
Boeing-Stearman Kaydet	USA	trainer	WW II	Versions: PT–13, PT–17
Boeing-Vertol 107–11 (CH–46)	USA	helicopter	1958[f]	
Boeing-Vertol 114 (CH–47) Chinook	USA	helicopter	1961[d]	Version: CH–47C
Boulton Paul P.108 Balliol	UK	trainer	late 1940s	
Breguet 1050 Alizé	France	ASW aircraft	1959	
Bristol Freighter 170	UK	transport	1940s	Versions: Mk 21/3, Mk31M
Bristol Beaufighter	UK	long-range day and night fighter	WW II	Version: Mk 10
Britten-Norman BN–2 Islander	UK	transport	1967	
Bücker Bü 181 Bestmann	Germany	trainer	WW II	
Canadair CF–5	Canada	fighter		Northrop F–5 produced under licence from USA; versions: A, D
Canadair CL–13 Sabre	Canada	fighter		NA F–86 produced under licence from USA; versions: B, Mk 3, Mk 4, Mk 6
Canadair CL–41 Tutor	Canada	trainer	1960	
Canadair CL–215	Canada	multi-purpose amphibian	1967[d]	
Canadair DC–4M	Canada	transport		Douglas DC–4 produced under licence from USA
Canadair F–104 Starfighter	Canada	supersonic fighter		Lockheed F–104 produced under licence from USA; version: G
Canadair T–33	Canada	trainer		Lockheed T–33 produced under licence from USA; versions: A, N
Cavalier F–51 Mustang	USA	fighter		Production and refurbishing for MAP of NA F–51

Firm: Designation	Country	Description	Date[a]	Comments
Canadian Car & Foundry				
CCF T–6 Harvard	Canada	trainer		NA T–6 produced under licence in Canada
Cessna 150	USA	cabin monoplane	1958	
Cessna 170	USA	cabin monoplane	late 1940s	
Cessna 172 (T–41)	USA	cabin monoplane (trainer)	1962	Versions: T–41A, T–41D
Cessna 177 Cardinal	USA	cabin monoplane	1967	
Cessna 180	USA	trainer	1953[h]	
Cessna 182	USA	cabin monoplane	1956[h]	Version: Skylane
Cessna 185 (U–17) Skywagon	USA	cabin monoplane	1961	Version: U–17A
Cessna 206	USA	utility aircraft	1960s	
Cessna 210 Turbo Centurion	USA	cabin monoplane	1966	
Cessna 310	USA	cabin monoplane	1953	Versions: K, L, P
Cessna 318 (T–37)	USA	jet trainer	1955	Versions: T–37B, C. Date refers to T–37B
Cessna 320 Skyknight	USA	cabin monoplane	1962	
Cessna 321 (0–2)	USA	monoplane	early 1950s	Version: A
Cessna 337 Skymaster	USA	cabin monoplane	1962	Version: C
Cessna 401	USA	executive transport	1965[f]	Version: A
Cessna 402	USA	transport	1965[f]	Version: A
Cessna 411/414	USA	business transport	1964	
Cessna A–37	USA	COIN attack	1966	Development of Cessna T–37; version: B
Cessna AT–17 Bobcat	USA	trainer	1941	
Cessna L–19 (0–1) Birddog	USA	light aircraft	1950	Versions: 0–1A, E
Cessna T.207 Turbo Skywagon	USA	utility aircraft	1969	Version of Skywagon
Chance Vought F–4U Corsair	USA	fighter	1942	Versions: 5, 5N
Commonwealth Aircraft Corporation				
CAC CA–27 Avon Sabre	Australia	fighter	1953	Version of NA F–86; versions: Mk 30, Mk 31, Mk 32
Convair C–131	USA	transport	1948[i]	Version: D
Convair CV–240	USA	transport	1948	
Convair CV–440	USA	transport	mid-1950s	
Convair F–102 Delta Dagger	USA	interceptor	1953	Versions: A; trainer: TF–102
Convair PBY–2 Pirateer	USA	bomber/reconnaissance	WW II	
Convair PBY–5 Catalina	USA	naval patrol bomber	1936–46	Version: A
Convair Stinson L–5	USA	monoplane	WW II	
Convair Vultee B–13 Valiant	USA	trainer	1939	Version: BY–13A
Curtiss C–46	USA	transport	1940[j]	Version: D
Curtiss SB2C–5 Helldiver	USA	bomber	1940	

Firm: Designation	Country	Description	Date[a]	Comments
Dassault M.D.315 Flamant	France	light transport	1947[i]	
Dassault M.D.450 Ouragan	France	fighter-interceptor	1949[f]	
Dassault Falcon	France	transport	1963	
Dassault Mirage III	France	fighter	1962 (B)	Versions: trainer: B, D; all-weather interceptor/ground attack: C; long-range intruder: E; reconnaissance: R
Dassault Mirage 5	France	fighter	1966	Versions: trainer: D; reconnaissance: R
Dassault Mirage F.1	France	fighter	1972	
Dassault Mystère IV A	France	interceptor/ ground attack	1952	
Dassault Super Mystère B.2	France	interceptor/ ground attack	1957	
DH (De Havilland)				*See* Hawker Siddeley
De Havilland of Canada				
DHC–1 Chipmunk	Canada	trainer	post-WWII	Version: T.10
DHC–2 Beaver	Canada	STOL transport	1948	
DHC–3 Otter	Canada	STOL transport	1952	
DHC–4 Caribou	Canada	STOL transport	1960	Version: A
DHC–5 Buffalo	Canada	STOL transport	1964	
DHC–6 Twin Otter	Canada	STOL transport	1965	Version: Series 100
Dornier Do–27	FR Germany	monoplane	1956	Version: B
Dornier Do–28	FR Germany	monoplane	1959	Version: B–1
Dornier Do–28 Skyservant	FR Germany	STOL transport	1967	New design based on Do–28
Douglas				*See* McDonnell-Douglas
English Electric				*See* BAC
Fairchild AU–23A Peacemaker	USA	STOL transport	. . .	COIN version of Pilatus Porter produced under licence from Switzerland
Fairchild C–119 Packet	USA	transport	1947	Development of C–82 Packet (1944); versions: G, K; gunship AC–119
Fairchild C–123 Provider	USA	transport	1954	Version: B
Fairchild Argus	USA	cabin monoplane	WW II	
Fairchild PT–19	USA	trainer	WW II	
Fairchild-Hiller FH–227 Friendship	USA	transport	mid-1960s	Version of Fokker F.27 produced under licence from the Netherlands
Fairchild-Hiller FH–1100	USA	helicopter	1965	

136

Firm: Designation	Country	Description	Date[a]	Comments
Fairchild-Hiller Turbo Porter	USA	STOL transport	1966	Produced under licence from Switzerland as Heli-Porter
Fairey Firefly	UK	fighter	1941	Versions: F.1; trainer: T.T.1, T.T.4
Fairey Gannet	UK	ASW aircraft	1953	Versions: AS.4, T.5
Fiat F–86K	Italy	fighter	. . .	NA F–86, built under licence in Italy
Fiat G.46	Italy	trainer	around 1950	
Fiat G.59	Italy	trainer	late 1940s	Version: 4B
Fletcher FD–25 Defender	USA	trainer/ground support	late 1940s	Versions: A, B
Fokker Instructor	Netherlands	trainer	late 1940s	Versions: S–11, S–12
Fokker–VFW F–27 Friendship	Netherlands	transport	1958	Versions: M, Mk 2, Mk 400, Mk 600
Fokker–VFW F–28	Netherlands	transport	1968	
Folland				See H.5
Fong Shou No. 2	China	transport	1957[g]	An–2 built under licence in China
Fouga				See Aérospatiale
Fuji-Beech T–34 Mentor	Japan	trainer	. . .	Beech T–34 produced under licence from USA

Government Aircraft Factories

Firm: Designation	Country	Description	Date[a]	Comments
GAF Nomad	Australia	STOL aircraft	1971[f]	
General Dynamics F–111	USA	fighter	1963	
Gloster Meteor	UK	fighter	WW II	Versions: F.8, NF.13; trainer: T.7; reconnaissance: FR.9
Grumman F–8F Bearcat	USA	fighter	mid-1940s	Versions: 1B, 1D
Grumman F–9F Panther	USA	fighter	1948	Constructed for use on carriers; development: F–9F Cougar (1954)
Grumman F–14 Tomcat	USA	fighter	1972[g]	
Grumman G–89 (S–2) Tracker	USA	naval attack/ASW	1952[d]	Constructed for use on carriers; version: S–2A; trainer: TS–2
Grumman G–159 Gulfstream	USA	transport	1958	
Grumman HU–16 Albatross	USA	maritime reconnaissance/ASW	1949	Versions: A, B
Grumman Goose	USA	general utility amphibian	1939	
HS (De Havilland) 89A Dragon Rapide	UK	transport	1934–46	
HS (De Havilland) 114 Heron	UK	transport	1950	Version: 2D
HS (De Havilland) Mosquito	UK	bomber	1941	Version: NF.38
HS (De Havilland) Sea Venom	UK	all-weather fighter	1954	Constructed for use on carriers
HS (De Havilland) Tiger Moth	UK	trainer	WW II	

137

Firm: Designation	Country	Description	Date[a]	Comments
HS (De Havilland) Vampire	UK	fighter	mid-1940s	Versions: F.1, F.3 (long-range ground attack: FB.5, FB.9, FB.50, FB.52, N.F.54, Mk 5, Mk 52; trainer: T.11, T.55; Sea Vampire T.22
HS (De Havilland) Venom	UK	fighter/fighter-bomber	around 1950	Versions: FB.4, FB.50
HS (Hawker) Fury	UK	fighter/fighter-bomber	late 1940s	
HS (Hawker) Sea Fury	UK	naval fighter/ fighter bomber	late 1940s	Versions: FB.11, FB.60; trainer: T.61
HS (Hawker) Hunter	UK	fighter	1953	Versions: F.6 (Mk 6), F.52, F.56, F.59; ground attack: FA.9, FB.9, FGA.9, FGA.57, FGA.59, FGA.71, FGA.73, FGA.74, FGA.78, F.57 (Mk 57); reconnaissance: FR.6, FR.59, FR.7; trainer: T.6, T.7, T.62, T.60, T.66B, T.67, T.69, T.75, T.79
Hughes 269 (200)	USA	helicopter	1961	Versions: A, HM; Hughes 200 commercial version, 269 military
Hughes 300	USA	helicopter	1964	Development of model 269
Hughes 369 (OH–6)/500	USA	helicopter	1965	Versions: A, M; Hughes 500 commercial version, 369 military
Hunting				*See* BAC
Israel Aircraft Industries				
AIAI Arava	Israel	STOL transport	1969[d]	
IAI Commodore Jet	Israel	transport	1971	Development of NA Rockwell Jet Commander
I1–10	USSR	monoplane	1945	
I1–12	USSR	transport	late 1940s	
I1–14	USSR	transport	around 1950	
I1–18	USSR	transport	1959[c]	
I1–28	USSR	bomber	1950	Version: trainer: U
Junker Ju 52/3 M	Germany	transport	WW II	
Kaman HH–43 Huskie	USA	helicopter	1958	Versions: B, F
Kamov Ka–26	USSR	helicopter	1965[f]	
Kawasaki-Bell 47	Japan	helicopter	1953	Bell 47, produced under licence in Japan
Kawasaki-Bell KH–4	Japan	helicopter	1962[d]	Developed version of Bell 47G–3B

138

Firm: Designation	Country	Description	Date[a]	Comments
Kawasaki-Vertol KV–107–11	Japan	helicopter	. . .	Boeing-Vertol 107, produced under licence in Japan
L–29 Delfin	Czechoslova-kia	trainer	1963	
L–39	Czechoslova-kia	trainer	1972	
La–9	USSR	fighter	WW II	
La–11	USSR	fighter	early 1950s	
Li–2	USSR	transport	1940s	
Lockheed 12	USA	transport	. . .	
Lockheed 488 Electra	USA	transport	1959[c]	
Lockheed C–130 Hercules	USA	transport	1952	Versions: B, E; L 100–20 (Civil)
Lockheed C–140 Jet Star	USA	transport	1960	
Lockheed F–80C Shooting Star	USA	fighter	1943[f]	
Lockheed F–104 Star-fighter	USA	fighter	1956	Versions: A, B, G; trainer: TF–104; reconnaissance: RF–104
Lockheed L–188 Electra	USA	transport	1959[c]	
Lockheed L–1049 Super Constellation	USA	transport	1953	
Lockheed LASA–60	Mexico	cabin monoplane	1959[k]	Produced under licence in Mexico
Lockheed P–2V Neptune	USA	maritime reconnaissance bomber	1944	Versions: E, H, V–5, V–7
Lockheed P–3 Orion	USA	ASW aircraft	1958	Version: C
Lockheed T–33	USA	trainer	around 1950	Versions: A, A–N; reconnaissance: RT–33; attack: AT–33
Lockheed U–2	USA	reconnaissance and research monoplane	1955	
Lockheed Constellation	USA	transport	1941	
Lockheed Lodestar	USA	transport	WW II	Version: C–60
Malmö Flygindustrier MFI–9B Militrainer	Sweden	monoplane	1964	
Makina Ve Kimya Endustrisi Kurumu MKEK Ugur	Turkey	trainer	late 1950s	
Macchi				*See* Aermacchi
Martin B–57 Canberra	USA	long-range bomber	1953	English Electric Canberra produced under licence; versions: B, B/D; reconnaissance: RB–57, B/D
Martin PBM–5 Mariner	USA	patrol bomber/ naval transport	1938	Version: A
Messersmitt-Bölkow-Blohm MBB Bo 105	FR Germany	helicopter	1970[g]	
(McDonnell-)Douglas A–1 Skyraider	USA	naval attack	1945	Versions: D, H, E/H

Firm: Designation	Country	Description	Date[a]	Comments
McDonnell-Douglas A–4 Skyhawk	USA	attack bomber	1953	Versions: B, E, F, H, N; trainer: TA–4
(McDonnell-) Douglas B–26 Invader	UK	bomber	1947	Versions: B, C, RB–26 (reconnaissance)
(McDonnell-) Douglas C–47 (DC–3)	USA	transport	WW II	Military version of DC–3; versions: EC–47, RC–47, AC–47 (gunship)
(McDonnell-) Douglas C–54 (DC–4)	USA	transport	1942	Military version of DC–4
(McDonnell-) Douglas C–118 (DC–6)	USA	transport	1955	Military version of DC–6; versions: C–118A, DC–6B
(McDonnell-)Douglas DC–7	USA	transport	1954[c]	
(McDonnell-) Douglas F–101 Voodoo	USA	fighter	1951–52	Versions: reconnaissance: RF–101 A, C
McDonnell-Douglas F–4 Phantom	USA	all-weather fighter	late 1950s	Version: E; reconnaissance: RF–4
(McDonnell-) Douglas F4D Skyray	USA	interceptor/ fighter	1951[f]	Constructed for use on carriers
Max Holste M.H. 1521 Broussard	France	monoplane	1954	Versions: C, M
Meridionali-Vertol CH–47	Italy	helicopter	1970	Produced under licence from USA
Mi–1	USSR	helicopter	1950	
Mi–4	USSR	helicopter	1952	
Mi–6	USSR	helicopter	1957[h]	
Mi–8	USSR	helicopter	1961	
MiG–15	USSR	fighter	around 1950	Versions: trainer: UTI; also built in China
MiG–17	USSR	interceptor/ fighter	1953	Versions: C, D, SB; also built in China as F4
MiG–19	USSR	interceptor/ fighter	1955[l]	Version: P; also built in China as F6
MiG–21	USSR	fighter	1956[l]	Versions: trainer: UTI, C, D, J, M, MF, FL
Mitsubishi Mu–2	Japan	STOL transport	1963	
Mitsubishi-Sikorsky S–62	Japan	helicopter	...	Sikorsky S–62 produced under licence in Japan
Morane-Saulnier M.S.500 Criquet	France	monoplane	WW II	
Morane-Saulnier M.S. 733 Alcyon	France	trainer	around 1950	
Morane-Saulnier M.S.760 Paris	France	monoplane	1958	Version: A

North American

NA B–25 Mitchell	USA	bomber	1940	Versions: D, J
NA F–51 Mustang	USA	fighter	WW II	*See also:* Cavalier versions: D, K
NA F–86 Sabre	USA	fighter	1952	Versions: D, F, K, L; reconnaissance: RF–86
NA F–100	USA	fighter	1955	Versions: A, C, D, F

Firm: Designation	Country	Description	Date[a]	Comments
NA T–6 Texan (Harvard)	USA	trainer	1939	Harvard built in Britain; versions: G, Harvard 2B
NA T–28	USA	trainer	1950	Versions: A, D
NA-Rockwell OV–10 Bronco	USA	COIN aircraft	1966	Version: A
NA-Rockwell T–2 Buckeye	USA	trainer	1958	Versions: B, D
NA-Rockwell Aero Commander 100	USA	light aircraft	early 1960s	
NA-Rockwell Aero Commander 500	USA	light aircraft	early 1960s	Versions: B, U (also called Shrike Commander)
NA-Rockwell Aero Commander 520	USA	light aircraft	1951	
NA-Rockwell Aero Commander 560	USA	light aircraft	1955	
NA-Rockwell Aero Commander 680	USA	light aircraft	1961	
NA-Rockwell Aero Grand Commander	USA	light aircraft	1963	
NA-Rockwell Aero Courser Commander	USA	light aircraft	1962[d]	Similar to Shrike Commander
NA-Rockwell Aero Turbo Commander	USA	light aircraft	1965	
Nihon Aircraft Manufacturing				
NAMC YS–11	Japan	transport	1964	
Nord				*See* Aérospatiale
Northrop F–5 Freedom Fighter	USA	fighter	1958	Versions: trainer: B; reconnaissance: RF–5A
Northrop F–5E Tiger II	USA	fighter	1972	Development of F–5A particularly for developing countries
On Mark B–26K Counter Invader	USA	COIN bomber	1963	Development of Douglas B–26
Pazmany PL–1	USA	light plane	1962	
Pazmany PL–2	USA	light plane	1969	
Percival Prentice	UK	trainer	1946[f]	Version: T.1
Piaggio P.136	Italy	flying boat	late 1940s	Version: L
Piaggio P.148	Italy	trainer	1950	
Piaggio P.149	Italy	monoplane	1953	Version: D
Piaggio P.166	Italy	light transport	1958	
Pilatus P–3	Switzerland	trainer	1960[g]	
Pilatus Porter PC–6	Switzerland	STOL transport	1959	
Pilatus Turbo-Porter	Switzerland	STOL transport	1961[d]	
Piper L–4 Cub	USA	cabin monoplane	WW II	Version: J
Piper PA–11	USA	trainer	1940s	
Piper L–18 Super Cub (L–21)	USA	cabin monoplane	1949	Versions: B, C
Piper PA–20 Pacer	USA	cabin monoplane	around 1950	Version: A
Piper PA–22 Tri Pacer	USA	cabin monoplane	1951	Development of Pacer
Piper PA–28 Cherokee	USA	monoplane	1961	
Piper PA–31 Turbo Navajo	USA	transport	1964	

141

Firm: Designation	Country	Description	Date[a]	Comments
Piper Apache	USA	cabin monoplane	1952	
Piper Aztec	USA	transport	1960	Versions: C, D
Po–2	USSR	trainer	pre-WW II	
Potez				*See* Aérospatiale
Reims-Cessna 150	France	cabin monoplane	...	Produced under licence from USA
Reims-Cessna 337 Skymaster	France	cabin monoplane	...	Produced under licence from USA
Republic F–47 Thunderbolt	USA	fighter/fighter bomber	1942	Version: D
Republic F–84	USA	fighter	1946	Versions: F, G; reconnaissance: RF–84
Republic F–105 Thunderchief	USA	fighter	1958	
Saab 91 Safir	Sweden	cabin monoplane	1945[f]	Versions: B, C, D
Saab B–17	Sweden	bomber	1940	
Saab MF1–15	Sweden	light aircraft	1969[f]	
Scottish Aviation Bulldog 120				*See* Beagle
Scottish Aviation Pioneer	UK	transport	1953	
Scottish Aviation Twin Pioneer	UK	transport	1956	Version: C.C. Mk 2
Shenyang F–4 (MiG–17)	China	fighter	...	MiG–17 produced under licence from USSR
Shenyang F–6 (MiG–19)	China	fighter	...	MiG–19 produced under licence from USSR
Shenyang Yak–18	China	trainer	...	Yak–18 produced under licence from USSR
Short S.A. 6 Sealand	UK	flying boat	1948	
Short Skyvan	UK	transport	1965	
Siai (Savoia)-Marchetti SM–79	Italy	cabin monoplane	WW II	
Siai-Marchetti SF.260	Italy	cabin monoplane	1966	Version: X
Siat Flamingo	FR Germany	light aircraft	1964	
Sikorsky S–51	USA	helicopter	1946	
Sikorsky S–52	USA	helicopter	1947	
Sikorsky S–55 (H–19)	USA	helicopter	1949[d]	
Sikorsky S–58 (CH–34)	USA	helicopter	1954	
Sikorsky S–61 (CH–3)	USA	ASW helicopter	1959	Versions: A, B, SH.3 Sea King, A–4, D–4
Sikorsky S–62 (CH–52)	USA	helicopter	1960	Version: A
Sikorsky S–64 (CH–54)	USA	helicopter	1963	
Sikorsky S–65 (CH–53)	USA	helicopter	1964[d]	Version: A
Silvercraft SH–4	Italy	helicopter	1970[c]	
Soko Galeb	Yugoslavia	trainer	1963	
Siko Jastred	Yugoslavia	light attack	1963	
Sokol Falcon M–1–D	Czechoslovakia	trainer	early 1950s	Version: B
Su–7	USSR	fighter/ground attack	1956[l]	Version: B
Su–20	USSR	fighter	1967[l]	
Sud				*See* Aérospatiale

Firm: Designation	Country	Description	Date[a]	Comments
Supermarine Spitfire	UK	fighter	1934	Versions: F.22, Mk 9
Temco T–35 Buckaroo	USA	trainer	early 1950s	Version: A
Transall C–160	FR Germany/			
	France	transport	1964	
Tu–2	USSR	bomber	WW II	
Tu–16	USSR	bomber	1954[l]	
Tu–20	USSR	bomber	1955[l]	
Tu–124	USSR	transport	1960[d]	
Vertol				*See also:* Boeing-Vertol
Vertol H–21 Shawnee	USA	helicopter	1957	
Vickers				*See* BAC
Westland W.G. 13 Lynx	UK	helicopter	1970[m]	Anglo-French co-operation
Westland Commando	UK	helicopter	1971[h]	Based on Sea King
Westland Dragonfly	UK	helicopter	1947	Sikorsky S–51 produced under licence
Westland Scout	UK	helicopter	1960	Version: Mk 1
Westland Sea King	UK	helicopter	1970	
Westland Wasp	UK	helicopter	1960	Version of Scout for navy; version: AS.1
Westland Wessex	UK	helicopter	1959	Development of Sikorsky S–58; versions: Mk 53, Mk 54
Westland Widgeon	UK	helicopter	1955	
Westland Whirlwind	UK	helicopter	1959	Versions: Series 1, 2, 3, 38
Westland-Bell 47G	UK	helicopter	. . .	Agusta-Bell 47G–3B produced under licence in UK
Yak–9P	USSR	fighter	WW II	
Yak–11	USSR	trainer	1950	
Yak–12	USSR	monoplane	late 1940s	Version: M
Yak–17 UTI	USSR	trainer	. . .	
Yak–18	USSR	trainer	1946	
Zlin 226 Bohatir	Czechoslova-kia	trainer	1955	

Missiles

Firm: Designation	Country	Description	Date[a]	Comments
Aérospatiale (Nord) AS.11	France	ASM		Version of SS.11
Aérospatiale (Nord) AS.12	France	ASM		Version of SS.12
Aérospatiale (Nord) AS.20	France	ASM, 7 km	(pre1960)	
Aérospatiale (Nord) AS.30	France	ASM, 12 km	late 1950s	
Aérospatiale (Nord) Entac	France	anti-tank, 2 km	1957	Versions: model 38, 58
Aérospatiale/MBB Roland	France/FR Germany	SAM, 6 km	1968[q]	Version: Mk 2 (all-weather)
Aérospatiale (Nord) MM–38 Exocet	France	naval SSM, (37 km)	1971[r]	
Aérospatiale (Nord) SS.10	France	SSM, 1.5 km	1957	
Aérospatiale (Nord) SS.11	France	SSM, 3 km	1962	
Aérospatiale (Nord) SS.12 (M)	France	SSM, 6 km	1966	
AS–1 "Kennel"	USSR	ASM, 90 km	1961[l]	

Firm: Designation	Country	Description	Date[a]	Comments
AS–5 "Kelt"	USSR	AMM, 90 km	1968[l]	Similar to "Kennel" but larger radar
AT–1 "Snapper"	USSR	anti-tank, 2.3 km	1964[l]	
AT–3 "Sagger"	USSR	anti-tank, 2.3 km	1965[l]	
British Aircraft Corporation				
BAC Bloodhound	UK	SAM, 80 km	1958[c]	Version: Mk 2
BAC Rapier	UK	SAM, 3 km	1967	
BAC Swingfire	UK	ATM, 4 km	1969[c]	
BAC Thunderbird I	UK	SAM, 35 km	1960	
BAC Vigilant	UK	anti-tank 1.6 km	1960	
Contraves Sea Killer	Italy	naval SSM, 3–10 km	late 1960s	Range refers to Mk 1
Dassault MD–660	France	SSM, (450 km)	1968[g]	Developed on Israeli order; capable of carrying nuclear warhead
"Frog–3"	USSR	artillery rocket (50 km)	around 1960	Capable of carrying nuclear warhead
"Frog–5"	USSR			Similar to "Frog–3" but different warhead
"Frog–7"	USSR	7.5–92 km		Similar to "Frog–3" and "Frog–5" but a different launch vehicle
Government Aircraft Factories				
GAF Ikara	Australia	ASW, (20 km)	early 1960s	
Hawker Siddeley Dynamics				
HSD Firestreak	UK	AAM, 1.2–8 km	1958	
HSD Redtop	UK	AAM, 11 km	early 1960s	
HSD Sea Dart	UK	naval SAM, 27–36 km	1965[g]	
Hughes HM–55 Falcon	USA	AAM, 8 km	1954	
Hughes Phoenix	USA	AAM, 126 km	1970	
Hughes Maverick	USA	ASM	1971	
Hughes TOW	USA	anti-tank, 3 km	1968	Also helicopter mounted
Israeli Aircraft Industries				
IAI Gabriel	Israel	naval SSM 15–20 km	late 1960s	
K–13 "Atoll"	USSR	AAM, . . .	(1956)[p]	Range: probably similar performance to NWC Sidewinder
Martin Bullpup	USA	ASM, 11 km	1962	Capable of carrying nuclear warhead
Matra R.530	France	AAM, 18 km	1963–64	
Matra R.550 Magic	France	AAM, 200–2000 m	1974[r]	
Matra/HSO Martel	France/UK	ASM, 30 km	1968[g]	
Matra/OTO Melara Otomat	France/Italy	naval SSM, 60–80 km	1971[q]	
Matra/Thomson–CSF Crotale	France	SAM, 8 km	1972[p]	Developed on S. African order: referred to as Cactus in S. Africa

Firm: Designation	Country	Description	Date[a]	Comments
MBB Bo 810 Cobra 2000	FR Germany	anti-tank, 1.6 km	1960	
Nord				*See* Aérospatiale
Naval Weapons Center				
NWC Shrike	USA	16 km	1964	
NWC Sidewinder	USA	AAM, 3.4 km	1954	
Raphael Shafrir	Israel	AAM	late 1960s	
Raytheon MIM–23 Hawk	USA	SAM, 35 km	1959	Versions: A, B
Raytheon Sparrow III	USA	AAM, 13 km	1958	Version: B
SA–2	USSR	SAM, 40 km	1957[e]	
SA–3	USSR	SAM, 25 km	. . .	
SA–4	USSR	SAM, 24 km	1964	Similar to MIM–23 Hawk
SA–6	USSR	SAM	1967	
SA–7	USSR	SAM, 3.5 km	. . .	Used against low-flying aircraft
"Samlet"	USSR	SSM		Version of AS–1 "Kennel"
Short Blowpipe	UK	SAM . . .	1972	Can also be fired from a submerged submarine
Short Seacat	UK	naval SSM, 4 km	1962	
Short Tigercat	UK	SAM		Version of Seacat
SS IC "Scud"	USSR	SSM, 150 km	early 1960s	Range and date refer to version A
SS–N–2 "Styx"	USSR	naval SSM, 35 km	. . .	
Usamicon MGR–1 Honest John	USA	artillery rocket, 19,3 km	1960	Capable of carrying nuclear warhead
Western Electric Nike Ajax	USA	SAM, 40 km	early 1950s	
Western Electric Nike Hercules	USA	SAM, 100 km	1958	

Armoured fighting vehicles[s]

Firm: Designation	Country	Description	Date[a]	Comments
Abbott	UK	105 mm self-propelled howitzer	1967	
AEC Mk 3	UK	AC, 12.5 ton	WW II	
AML				*See* Panhard
AMX–13	France	light tank, 15 ton	1950[f]	
AMX–30	France	main battle tank, 36 ton	1966	
AMX–105 A	France	105 mm propelled howitzer, 16 ton	1952	
AMX–155	France	155 mm self-propelled howitzer, 16 ton	1964	
BA–64	USSR	AC, 2.5 ton	WW II	
BMP–76	USSR	APC, 12–14 ton	1967[f]	
BRDM	USSR	APC, 6.5 ton	1959	
BTR 50 P	USSR	tracked APC	1955[c]	
BTR 152	USSR	APC, 7 ton	1946	
BTR 40	USSR	APC, 5.3–10 ton	1948[f]	
BTR 60	USSR	APC, 9.5–10 ton	1961[f]	

Firm: Designation	Country	Description	Date[a]	Comments
Centurion	UK	main battle tank, 50–52 ton	1950 (Mk III)	Versions: Mk III, Mk 9, Mk 10 (1958)
Charioteer	UK	main battle tank, 28.5 ton	1951	Version: 6
Chieftain	UK	main battle tank, 52 ton	1966	
Churchill	UK	main battle tank, 38.5–40 ton	WW II	
Comet	UK	main battle tank, 33.5 ton	WW II	
Cromwell	UK	main battle tank, 27 ton	WW II	
Ferret	UK	AC, 4.2–5.4 ton	1951[i]	
Fox	UK	AC, 5.7 ton	1970	
Humber Mk IV	UK	AC, 7.1 ton	1942[c]	
HW–K11	FR Germany	APC, 11 ton	1962[f]	
JS II	USSR	main battle tank, 45 ton	WW II	
JS III	USSR	main battle tank, 46 ton	1945	
JSU–100	USSR	tank destroyer, 30 ton	WW II	
JSU–122	USSR	tank destroyer, 46 ton	1944	
JSU–152	USSR	tank destroyer, 46 ton	1944	
Leopard	FR Germany	main battle tank, 40 ton	1966	
M–2	USA	APC, halftrack, 6–9 ton	WW II	
M–3	USA	APC, halftrack, 9 ton approx	1941	
M–3 Stuart	USA	light tank, 12 ton	1941	
M–3A1 White	USA	AC, 4 ton	1942	
M–4 Sherman	USA	main battle tank, 34 ton	WW II	Version: Mk 3
M–5 Stuart	USA	light tank, 15 ton	1944	
M–5	USA	APC, halftrack, 9 ton approx	...	Later version of M–2 and M–3
M–6 Staghound	USA	AC, 13 ton	WW II	
M–9	USA	APC, halftrack, 9 ton approx	...	Later version of M–2 and M–3
M–8 Greyhound	USA	AC, 7.5 ton	WW II	
M–10	USA	based on M–4, 30 ton	1942	
M–18	USA	tank destroyer, 17 ton	WW II	
M–20	USA	AC, 7 ton	1943	Command version of M–8
M–24 Chaffee	USA	light tank, 18 ton	1945	
M–26 Pershing	USA	main battle tank, 40 ton	1944	
M–36	USA	tank destroyer, 30 ton	WW II	
M–41 Walker Bulldog	USA	tank, 25.4 ton	1951	

Firm: Designation	Country	Description	Date[a]	Comments
M–42	USA	self-propelled AA-gun, 24 ton	1942	
M–44	USA	155 mm tracked self-propelled howitzer 28.4 ton	1953	
M–47 Patton	USA	main battle tank, 44 ton	1951	
M–48 Patton	USA	main battle tank, 45 ton	1952	
M–52	USA	105 mm tracked self-propelled howitzer, 24.5 ton	1953	
M–56	USA	tank destroyer, 7.5 ton	1957	
M–59	USA	APC, 18 ton	1954	
M–60	USA	main battle tank, 46–48 ton	1961	Version: A1 (1965)
M–74	USA	armoured recovery vehicle	1955	Version of M–4
M–75	USA	APC, 21 ton	1952	
M–107	USA	175 mm self-propelled howitzer, 28.5 ton	1962	
M–108	USA	105 mm self-propelled howitzer, 21 ton	1964	
M–109	USA	155 mm self-propelled howtizer, 24.5 ton	1964	
M–110	USA	203 mm self-propelled howitzer, 25 ton	1962	
MAC–1	USA	AC, 6.5 ton	1963	
Marder	FR Germany	APC	1970s	
Mowag Roland	Switzerland	APC, 4.7 ton	1960s	
Nahuel (Tiger) DL–43	Argentina	tank	1943	10 produced in Argentina 1943–44
M–113	USA	APC, 10–11 ton	1959	
OT–62	Czechoslovakia	APC, 13 ton	1963	
OT–64	Czechoslovakia	APC, 12.5 ton	1964[g]	
Panhard AML 245				Subtypes: AML–60 and AML–90
Panhard AML–60	France	AC, 4.8 ton	1962	
Panhard AML–90	France	AC, 5.5 ton	1965	
Panhard AML–VTT	France	APC, 5.5 ton	1970s	
Panhard EBR–75	France	AC, 13.5 ton	1951	
PT–76	USSR	light tank, 16 ton	1955	
Saladin	UK	AC, 11 ton	1958	
Saracen	UK	APC, 10–11 ton	1953	
Saviem	France	APC, 12–13 ton	. . .	
Scorpion	UK	light tank	1970s	

147

Firm: Designation	Country	Description	Date[a]	Comments
Shorland	UK	light AC, 3.36 ton	1965[f]	Versions: Mk 2, Mk 3
Su–76	USSR	self-propelled gun, 11.5 ton	WW II	
Su–100	USSR	tank destroyer, 32 ton	1945	
Super Sherman	Israel	main battle tank, (34 ton)	1958	
T–10	USSR	main battle tank, 50 ton	1957	
T–34	USSR	main battle tank, 32 ton	WW II	Version: T–34/85 (1945)
T–54	USSR	main battle tank, 36 ton	1955	
T–55	USSR	main battle tank, 36 ton	1961	Version of T–54
T–59	China	main battle tank, 32 ton	1963	T–54 manufactured in China
T–62	USSR	main battle tank, 37 ton	1963	
UR–416	FR Germany	AC, 5 ton		
V–100 Commando	USA	AC, 5.7 ton	1962	
Valentine	UK	light tank, 16 ton	1942	
Vickers	UK	main battle tank, 37 ton	1965	Version: Vijayanta (India)
6–M	Canada	APC		

Notes:

[a] Unless otherwise specified, the date refers to the date on which production of the first version was started.

[b] First Italian-produced.

[c] Entered service.

[d] First flight.

[e] Flight rules started.

[f] First prototype.

[g] First delivery.

[h] First announced.

[i] Civil version Convair-Liner 240.

[j] Ordered in quantity.

[k] First US prototype.

[l] First seen publicly.

[m] Prototype flight expected.

[n] In the description of missiles, the range is also given.

[o] MiG-21 first seen.

[p] Full production scheduled.

[q] Test firings begun.

[r] Expected to be ready for service.

[s] In the description of armoured fighting vehicles, the weight is also given.

[t] First version.

[u] Average.

Appendix 2

The value tables

The arms trade registers were valued, by type of weapon, at a standard set of prices worked out for the purpose.* (For a more detailed description of the methods used, see appendix 3, p. 170.)

The values are presented in three sections: first the aggregate values of arms exports by supplier and of imports by recipient area. The totals are presented including and excluding Viet-Nam. In the tables in section II, the arms supplies of the main exporters are broken down by recipient area. The main suppliers to each third world area are presented in section III, which also includes a number of charts showing the trend in major weapon imports by selected countries and groups of countries.

Two main differences from previous tables should be noted. First, values have been brought up to 1973 constant prices. Second, Greece and Turkey have been excluded from the values. (They appear, however, in the registers and a separate table on their major arms imports by main supplier is included in section III of the tables.)

Table conventions
* Less than the smallest digit shown
– Nil

---

* The figures for appendix 2 were prepared by Ernst Falta.

Tables

I. Aggregate tables

Table 2A.1. Major weapons exports to areas listed in table 2A.2, by main suppliers,

Country	1950	51	52	53	54	55	56	57	58	59
USA	91	109	103	73	280	302	326	346	379	247
USSR	25	43	28	176	6	62	145	252	193	108
UK	96	64	46	165	166	175	198	180	358	183
France	3	3	1	41	66	67	120	70	129	47
Canada	14	4	1	*	–	1	39	4	4	66
China	23	23	–	–	–	–	–	1	191	133
Czechoslovakia	–	–	–	–	–	43	58	6	23	58
FR Germany	*	*	–	1	4	7	9	5	7	26
Italy	7	29	–	2	–	2	31	29	28	*
Japan	–	–	–	1	15	–	9	11	23	12
Netherlands	35	14	6	2	1	85	1	2	1	4
Sweden	*	1	16	5	6	6	6	–	37	*
Other ind. west	–	–	–	7	*	5	*	–	–	–
Other ind. east	–	–	–	–	–	–	2	*	29	24
Other third world	–	–	–	15	1	1	3	5	11	2
Total[b]	**294**	**289**	**201**	**488**	**547**	**755**	**947**	**912**	**1 413**	**911**

[a] Excluding North and South Viet-Nam.

[b] Items may not add up to totals due to rounding.
Source: SIPRI worksheets.

Table 2A.2. Major weapons imports by recipient areas, 1950–1973

Region	1950	51	52	53	54	55	56	57	58	59
Far East, excl Viet-Nam	147	152	87	209	174	222	227	211	506	396
South Asia	44	20	19	92	104	108	176	254	488	148
Middle East	35	55	12	70	81	186	350	300	249	238
North Africa	–	–	–	–	–	–	6	5	4	6
Sub-Saharan Africa	*	5	4	16	18	12	1	1	3	46
South Africa	8	–	16	15	17	15	54	22	18	17
Central America	6	5	27	12	10	18	15	6	11	14
South America	54	52	35	73	144	195	118	112	134	45
Total,[a] **excl Viet-Nam**	**294**	**289**	**201**	**488**	**547**	**755**	**947**	**912**	**1 413**	**911**
Viet-Nam, North and South	–	–	–	–	9	9	11	7	48	9
Total [a]	**294**	**289**	**201**	**488**	**556**	**765**	**957**	**919**	**1 461**	**920**

[a] Items may not add up to totals due to rounding.
Source: SIPRI worksheets.

1950–1973[a]   *US $ mn, at constant (1973) prices*

60	61	62	63	64	65	66	67	68	69	70	71	72	73
530	263	240	353	264	374	373	310	497	784	724	740	360	749
158	374	773	326	276	398	590	861	571	588	786	1 003	570	1 175
196	185	95	135	137	203	148	155	225	266	142	300	283	242
35	38	92	148	105	74	107	52	220	131	156	211	269	411
11	14	*	10	9	14	9	9	36	14	28	42	30	3
125	–	–	–	–	7	27	13	4	–	6	66	101	21
45	5	5	12	7	3	6	9	30	17	24	11	10	1
23	5	2	10	20	10	64	3	8	13	1	19	28	2
7	–	*	15	15	5	1	16	51	41	33	32	39	43
–	11	18	1	1	5	9	23	38	2	*	*	–	–
1	2	2	*	9	17	1	–	4	19	7	26	20	30
1	*	–	–	–	–	1	–	–	*	–	–	4	1
1	2	1	2	*	23	18	45	6	8	3	37	10	16
*	–	8	*	–	*	–	1	–	1	–	4	–	–
3	2	8	3	2	3	19	12	7	16	6	11	14	16
1 135	**900**	**1 245**	**1 015**	**844**	**1 135**	**1 372**	**1 507**	**1 697**	**1 898**	**1 916**	**2 502**	**1 738**	**2 711**

US $ mn, at constant (1973) prices

60	61	62	63	64	65	66	67	68	69	70	71	72	73
583	153	272	237	300	260	380	152	203	448	207	320	124	231
205	221	144	169	61	163	299	207	227	239	229	381	313	221
123	150	439	301	296	337	336	813	962	927	1 118	1 345	823	1 691
9	12	30	26	30	62	93	103	64	67	92	94	128	111
27	43	36	36	52	72	71	62	42	55	93	102	68	116
4	3	12	118	39	142	70	60	34	35	59	53	19	28
45	162	228	74	26	14	16	13	6	8	4	36	27	43
139	156	83	55	39	84	106	98	159	121	113	170	237	270
1 135	**900**	**1 245**	**1 015**	**844**	**1 135**	**1 372**	**1 507**	**1 697**	**1 898**	**1 916**	**2 502**	**1 738**	**2 711**
24	56	57	43	70	57	181	378	362	228	331	333	917	63
1 159	**957**	**1 302**	**1 058**	**914**	**1 192**	**1 553**	**1 885**	**2 059**	**2 126**	**2 247**	**2 835**	**2 656**	**2 773**

Chart 2A.1. Total exports of major weapons to third world countries

US $ mn, at constant (1973) prices, five-year moving averages

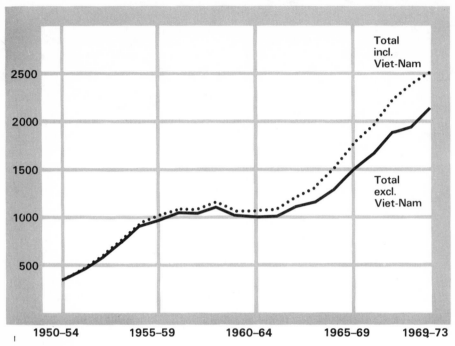

Source: SIPRI worksheets.

II. Values of exports from major weapon-producing countries, by region

Table 2A.3. USA: major weapons exports, by region

Region	1950	51	52	53	54	55	56	57	58	59
Far East, excl Viet-Nam	63.4	69.3	54.1	26.0	157.5	164.4	169.4	156.8	174.8	151.6
South Asia	–	–	–	11.7	41.5	40.4	56.3	56.4	91.5	18.3
Middle East	5.6	4.5	2.1	7.0	14.2	20.1	51.6	57.2	75.7	38.0
North Africa	–	–	–	–	–	–	–	–	–	1.4
Sub-Saharan Africa	–	–	–	5.8	5.7	1.3	0.6	0.3	0.6	2.8
South Africa	2.6	–	–	–	–	4.4	2.0	1.3	1.9	–
Central America	6.4	5.4	12.4	12.2	5.0	12.1	9.7	3.8	4.6	10.9
South America	13.0	30.2	34.0	10.4	56.5	59.1	36.0	70.4	29.3	23.8
Total [a]	**91.0**	**109.5**	**102.6**	**73.1**	**280.4**	**301.9**	**325.7**	**346.1**	**378.6**	**246.8**
Viet-Nam	–	–	–	–	4.6	3.4	4.1	*	1.6	2.4
Total, incl Viet-Nam	**91.0**	**109.5**	**102.6**	**73.1**	**284.9**	**305.3**	**329.8**	**346.1**	**380.2**	**249.2**

[a] Items may not add up to totals due to rounding.
Source: SIPRI worksheets.

Figure 2A.1. Distribution of major weapons exports, by supplier, 1950–1974 [a]

Value $ 28 373 mn, at constant (1973) prices

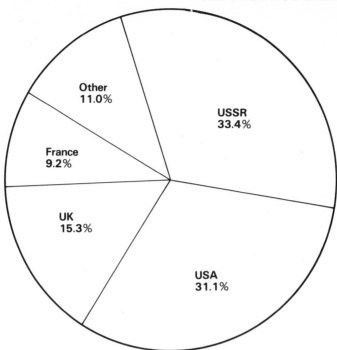

[a] Excluding Viet-Nam.

US $ mn, at constant (1973) prices

60	61	62	63	64	65	66	67	68	69	70	71	72	73
383.3	87.8	95.6	106.6	155.2	114.8	180.8	66.6	87.7	371.5	135.5	187.7	74.9	152.2
20.1	34.3	77.0	84.9	20.5	2.5	4.4	4.4	–	0.3	–	2.6	0.5	14.0
29.0	23.3	22.6	80.4	43.8	203.3	79.1	145.5	325.2	333.7	496.7	462.7	207.8	540.0
1.1	0.1	0.7	1.0	1.2	0.4	19.0	21.3	8.2	26.0	35.1	4.9	–	0.3
5.5	5.2	4.4	9.0	13.9	3.8	29.7	9.1	3.3	2.0	5.0	13.9	7.2	2.6
–	–	0.9	30.7	–	0.1	2.4	26.3	–	–	–	–	–	–
9.4	13.8	4.0	4.3	4.5	3.8	7.6	6.0	5.4	2.6	4.0	16.2	1.3	8.2
82.0	98.9	34.7	35.8	24.9	45.3	50.1	31.1	67.1	45.0	47.8	51.9	68.6	31.5
530.5	**263.4**	**240.0**	**352.8**	**264.0**	**374.0**	**373.1**	**310.3**	**496.9**	**783.6**	**724.1**	**739.9**	**360.3**	**748.9**
14.8	36.9	41.3	40.4	20.3	38.8	20.3	57.4	79.5	170.3	238.0	161.9	531.3	62.8
545.2	**300.4**	**281.3**	**393.2**	**284.3**	**412.8**	**393.4**	**367.8**	**576.4**	**953.8**	**962.1**	**731.1**	**891.6**	**811.7**

Table 2A.4. USSR: major weapons exports, by region

Region	1950	51	52	53	54	55	56	57	58	59
Far East, excl Viet-Nam	25.4	42.6	28.2	176.4	6.0	37.0	48.4	40.3	49.1	3.9
South Asia	–	–	–	–	–	2.6	1.8	12.0	7.3	12.6
Middle East	–	–	–	–	–	22.3	94.4	200.1	136.6	88.0
North Africa	–	–	–	–	–	–	–	–	–	–
Sub-Saharan Africa	–	–	–	–	–	–	–	–	–	0.4
South Africa	–	–	–	–	–	–	–	–	–	–
Central America	–	–	–	–	–	–	–	–	–	3.3
South America	–	–	–	–	–	–	–	–	–	–
Total	**25.4**	**42.6**	**28.2**	**176.4**	**6.0**	**62.0**	**144.6**	**252.5**	**193.0**	**108.2**
Viet-Nam	–	–	–	–	0.6	3.0	3.9	3.4	3.6	3.3
Total,[a] incl Viet-Nam	**25.4**	**42.6**	**28.2**	**176.4**	**6.6**	**65.0**	**148.5**	**255.9**	**196.6**	**111.4**

[a] Items may not add up to totals due to rounding.
Source: SIPRI worksheets.

Table 2A.5. UK: major weapons exports, by region

Region	1950	51	52	53	54	55	56	57	58	59
Far East, excl Viet-Nam	0.1	0.2	0.2	0.2	4.0	12.3	4.8	6.6	7.3	9.8
South Asia	44.1	20.2	19.1	38.9	23.4	63.3	115.6	135.3	270.1	111.5
Middle East	21.1	31.1	6.8	42.0	49.9	39.9	31.4	9.8	13.2	5.4
North Africa	–	–	–	–	–	–	–	1.3	–	*
Sub-Saharan Africa	–	4.6	3.9	10.4	11.8	10.4	0.4	0.4	1.8	40.4
South Africa	5.1	–	15.7	14.8	16.6	10.9	19.5	19.5	15.1	14.8
Central America	*	–	–	–	–	–	–	2.0	3.9	*
South America	25.1	7.7	–	58.3	60.2	38.5	26.8	5.5	46.3	9.6
Total [a]	**95.6**	**63.8**	**45.8**	**164.6**	**166.0**	**175.3**	**198.4**	**180.2**	**357.7**	**182.7**

[a] Items may not add up to totals due to rounding.
Source: SIPRI worksheets.

Table 2A.6. France: major weapons exports, by region

Region	1950	51	52	53	54	55	56	57	58	59
Far East, excl Viet-Nam	–	–	–	–	1.3	3.3	0.3	0.1	–	0.4
South Asia	–	–	–	38.8	38.8	–	–	46.8	110.8	–
Middle East	2.8	2.7	1.4	2.4	16.6	59.6	104.0	17.7	11.6	42.2
North Africa	–	–	–	–	–	–	6.0	4.1	3.8	4.8
Sub-Saharan Africa	–	–	–	–	–	–	–	–	–	–
South Africa	–	–	–	–	–	–	–	–	–	–
Central America	–	–	–	–	–	–	–	–	2.9	–
South America	–	–	–	–	9.7	3.8	9.4	1.0	–	–
Total [a]	**2.8**	**2.7**	**1.4**	**41.2**	**66.3**	**66.8**	**119.8**	**69.5**	**129.1**	**47.4**
Viet-Nam	–	–	–	–	4.0	2.9	2.8	*	2.4	2.4

[a] Items may not add up to totals due to rounding.
Source: SIPRI worksheets.

US $ mn, at constant (1973) prices

60	61	62	63	64	65	66	67	68	69	70	71	72	73
14.9	39.1	158.8	79.8	82.9	112.0	112.4	29.1	75.8	47.5	47.5	83.1	10.2	5.6
51.5	58.7	47.0	53.6	20.1	108.4	190.8	120.4	90.0	188.9	161.0	233.3	127.9	120.4
56.9	109.9	317.3	113.7	134.1	95.7	159.6	622.0	385.2	324.6	493.6	653.6	397.5	969.3
–	5.9	26.0	14.3	19.7	57.9	59.2	63.5	15.4	3.9	24.4	17.3	1.2	0.1
4.7	16.1	1.2	3.5	1.3	17.3	10.8	19.4	5.1	19.1	55.2	6.1	7.1	50.6
–	–	–	–	–	–	–	–	–	–	–	–	–	–
29.8	143.8	223.2	60.9	18.3	6.8	7.4	6.1	–	3.6	–	9.3	25.5	27.3
–	–	–	–	–	–	–	–	–	–	4.7	–	–	1.9
157.8	**373.5**	**773.4**	**325.0**	**276.4**	**398.1**	**590.2**	**860.6**	**571.4**	**587.8**	**786.4**	**1 002.7**	**569.5**	**1 175.1**
6.7	17.0	13.3	2.5	10.7	17.7	151.6	320.7	282.3	50.3	82.1	155.6	367.0	–
164.5	**390.5**	**786.7**	**328.3**	**287.1**	**415.8**	**741.8**	**1181.3**	**853.7**	**638.1**	**868.5**	**1 158.3**	**936.5**	**1 175.1**

US $ mn, at constant (1973) prices

60	61	62	63	64	65	66	67	68	69	70	71	72	73
3.1	9.4	7.8	30.0	33.7	5.6	23.3	36.8	17.4	2.2	20.0	40.2	16.8	20.1
132.9	109.2	17.8	14.3	12.3	45.0	37.7	74.0	37.7	38.0	31.8	48.4	63.7	36.7
11.3	5.6	22.8	28.9	41.8	13.3	45.3	30.1	119.4	173.0	65.2	156.1	158.9	115.1
2.9	2.9	–	0.3	1.2	1.2	10.7	7.8	8.7	23.1	5.2	*	0.6	16.9
5.6	4.6	16.2	9.1	15.9	16.9	12.1	6.1	6.8	6.8	1.2	17.9	12.8	4.0
3.3	–	6.6	37.7	28.7	87.4	1.2	–	–	1.6	3.3	10.2	–	0.9
–	–	–	0.1	0.1	1.1	–	–	–	–	–	10.7	*	–
36.9	52.4	23.7	14.6	2.9	32.2	17.3	–	34.6	21.6	14.9	17.0	29.7	48.0
196.1	**184.5**	**95.0**	**135.1**	**136.6**	**202.7**	**147.6**	**154.9**	**224.7**	**266.4**	**141.6**	**300.5**	**282.6**	**241.7**

US $ mn, at constant (1973) prices

60	61	62	63	64	65	66	67	68	69	70	71	72	73
0.4	1.9	7.9	5.3	7.8	11.9	2.5	–	0.3	7.2	1.2	1.9	2.0	35.7
–	19.1	–	6.2	–	–	1.6	1.6	76.7	4.8	21.3	15.8	28.9	49.3
11.3	6.4	71.2	72.4	71.3	15.8	14.9	11.8	96.1	42.4	22.7	36.1	15.0	25.9
3.9	0.1	1.2	6.1	8.3	0.1	4.0	7.0	5.2	8.2	24.3	71.8	122.7	86.0
5.8	4.4	2.7	5.8	2.7	5.3	5.8	9.4	14.3	10.6	14.6	34.2	10.6	10.4
–	2.3	3.7	48.7	10.5	38.6	66.7	19.5	15.5	26.7	51.5	39.7	17.8	23.2
–	–	–	0.2	2.1	1.9	–	–	–	0.3	–	–	–	–
13.4	3.9	5.7	3.4	2.3	–	11.3	2.5	11.9	31.1	20.0	11.3	71.8	172.6
34.8	**38.2**	**92.4**	**148.0**	**105.1**	**73.7**	**106.8**	**51.8**	**220.1**	**131.4**	**155.6**	**220.0**	**268.7**	**411.1**
2.4	–	–	–	–	–	–	–	–	–	–	–	–	–

Chart 2A.2. Exports of major weapons to third world countries: four main suppliers (excl. Viet-Nam)

US $ mn, at constant (1973) prices, five-year moving averages

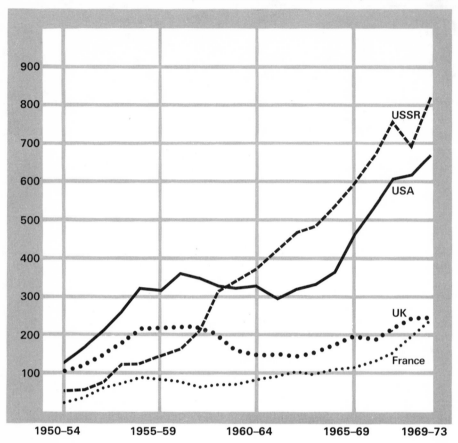

Source: SIPRI worksheets.

Table 2A.7. Canada: major weapons exports, by region[a]

US $ thousand, at constant (1973) prices

Region	1950–1954 $ 000 annual average	1950–1954 Per cent	1955–1959 $ 000 annual average	1955–1959 Per cent	1960–1964 $ 000 annual average	1960–1964 Per cent	1965–1969 $ 000 annual average	1965–1969 Per cent	1969–1973 $ 000 annual average	1969–1973 Per cent	1950–1973 $ 000 annual average	1950–1973 Per cent
Far East, excl Viet-Nam	520	14.0	190	0.8	455	5.2	5 395	32.9	2 730	11.6	1 560	10.4
South Asia	80	2.1	845	3.7	3 520	40.0	780	4.8	225	1.0	1 135	7.5
Middle East	4.5	1.2	12 905	56.6	285	3.2	1 205	7.3	1 950	8.3	3 250	21.6
North Africa	–	–	–	–	–	–	–	–	275	1.2	55	0.4
Sub-Saharan Africa	–	–	145	0.6	2 320	26.4	2 855	17.4	2 840	12.1	1 700	11.3
South Africa	–	–	7 280	31.9	365	4.2	–	–	–	–	1 595	10.6
Central America	–	–	60	0.3	1 560	17.8	75	0.5	75	0.3	370	2.4
South America	3 090	82.8	1 385	6.1	285	3.3	5 985	36.5	15 710	66.8	5 440	36.1
Total	**3 730**	**100.0**	**22 810**	**100.0**	**8 790**	**100.0**	**16 395**	**100.0**	**23 535**	**100.0**	**15 080**	**100.0**

[a] Figures are rounded to the nearest 5.
Source: SIPRI worksheets.

Table 2A.8. China: major weapons exports, by region

US $ thousand, at constant (1973) prices

Region	1950–1954 $ 000 annual average	1950–1954 Per cent	1955–1959 $ 000 annual average	1955–1959 Per cent	1960–1964 $ 000 annual average	1960–1964 Per cent	1965–1969 $ 000 annual average	1965–1969 Per cent	1969–1973 $ 000 annual average	1969–1973 Per cent	1950–1973 $ 000 annual average	1950–1973 Per cent
Far East, excl Viet-Nam	11 830	100.0	84 790	100.0	32 395	100.0	4 325	43.2	–	–	27 780	75.0
South Asia	–	–	–	–	–	–	6 005	60.0	30 610	78.8	7 630	20.6
Sub-Saharan Africa	–	–	–	–	–	–	675	6.8	8 260	21.3	1 860	5.0
Total[a]	**11 830**	**100.0**	**84 790**	**100.0**	**32 395**	**100.0**	**10 010**	**100.0**	**38 870**	**100.0**	**37 060**	**100.0**

[a] Items may not add up to totals due to rounding.
Source: SIPRI worksheets.

Table 2A.9. Czechoslovakia: major weapons exports, by region

US $ thousand, at constant (1973) prices

Region	1950–1954 $ 000 annual average	1950–1954 Per cent	1955–1959 $ 000 annual average	1955–1959 Per cent	1960–1964 $ 000 annual average	1960–1964 Per cent	1965–1969 $ 000 annual average	1965–1969 Per cent	1969–1973 $ 000 annual average	1969–1973 Per cent	1950–1973 $ 000 annual average	1950–1973 Per cent
Far East, excl Viet-Nam	–	–	15 290	40.6	9 711	65.9	–	–	–	–	5 210	33.6
South Asia	–	–	–	–	–	–	1 735	13.5	5 720	45.6	1 280	8.3
Middle East	–	–	22 040	58.6	3 015	20.5	5 655	44.1	4 910	39.1	7 095	45.8
North Africa	–	–	–	–	–	–	2 340	18.2	990	7.9	590	3.8
Sub-Saharan Africa	–	–	310	0.8	–	–	3 105	24.2	935	7.5	905	5.9
Central America	–	–	–	–	2 010	13.6	–	–	–	–	420	2.7
Total[a]	**–**	**–**	**37 640**	**100.0**	**14 735**	**100.0**	**12 835**	**100.0**	**12 550**	**100.0**	**15 500**	**100.0**

[a] Items may not add up to totals due to rounding.
Source: SIPRI worksheets.

Table 2A.10. FR Germany: major weapons exports, by region

US $ thousand, at constant (1973) prices

Region	1950–1954 $ 000 annual average	1950–1954 Per cent	1955–1959 $ 000 annual average	1955–1959 Per cent	1960–1964 $ 000 annual average	1960–1964 Per cent	1965–1969 $ 000 annual average	1965–1969 Per cent	1969–1973 $ 000 annual average	1969–1973 Per cent	1950–1973 $ 000 annual average	1950–1973 Per cent
Far East, excl Viet-Nam	685	60.5	6 495	60.0	2 520	21.4	215	1.1	1 385	11.0	2 355	21.2
South Asia	–	–	–	–	–	–	5 140	26.2	–	–	1 070	9.6
Middle East	10	0.7	1 025	9.5	3 140	26.6	9 880	50.3	2 655	21.0	2 930	26.4
North Africa	–	–	–	–	975	8.3	2 230	11.4	–	–	670	6.0
Sub-Saharan Africa	–	–	–	–	3 305	28.1	815	4.2	660	5.2	995	9.0
South Africa	–	–	20	0.2	–	–	–	–	–	–	5	0.04
Central America	–	–	–	–	235	2.0	–	–	–	–	50	0.4
South America	440	38.8	3 280	30.3	1 615	13.7	1 350	6.9	7 930	62.8	3 045	27.4
Total[a]	**1 135**	**100.0**	**10 820**	**100.0**	**11 795**	**100.0**	**19 630**	**100.0**	**12 630**	**100.0**	**11 115**	**100.0**

[a] Items may not add up to totals due to rounding.
Source: SIPRI worksheets.

Table 2A.11. Italy: major weapons exports, by region

US $ thousand, at constant (1973) prices

Region	1950–1954 $ 000 annual average	1950–1954 Per cent	1955–1959 $ 000 annual average	1955–1959 Per cent	1960–1964 $ 000 annual average	1960–1964 Per cent	1965–1969 $ 000 annual average	1965–1969 Per cent	1969–1973 $ 000 annual average	1969–1973 Per cent	1950–1973 $ 000 annual average	1950–1973 Per cent
Far East, excl Viet-Nam	–	–	4 580	25.3	5 895	78.5	405	1.8	730	1.9	2 420	13.6
South Asia	500	6.3	2 095	11.6	130	1.8	2 210	9.7	–	–	1 030	5.8
Middle East	4 375	55.8	1 145	6.3	80	1.1	7 920	34.7	21 910	58.3	6 260	35.1
North Africa	–	–	–	–	–	–	1 690	7.4	1 885	5.0	745	4.2
Sub-Saharan Africa	–	–	–	–	505	6.7	2 385	10.5	4 025	10.7	1 210	6.8
South Africa	–	–	–	–	–	–	7 835	34.3	3 920	10.4	2 175	12.2
South America	2 965	37.8	10 265	56.8	895	11.9	390	1.7	5 105	13.6	4 005	22.5
Total[a]	**7 840**	**100.0**	**18 085**	**100.0**	**7 505**	**100.0**	**22 835**	**100.0**	**37 570**	**100.0**	**17 845**	**100.0**

[a] Items may not add up to totals due to rounding.
Source: SIPRI worksheets.

III. Regional imports of major weapons, by supplier

Figure 2A.2. Distribution of major weapons imports, by recipient region, 1950–1974

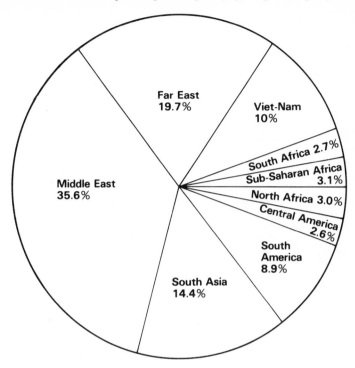

Table 2A.12. Far East: imports of major weapons, by supplier

US $ *mn, at constant (1973) prices*

	1950–1954		1955–1959		1960–1964		1965–1969		1969–1973		1950–1973	
Supplier	$ mn annual average	Per cent	$ mn annual average	Per cent	$ mn annual average	Per cent	$ mn annual average	Per cent	$ mn annual average	Per cent	$ mn annual average	Per cent
USA	74.1	48.2	163.4	52.3	165.7	53.6	164.3	56.9	184.4	69.3	141.1	54.6
USSR	55.7	36.2	35.8	11.5	75.1	24.3	85.4	29.6	38.8	14.6	58.6	22.7
UK	1.0	0.6	6.4	2.0	16.8	5.4	17.1	5.9	19.9	7.6	12.6	4.9
France	0.3	0.2	0.8	0.3	4.6	1.5	4.4	1.5	9.6	3.6	3.8	1.5
China	9.1	5.9	65.2	20.9	24.9	8.1	3.3	1.2	–	–	21.4	8.3
Other	13.7	8.9	40.8	13.1	21.9	7.1	14.2	4.9	13.4	5.0	20.9	8.0
Total[a]	153.8	100.0	312.3	100.0	309.1	100.0	288.6	100.0	366.0	100.0	258.4	100.0

[a] Items may not add up to totals due to rounding.
Source: SIPRI worksheets.

Chart 2A.3. Supplies of major weapons to the Far East

US $ mn, at constant (1973) prices, five-year moving averages

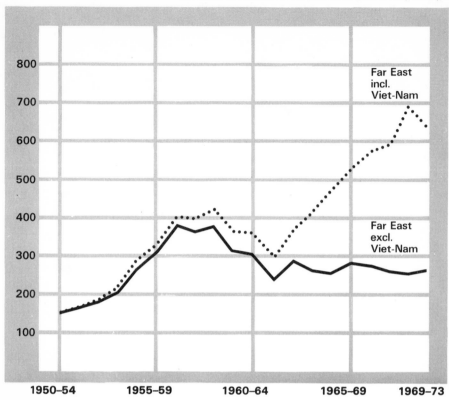

Source: SIPRI worksheets.

Table 2A.13. South Asia: imports of major weapons, by supplier

US $ mn, at constant (1973) prices

Supplier	1950–1954		1955–1959		1960–1964		1965–1969		1969–1973		1950–1973	
	$ mn annual average	Per cent	$ mn annual average	Per cent	$ mn annual average	Per cent	$ mn annual average	Per cent	$ mn annual average	Per cent	$ mn annual average	Per cent
USA	10.6	*19.1*	52.6	*22.4*	47.4	*29.6*	2.3	*1.1*	3.5	*1.3*	24.2	*12.9*
USSR	–	–	7.3	*3.1*	46.2	*28.9*	139.7	*61.5*	166.3	*60.2*	67.0	*35.5*
UK	29.2	*52.5*	139.2	*59.3*	57.3	*35.8*	46.5	*20.5*	43.7	*15.9*	64.2	*34.0*
France	15.5	*27.8*	31.5	*13.5*	5.1	*3.2*	16.9	*7.5*	24.0	*8.7*	19.2	*10.2*
Other	0.6	*1.1*	4.3	*1.9*	4.2	*2.6*	21.7	*9.6*	39.1	*14.2*	14.3	*7.6*
Total[a]	55.9	100.0	234.8	100.0	160.1	100.0	227.1	100.0	276.6	100.0	188.9	100.0

[a] Items may not add up to totals due to rounding.
Source: SIPRI worksheets.

Chart 2A.4. Supplies of major weapons to India and Pakistan
US $ mn, at constant (1973) prices, five-year moving averages

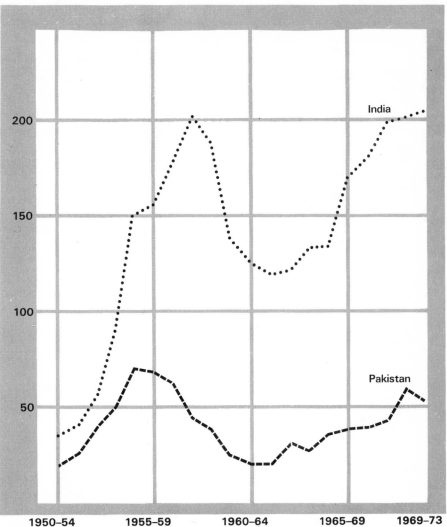

Source: SIPRI worksheets.

Table 2A.14. Middle East: imports of major weapons, by supplier

US $ mn, at constant (1973) prices

Supplier	1950–1954 $ mn annual average	Per cent	1955–1959 $ mn annual average	Per cent	1960–1964 $ mn annual average	Per cent	1965–1969 $ mn annual average	Per cent	1969–1973 $ mn annual average	Per cent	1950–1973 $ mn annual average	Per cent
USA	6.7	13.2	48.5	18.4	39.8	15.2	217.4	32.2	408.2	34.6	136.2	29.1
USSR	–	–	108.3	41.0	146.4	55.9	317.4	47.0	567.7	48.1	223.9	47.8
UK	30.2	59.7	20.0	7.6	22.2	8.5	76.2	11.3	133.7	11.3	51.6	11.0
France	5.2	10.3	47.0	17.8	46.5	17.8	36.2	5.4	28.4	2.4	32.3	6.9
Other	8.5	16.9	40.6	15.4	7.0	2.7	27.8	4.1	42.7	3.6	24.2	5.1
Total[a]	**50.6**	**100.0**	**264.4**	**100.0**	**261.9**	**100.0**	**675.1**	**100.0**	**1 180.7**	**100.0**	**468.2**	**100.0**

[a] Items may not add up to totals due to rounding.
Source: SIPRI worksheets.

Chart 2A.5. Supplies of major weapons to the Middle East, by selected recipients
US $ mn, at constant (1973) prices, five-year moving averages

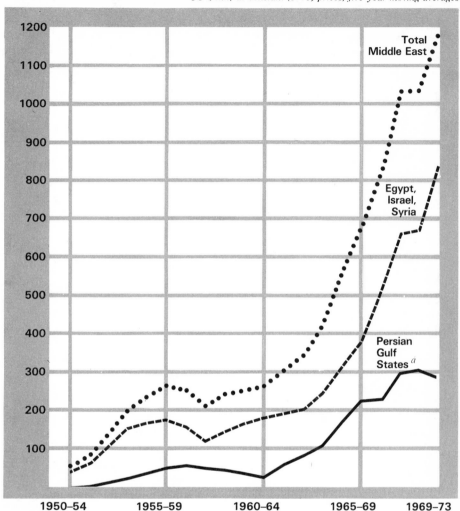

^{a} Abu Dhabi, Bahrain, Dubai, Iran, Kuwait, Oman, Qatar, Saudi Arabia, Sharya.
Source: SIPRI worksheets.

Chart 2A.6. Supplies of major weapons to Egypt and Israel

US $ mn, at constant (1973) prices, five-year moving averages

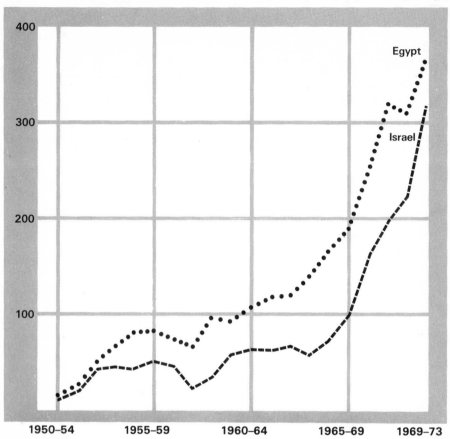

Source: SIPRI worksheets.

Table 2A.15. North Africa: imports of major weapons, by supplier

US $ mn, at constant (1973) prices

Supplier	1950–1954 $ mn annual average	1950–1954 Per cent	1955–1959 $ mn annual average	1955–1959 Per cent	1960–1964 $ mn annual average	1960–1964 Per cent	1965–1969 $ mn annual average	1965–1969 Per cent	1969–1973 $ mn annual average	1969–1973 Per cent	1950–1973 $ mn annual average	1950–1973 Per cent
USA	–	–	0.3	6.6	0.8	3.9	15.0	19.3	13.3	13.5	5.0	12.8
USSR	–	–	–	–	13.2	61.4	40.0	51.5	9.4	9.5	12.9	32.8
UK	–	–	0.3	6.1	1.5	6.9	10.3	13.3	9.2	9.3	3.5	8.8
France	–	–	3.7	87.2	3.9	18.3	4.9	6.4	62.6	63.7	15.3	39.0
Other	–	–	*	0.2	2.0	9.5	7.5	9.6	3.9	4.0	2.6	6.6
Total[a]	–	–	4.3	100.0	21.4	100.0	77.7	100.0	98.3	100.0	39.2	100.0

[a] Items may not add up to totals due to rounding.
Source: SIPRI worksheets.

Table 2A.16. Sub-Saharan Africa: imports of major weapons, by supplier

US $ mn, at constant (1973) prices

Supplier	1950–1954 $ mn annual average	1950–1954 Per cent	1955–1959 $ mn annual average	1955–1959 Per cent	1960–1964 $ mn annual average	1960–1964 Per cent	1965–1969 $ mn annual average	1965–1969 Per cent	1969–1973 $ mn annual average	1969–1973 Per cent	1950–1973 $ mn annual average	1950–1973 Per cent
USA	2.3	26.2	1.1	8.8	7.6	19.6	9.6	15.9	6.1	7.1	5.5	13.4
USSR	–	–	0.1	0.7	5.4	13.8	14.3	23.7	27.6	31.9	9.1	22.2
UK	6.1	70.1	10.7	84.0	10.3	26.5	9.7	16.1	8.5	9.8	9.2	22.4
France	–	–	–	–	4.3	11.0	9.1	15.0	16.1	18.5	5.7	13.9
Other	0.3	3.8	0.8	6.6	11.3	29.1	17.7	29.4	28.4	32.7	11.5	28.2
Total[a]	8.8	100.0	12.7	100.0	38.8	100.0	60.4	100.0	86.7	100.0	40.9	100.0

[a] Items may not add up to totals due to rounding.
Source: SIPRI worksheets.

Table 2A.17. South Africa: imports of major weapons, by supplier

US $ mn, at constant (1973) prices

Supplier	1950–1954 $ mn annual average	1950–1954 Per cent	1955–1959 $ mn annual average	1955–1959 Per cent	1960–1964 $ mn annual average	1960–1964 Per cent	1965–1969 $ mn annual average	1965–1969 Per cent	1969–1973 $ mn annual average	1969–1973 Per cent	1950–1973 $ mn annual average	1950–1973 Per cent
USA	0.5	4.8	1.9	7.7	6.3	17.9	5.8	8.5	–	–	3.0	8.5
UK	10.4	95.3	15.9	63.3	15.2	43.1	18.0	26.4	3.2	8.2	13.0	36.4
France	–	–	–	–	13.1	36.9	33.4	48.9	31.8	81.7	15.2	42.5
Italy	–	–	–	–	–	–	7.8	11.5	3.9	10.1	2.2	6.1
Other	–	–	4.3	29.0	0.8	2.2	3.3	4.8	–	–	2.4	6.6
Total[a]	11.0	100.0	25.7	100.0	35.4	100.0	68.3	100.0	38.9	100.0	35.8	100.0

[a] Items may not add up to totals due to rounding.
Source: SIPRI worksheets.

Chart 2A.7. Supplies of major weapons to North Africa,[a] Sub-Saharan Africa and South Africa

US $ mn, at constant (1973) prices, five-year moving averages

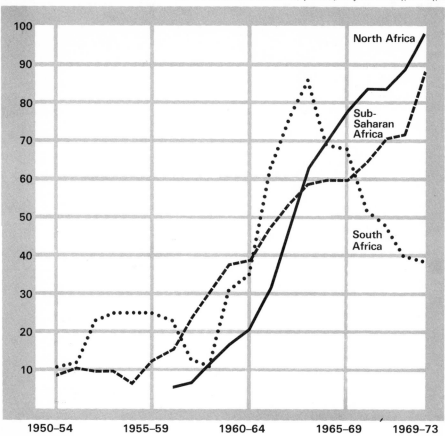

[a] North African averages are calculated from 1956, when imports began.
Source: SIPRI worksheets.

Table 2A.18. Central America: imports of major weapons, by supplier

US $ mn, at constant (1973) prices

Supplier	1950–1954		1955–1959		1960–1964		1965–1969		1969–1973		1950–1973	
	$ mn annual average	Per cent	$ mn annual average	Per cent	$ mn annual average	Per cent	$ mn annual average	Per cent	$ mn annual average	Per cent	$ mn annual average	Per cent
USA	8.3	67.7	8.2	63.5	7.2	6.8	5.1	45.2	6.5	27.3	7.2	21.0
USSR	–	–	0.7	5.0	95.2	89.2	4.8	42.7	13.2	55.7	23.6	68.5
Other Europe	3.9	32.3	4.0	31.0	2.7	2.6	1.0	9.2	2.2	9.3	2.9	8.0
Other	–	–	0.1	0.5	1.6	1.5	0.3	3.0	1.8	7.6	0.8	2.1
Total[a]	**12.2**	**100.0**	**13.0**	**100.0**	**106.7**	**100.0**	**11.2**	**100.0**	**23.6**	**100.0**	**34.4**	**100.0**

[a] Items may not add up to totals due to rounding.
Source: SIPRI worksheets.

Table 2A.19. South America: imports of major weapons, by supplier

US $ mn, at constant (1973) prices

Supplier	1950–1954 $ mn annual average	Per cent	1955–1959 $ mn annual average	Per cent	1960–1964 $ mn annual average	Per cent	1965–1969 $ mn annual average	Per cent	1969–1973 $ mn annual average	Per cent	1950–1973 $ mn annual average	Per cent
USA	28.9	40.4	43.7	36.2	55.3	58.5	47.7	42.0	49.0	26.9	44.9	38.6
UK	30.3	42.3	25.3	21.0	26.1	27.7	21.1	18.6	26.2	14.4	26.0	22.4
France	1.9	2.7	2.9	2.4	5.8	6.1	11.4	10.0	61.4	33.7	16.1	13.8
Other Europe	4.4	6.2	40.2	33.3	3.1	3.3	19.8	17.5	27.9	15.3	19.0	16.3
Other	6.0	8.4	8.8	7.3	4.3	4.5	13.5	11.9	17.7	9.7	10.4	8.9
Total[a]	71.5	100.0	120.9	100.0	94.5	100.0	113.5	100.0	182.2	100.0	116.3	100.0

[a] Items may not add up to totals due to rounding.
Source: SIPRI worksheets.

Table 2A.20. Greece and Turkey: imports of major weapons by supplier

US $ mn, at constant (1973) prices

Supplier	1950–1954 $ mn annual average	Per cent	1955–1959 $ mn annual average	Per cent	1960–1964 $ mn annual average	Per cent	1965–1969 $ mn annual average	Per cent	1969–1973 $ mn annual average	Per cent	1950–1973 $ mn annual average	Per cent
USA	93.6	89.8	169.4	83.3	56.5	48.5	111.3	77.0	64.2	55.2	96.3	71.4
UK	*	*	12.7	6.3	0.3	0.3	–	–	0.1	0.1	2.7	2.0
France	–	–	–	–	*	*	0.7	0.5	12.2	10.5	2.7	2.0
FR Germany	–	–	0.4	0.2	14.4	12.4	16.2	11.2	35.6	30.7	13.3	9.9
Other	10.6	10.2	20.8	10.2	45.2	38.9	16.3	11.3	4.2	3.6	19.9	14.8
Total[a]	104.3	100.0	203.4	100.0	116.4	100.0	144.6	100.0	116.3	100.0	134.9	100.0

[a] Items may not add up to totals due to rounding.
Source: SIPRI worksheets.

Table 2A.21. The spread of sophisticated aircraft[a] to third world countries.

*The first shaded year indicates the year when
a country first received sophisticated aircraft*

Country	1955	56	57	58	59	60	61	62	63	64	65	66	67	68	69	70	71	72	73	74	On order
Israel	■	■	■	■	■	■	■	■	■	■	■	■	■	■	■	■	■	■	■	■	■
India				■	■	■	■	■	■	■	■	■	■	■	■	■	■	■	■	■	■
Taiwan			■	■	■	■	■	■	■	■	■	■	■	■	■	■	■	■	■	■	■
Cuba								■	■	■	■	■	■	■	■	■	■	■	■	■	■
Egypt								■	■	■	■	■	■	■	■	■	■	■	■	■	■
Pakistan							■	■	■	■	■	■	■	■	■	■	■	■	■	■	■
Iraq									■	■	■	■	■	■	■	■	■	■	■	■	■
South Africa								■	■	■	■	■	■	■	■	■	■	■	■	■	■
Indonesia									■	■	■	■	■	■	■	■	■	■	■	■	■
Algeria										■	■	■	■	■	■	■	■	■	■	■	■
Iran										■	■	■	■	■	■	■	■	■	■	■	■
Korea, North										■	■	■	■	■	■	■	■	■	■	■	■
Korea, South											■	■	■	■	■	■	■	■	■	■	■
Philippines											■	■	■	■	■	■	■	■	■	■	■
Afghanistan												■	■	■	■	■	■	■	■	■	■
Argentina												■	■	■	■	■	■	■	■	■	■
Ethiopia												■	■	■	■	■	■	■	■	■	■
Morocco												■	■	■	■	■	■	■	■	■	■
Saudi Arabia												■	■	■	■	■	■	■	■	■	■
Thailand												■	■	■	■	■	■	■	■	■	■
Viet-Nam, North											■	■	■	■	■	■	■	■	■	■	■
Jordan												■	■	■	■	■	■	■	■	■	■
Syria												■	■	■	■	■	■	■	■	■	■
Viet-Nam, South											■	■	■	■	■	■	■	■	■	■	■
Kuwait													■	■	■	■	■	■	■	■	■
Lebanon													■	■	■	■	■	■	■	■	■
Libya													■	■	■	■	■	■	■	■	■
Peru													■	■	■	■	■	■	■	■	■
(Nigeria)														■	■	■	■	■	■	■	■
Sudan															■	■	■	■	■	■	■
Brazil																	■	■	■	■	■	■
Colombia																	■	■	■	■	■	■
Abu Dhabi																		■	■	■	■
Bangladesh																		■	■	■	■
Singapore																		■	■	■	■
(Uganda)																		■	■	■	■
Venezuela																			■	■	■
Somalia																				■	■
Ecuador																					■
Malaysia																					■
Singapore																					■
Zaïre																					■

[a] Super- and transonic aircraft. The following are known to have been supplied to third world countries: F–4 Phantom, F–5 Freedom Fighter, F–5E Tiger II, F–101 Voodoo, F–104 Starfighter, A–4 Skyhawk Mystère IV A, Super Mystère, Vautour II, Mirage III, Mirage 5, Mirage F1, Jaguar, Lightning, Buccaneer, MiG–21, MiG–23, Su–7 and Su–9.

Chart 2A.8. Licensed production of major weapons in third world countries, and third world major arms exports

US $ mn, at constant (1973) prices, five-year moving averages

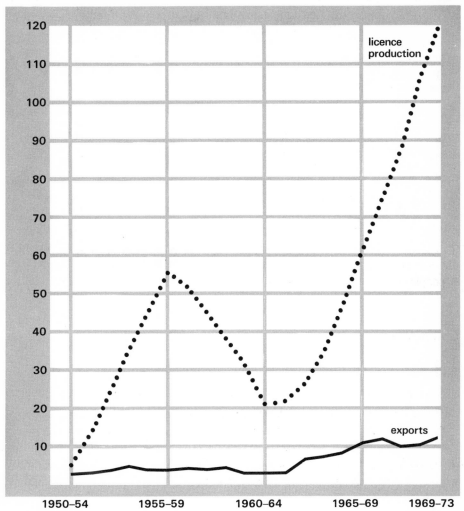

Source: SIPRI worksheets.

169

Appendix 3

Sources and methods

Sources of information

In collecting the basic information, three types of sources have been used. First, unofficial sources were used: for example, technical journals, press reports and other publications concerning defence equipment, military aid and alliances. Second, information was gathered from official sources: parliamentary statements, hearings and debates, official publications and press releases. Third, correspondents in different parts of the world interviewed officials, manufacturers, and other people connected with the arms trade, and read the relevant local publications.

Coverage

Weapons

The SIPRI statistics cover the deliveries of major weapons: ships, aircraft, armoured fighting vehicles and missiles. The coverage of warships, combat aircraft and tanks is probably reasonably good. Even if it were possible, very few countries attempt to conceal deliveries of these items. The coverage of smaller items such as light aircraft, helicopters, armoured cars and missiles is not quite so good, but probably sufficient to provide a basically accurate picture of the trade in these weapons.

Information on transfers of other weapons, especially small arms, is fragmentary and unreliable. Even if the types of small arms possessed by different countries could be established, it would be extremely difficult to discover the numbers, the dates of deliveries and the countries from which they were purchased. Small arms often have long production series, often change hands a number of times, and often take complicated routes to reach their destinations. For this reason, the tables are limited to the delivery of major weapons.

The tables include spares and equipment for aircraft and equipment which is part of the missile system. But they do not include a whole range of equipment that may be needed to acquire a particular weapon system. For instance, a country purchasing a fighter squadron will, in addition to spares and equipment for the aircraft itself, need to acquire various kinds of munitions for the aircraft, a radar tracking and warning system, ground equipment, repair and maintenance facilities, training for its pilots and technicians, etc. Thus the figures in the tables may appear rather low when compared with, for instance, figures for US grant aid or sales.

In a number of countries, the air force is responsible for some of the country's civil transport and for training pilots for civil planes. This is particularly true for many South American countries. The Brazilian Air Force, for instance, provides transport to remote areas where civil airlines do not operate, delivers food, mail and medical supplies, and is responsible for surveying much of the vast unmapped territory of Brazil. On the other hand, almost all training aircraft can be adapted for counterinsurgency action without great difficulty. The MFI-9 plane used by Swedish pilots in Biafra for strafing operations is a basic primary trainer. The Macchi M.B.326, produced under licence in Brazil and South Africa, is eminently suitable for counterinsurgency operations. The general principle has been to include in the registers all planes supplied to the armed forces of the countries concerned, with a note indicating when it was known that the planes were for civil use only. In the latter case they were not included in the value tables. Often, however, it was not known, and it should be borne in mind in considering the statistics that transport and trainer aircraft may be used for both civil and military purposes.

Countries

The countries covered by the country registers and the tables are the non-arms producing countries. Many of the countries under consideration do have domestic defence industries, but they are still heavily dependent on imports in meeting their defence requirements. The two countries possessing the most developed domestic defence industries – Israel and South Africa – are still far from self-sufficiency.

Arms supplies to colonies or dependencies are included when these countries have armed forces separate from the metropolitan power – for example, the Central African Republic during the 1950s. Only weapons supplied to the indigenous armed forces in the third world are included. Thus, for instance, for the US supply of arms to Viet-Nam, only the major weapons supplied to South Viet-Namese forces are entered as arms trade; the weapons supplied to US troops do not appear in the tables. Soviet arms based in Egypt or Syria have also not been included.

Viet-Nam – North and South – is shown separately in the tables of major weapon imports, and totals are given including and excluding Viet-Nam. In the table of major weapon exports by supplier, both North and South Viet-Nam are excluded. Since the United States has been intervening directly in this conflict, while the Soviet Union was simply supplying arms to North Viet-Nam, any comparison of the arms supplies of the two great powers to the two sides would be inappropriate. The cost of the United States intervention, at around $24 billion in 1969, vastly exceeds the whole of the trade in major weapons recorded in the tables.

The third world areas listed in the tables are as follows:

Far East. All countries east of Pakistan, except China, Japan, Australia and New
    Zealand. Viet-Nam is shown separately.

Middle East. Abu Dhabi, Bahrein, Dubai, Egypt, Iran, Iraq, Israel, Jordan, Kuwait,
    Lebanon, Oman, Qatar, Saudi Arabia, Sharya, Southern Yemen, Syria, Yemen.

North Africa. Algeria, Libya, Morocco, Tunisia.

Sub-Saharan Africa. The rest of Africa, except for South Africa.

South Africa.

South Asia. Afghanistan, India, Pakistan, Sri Lanka.

Central America. All countries from Panama northwards up to the United States.

South America. The rest of Latin America.

Europe. Greece and Turkey appear in the register but have been excluded from
    the tables.

The figures

There may be some slight upward bias in the figures for recent years due to extra
information. This upward bias could account for approximately 10 per cent of the
total. But it is unlikely to be higher than this. It concerns primarily the smaller
items–helicopters, light aircraft and inexpensive military vehicles, whose values
are low compared with those of tanks and combat aircraft. It is unlikely that there
is any upward bias in the estimates for ships and missiles. The ship estimates are
based almost entirely on one source, *Jane's Fighting Ships.*[1] There were very few
transfers of missiles in the earlier years.

In order to obtain aggregate statistics of the trade in major weapons, it was
necessary first to reconcile conflicting data and to estimate the numbers and types
of weapons and the dates of the deliveries when such information was not available, and then to value individual transactions.

Reconciliation and estimation

There is little difficulty in obtaining reliable and unconflicting information about
the deliveries of warships, combat aircraft and main battle tanks. In value terms,
these amount to around 80 per cent of total arms deliveries. The problems of
reconciliation and estimation primarily concern armoured cars and armoured personnel carriers and other vehicles, missiles, light aircraft and helicopters. When
there was conflicting information, we have, if possible, made our decision on the
basis of general experience of the reliability of different sources.

For armoured fighting vehicles, other than main battle tanks, the main problem
has been the lack of sources. For certain countries whose armed forces are well
publicized, such as India, Pakistan, Egypt or Israel, the information on deliveries
of armoured fighting vehicles has been fairly good. These are the countries

[1]London, Sampson Low, Marston & Co., annual.

in the third world which have been the main importers of main battle tanks. For some countries (which, for the most part, imported light tanks or armoured cars) there is only information on the types the country possesses and the numbers of battalions or armoured divisions in that country. To estimate the dates and numbers of tank deliveries, we took into account the dates of production of particular types, or, in the case of second-hand equipment, the dates of replacement of the particular type in the supplier country, the dates of aid or sales agreements or other political and diplomatic ties between the supplier and the recipient countries, the dates at which the presence of these types was first reported, and the number of tanks, armoured cars, and armoured personnel carriers in an armoured battalion or division. Where we have not known the latter, we have assumed that the size of a battalion or division is the same as that of the main supplier, or in the case of ex-colonies, the same as that of the former metropolitan power.

Estimates for light aircraft – helicopters, trainers, liaison and light transport types – have followed a similar pattern. Here we have taken into account the size of squadrons and the relative requirements in an air force for combat aircraft and other types.

The problems concerning missiles are somewhat different. Once it is known that a country possesses a particular missile, it is fairly easy to pin down the date of delivery. The period between the initial date of production and the date the missile was reported is usually limited. The main problem concerns the estimation of numbers of missiles, which are small and easily concealed. For missiles launched from tanks, ships or aircraft, the estimates are based on the numbers of tanks, ships and aircraft a country possesses which are capable of delivering a particular missile. The remaining missiles are almost entirely anti-tank and anti-aircraft missiles. The deliveries of anti-aircraft missiles such as SA-2, Hawk or Bloodhound have tended to attract considerable attention. There is usually, therefore, fairly good information on the numbers of missile sites, launchers, or even of the missiles themselves.

Valuation

The purpose of valuing all items in a common unit is to be able to measure changes in the total flow of weapons and its geographical pattern. Various methods of valuation are conceivable. The obvious ones are military value and monetary value. Military value is generally unmeasurable because it depends on the circumstances in which the weapons may be used. Monetary value, on the other hand, measures something that is relatively precise and is interesting in itself – the quantity of resources used. It is therefore what we have used. The monetary values chosen may not correspond to actual prices paid. Actual prices paid vary considerably according to different pricing methods, the lengths of production series and the terms involved in individual transactions. We have tried to draw up a list of comparable prices in 1968 US dollars (now brought up to 1973 prices) based on actual prices and on criteria such as weight, speed and role. These criteria have been different for each of the four different types of weapons – ships, aircraft, missiles and armoured fighting vehicles. One consequence of this method of valuation is that our values of Soviet weapon exports tend to be higher than their quoted prices. For this reason, our figures of the relative flows of major weapons from the United States and the Soviet Union may be much closer together than other statistics comparing weapon flows from these two countries. There is an additional reason for the smaller difference between the two in our figures. Soviet weapon exports to developing countries include a smaller proportion of small arms than exports from the United States; a comparison of *total* weapon exports from the two countries would look somewhat different from a comparison of major weapon exports alone.

Ships

Ships were divided into 11 different categories.[2] For each category, we calculated a 1968 dollar price per ton, based on actual prices in 1968. We also assumed a technical improvement factor of 3.5 per cent per annum. This means that the price of a ship completed in 1967 is 3.5 per cent less than the price of a similar ship completed in 1968. This improvement factor has nothing to do with general price inflation; it is merely intended to measure the increase in the sophistication of ships.

A large proportion of the ships to the countries under consideration are second-hand. It was therefore necessary to take into account the depreciation of ship values. A simple exponential depreciation was taken, based on the length of life of ships in each of the 11 categories and a scrap value of 1 per cent. This yields a rather rapid depreciation in the first few years of a ship's life. For this reason, among others, the export of warships by the United Kingdom, which has exported many new ships to developing countries, is higher in value terms than the export of warships from either the United States or the Soviet Union, which have both exported large numbers of second-hand warships.

Aircraft

For aircraft we derived a price for each individual type of aeroplane. This price was based on two factors. First, it was based on actual prices, taking into account factors which cause these prices to vary such as the length of the production series, the sales or aid terms, and the support facilities, spares and extra equipment included in the price. Second, we used kilo prices for the empty weight of dif-

---

[2] The categories were:
1. Aircraft carriers
2. Submarines
3. Cruisers
4. Destroyers, 1 300 tons and over
5. Frigates, corvettes, patrol vessels, 600–1 300 tons
6. Patrol boats, torpedo boats, gunboats, etc. 300–500 tons
7. Patrol boats, torpedo boats, gunboats, etc. 100–300 tons
8. Patrol boats, torpedo boats, gunboats, etc. under 100 tons
9. Minesweepers
10. Minelayers
11. Landing ships, land craft, transports, supply ships, survey ships, oilers, tugs etc.

ferent categories of aircraft,[3] as a rule of thumb. These categories were roughly divided into older construction and fully modern construction. We included a certain percentage of the price for spares and equipment for each of the three categories of aircraft. Explosives, missiles and ground equipment were not included.

The problem of depreciation is much harder for aircraft than for ships. The life of an aircraft is shorter than that of a ship and the scrap value approaches zero. A simple exponential depreciation yielded too rapid a depreciation in early years. Many of the second-hand aircraft sold in the period had been part of a long production series. It was often impossible to discover the date the aircraft had been built, the extent they had been used, and the extent of refurbishing. Since second-hand aircraft are a rather small proportion of total aircraft deliveries[4] a blanket assumption of 10 per cent of the original price for each second-hand aeroplane was taken. An assumption of 50 per cent of the original price was made for planes having undergone a more thorough refurbishing.

Tanks

We calculated individual prices for each armoured fighting vehicle. The prices were based on the type and the date when the vehicle had first been used. The five types were: main battle tank, light tank, tank destroyer, armoured car, and armoured personnel carrier. Second-hand tanks were valued at 50 per cent of the original price.

Missiles

Here again, we calculated individual prices for each missile. The prices were based on type, date of production, range and guidance. There were seven types: artillery rockets, anti-tank missiles, surface-to-surface missiles, air-to-surface missiles, long-range surface-to-air missiles, short-range surface-to-air missiles and air-to-air missiles.

We had separate prices for missiles and their launchers, radar, computers and so on.

Joint and licensed production

Licensed production can vary from assembly to complete manufacture. In many

---

[3] These categories were:
(a) Combat aircraft (fighters, bombers)
   Supersonic
   Subsonic
   (i) conventional
   (ii) STOL (short take-off and landing)
(b) Helicopters
(c) Others (transport, trainers, etc.)
   (i) piston engined
   (ii) turbojet
   (iii) turbo fan jet

[4] Unless our sources indicated that a particular aircraft was second-hand or unless they gave a delivery date after the production line had closed down, we assumed that it was new. If we did not know when the production line had closed down, we took as the closing date the last date the aircraft appeared in *Jane's All the World's Aircraft*, (London, Sampson, Low, Marston & Co., annual).

cases, it is known what proportion of a particular weapon is imported and what proportion is produced at home and this has been noted in the registers. For the value tables, the full cost of importing the weapon has been included. The reason is that it has been shown to be more expensive, often even in terms of foreign exchange costs only, to produce a weapon under licence in a third world country than to import the same weapon. (This is discussed in greater detail in *The Arms Trade with the Third World*, chapter 22.)